D0848157

*Israel and
Conventional
Deterrence*

CORNELL STUDIES IN SECURITY AFFAIRS

edited by Robert J. Art *and* Robert Jervis

Strategic Nuclear Targeting, edited by Desmond Ball and Jeffrey Richelson

Japan Prepares for Total War: The Search for Economic Security, 1919–1941, by Michael A. Barnhart

Citizens and Soldiers: The Dilemmas of Military Service, by Eliot A. Cohen

Great Power Politics and the Struggle over Austria, 1945–1955, by Audrey Kurth Cronin

The Wrong War: American Policy and the Dimensions of the Korean Conflict, 1950–1953, by Rosemary Foot

The Soviet Union and the Failure of Collective Security, 1934–1938, by Jiri Hochman

The Warsaw Pact: Alliance in Transition? edited by David Holloway and Jane M. O. Sharp

The Illogic of American Nuclear Strategy, by Robert Jervis

Nuclear Crisis Management: A Dangerous Illusion, by Richard Ned Lebow

The Nuclear Future, by Michael Mandelbaum

Conventional Deterrence, by John J. Mearsheimer

The Sources of Military Doctrine: France, Britain, and Germany between the World Wars, by Barry R. Posen

Israel and Conventional Deterrence: Border Warfare from 1953 to 1970, by Jonathan Shimshoni

The Ideology of the Offensive: Military Decision Making and the Disasters of 1914, by Jack Snyder

The Militarization of Space: U.S. Policy, 1945–1984, by Paul B. Stares

Making the Alliance Work: The United States and Western Europe, by Gregory F. Treverton

The Origins of Alliances, by Stephen M. Walt

The Ultimate Enemy: British Intelligence and Nazi Germany, 1933–1939, by Wesley K. Wark

Israel and Conventional Deterrence

BORDER WARFARE FROM 1953 TO 1970

JONATHAN SHIMSHONI

Cornell University Press

ITHACA AND LONDON

First published 1988 by Cornell University Press.

International Standard Book Number 0-8014-2120-9
Library of Congress Catalog Card Number 87-47965

Printed in the United States of America

*Librarians: Library of Congress cataloging information
appears on the last page of the book.*

*The paper in this book is acid-free and meets the guidelines for
permanence and durability of the Committee on Production Guidelines
for Book Longevity of the Council on Library Resources.*

For Lea,
who makes it worthwhile

Contents

[vii]

Maps

Acknowledgments

This book could not have been written without the assistance of a large number of individuals and organizations. Each helped make it possible to sustain a long and arduous effort and to make what I hope is a positive contribution to the understanding of a complex problem.

I wrote the initial version of the book at Princeton University and give special thanks to Professors Richard Ullman and Barry Posen for the intensive and most helpful guidance they gave me at that time. In the course of thinking through and trying to express my ideas, I also enjoyed healthy criticism from, and stimulating discussions with, Edward Rhodes, Stephen Walt, and Harold Feiveson.

The Woodrow Wilson School of Princeton generously provided me with office space, financial assistance, a scholarly atmosphere, and much needed moral support, for which I am most grateful. At Princeton I was also the recipient of a research grant awarded by the Center of International Studies.

While I was doing research in Israel, the Dayan Center (Shiloach Institute) and the Jaffee Center for Strategic Studies, both at Tel-Aviv University, were very cooperative in making important material available.

Many friends provided critical assistance and encouragement to me and my family at various stages of the lengthy process. Among them I must mention Lori and Jerry Kantor, Joan and Mark Levin, Virginia Mason and Robert Willig, Ruth and Bernard Miller, Shmuel Reshef, my cousins Kenneth and Ellen Rosenthal, and Julian and Eileen Wolpert.

The editors of Cornell University Press and the series, especially

[xi]

Robert Art, gave detailed and enlightening comments for improving the manuscript.

Finally, my mother, Rose Shimshoni, was instrumental in the production of the final version. She contributed tirelessly—as typist, "processor," and ruthless (yet constructive) critic of both form and content. Indeed, her assistance made publication possible.

JONATHAN SHIMSHONI

Princeton, N.J.
Kibbutz Hamaapil, Israel

Israel and
Conventional
Deterrence

Introduction

Among scholars and laypeople—in the United States, at least—the discussion and study of deterrence have acquired the popularity of a national sport, and library shelves groan with the ever-growing weight of books about it. Yet it is a new interest and a young literature, concerned very little with questions of conventional deterrence. This is surprising, for the desire to dissuade opponents from instigating war is surely as old as violence itself, which is neither an invention nor an innovation of the nuclear era. But the main thrust and very genesis of deterrence theory as a discrete field of inquiry came with the emergence of the post–World War II condition of mutual nuclear confrontation; deterrence theory is, basically, *nuclear* deterrence theory.[1]

The Israeli security experience has also been a major focus for students of security, strategy, and doctrine, and they also have produced copious harvests of paper on the subject. Yet here too there has been a surprising dearth of interest in Israeli deterrence, even within the Israeli scholarly and executive communities, where most explicit attention has been devoted to winning wars and not to avoiding them.[2] The purpose

1. For a discussion of the sources of deterrence theory, see Robert Jervis, "Deterrence Theory Revisited," *World Politics* 31 (January 1979).
2. Studies of Israeli deterrence can be found in Shlomo Aronson, *Conflict and Bargaining in the Middle East: An Israeli Perspective* (Baltimore, 1978); Shai Feldman, *Israeli Nuclear Deterrence: A Strategy for the 1980s* (New York, 1982); Avner Yaniv, *Deterrence without the Bomb: The Politics of Israeli Strategy* (Lexington, Mass., 1987); sections of Yoav Ben-Horin and Barry Posen, *Israel's Strategic Doctrine*, R-2845-NA (Santa Monica, Calif., September 1981); Dan Horowitz, *Israel's Concept of Defensible Borders*, Jerusalem Papers on Peace Problems, no. 16 (Jerusalem, 1975); idem, *Hatfisa ha-Yisraelit shel Bitachon Leumi: Hakavua veha-Mishtaneh ba-Khashiva ha-Estrategit ha-Yisraelit* [Israel's concept of national security: The constant and the dynamic in Israeli strategic thought] (Jerusalem, 1973).

[1]

of this book is, therefore, twofold: to develop and enhance an understanding of conventional deterrence and to write part of a critical history of Israel's deterrence experience.

Where deterrence theory has not related purely to the nuclear context, it has generally been an undisciplined mixture, characterized either by attempts to generate general or multipurpose theory or else by use of "conventional" evidence for propositions about nuclear deterrence.[3] The central belief underlying this book is that there are critical logical and operational peculiarities to conventional deterrence that make it different in kind from nuclear deterrence. It therefore requires a distinct theory.

That nuclear and conventional deterrence are different is clearly not my discovery. Probably the best early discussion of the differences is Glenn Snyder's, in *Deterrence and Defense*.[4] Yet Snyder is discussing deterrence in a specific context: the East-West confrontation in Europe. Clearly, nuclear weapons are an inescapable part of any relationship across the East-West divide, intruding blatantly on the logic of conventional confrontation or coercion there. Twenty years later John Mearsheimer developed the discussion of deterrence in conventional situations.[5] He too chooses a very narrow context, in which large mobilized armies confront each other in disputes of unambiguously vital interests at clear and immediate risk. Neither writer, nor anyone else to my knowledge, has pursued a general understanding of the specific logic, concepts, and problems of deterrence in a conventional world.

What do I mean by "deterrence in a conventional world"? By "deterrence" I mean the dissuasion of one's opponent from either initiating or expanding (in time or extent) violence against oneself by threat of negative sanctions. "Conventional" is a more complicated idea. Restricting it to situations in which nuclear weapons simply do not exist would limit this study and its relevance to the past. Intent on maintaining relevance, I define a conventional situation as one in which neither defender nor challenger has immediate access to nuclear weapons, though their allies may be nuclear powers. I even suggest in Chapter 1 that under certain conditions "essential conventionality" can be maintained where one party has access to nuclear weapons, so long as the other does not.

3. For examples see Avner Yaniv, "Harta'ah ve-Haganah ba-Estrategiya ha-Yisraelit" [Deterrence and defense in Israeli strategy], *Medinah Memshal ve-Yakhasim Bein-Leumim* 24 (1985); Sharon Watkins, "Deterrence Theory: Expectations and Illusions," *Journal of Strategic Studies* 5 (December 1982); Robert Jervis, "Deterrence and Perception," *International Security* 7 (Winter 1982/83).

4. Glenn Snyder, *Deterrence and Defense* (Princeton, N.J., 1960).

5. John Mearsheimer, *Conventional Deterrence* (Ithaca, N.Y., 1983).

"Deterrence" has been used in a number of different ways: as policy goal, strategy, doctrine, and phenomenon. Admittedly, a major concern of mine is to improve policy and strategy. But in the reasonable scheme of things we should try to understand the objects of our strategies before dwelling on the policy process and the wisdom of specific steps, just as an economist must comprehend the nature and logic of monopolies, oligopolies, and contestability of markets before discussing regulation. Given the underdeveloped state of conventional deterrence theory, I take here a phenomenological approach. I do not ignore specific policies, for it is the nature of deterrence that policies are part of the phenomenon. But the wisdom and process of policy making or of specific approaches and strategies are not my real concerns.

The study of conventional deterrence should be of general interest for three reasons. First, and obviously, before 1945 deterrence was strictly conventional. New light may be thrown on the general history of security and conflict through the application of the paradigm of deterrence theory. Second, much of the world still relies on conventional deterrence and, with the slow rate of nuclear proliferation, seems destined to continue to do so for a long time. The third reason is perhaps the most exciting. I interpret the Strategic Defense Initiative ("Star Wars") as an attempt to make the dominant global relationships conventional again. An important yet so far ignored aspect of the SDI debate is the nature and logic of deterrence should SDI succeed. It behooves its proponents to examine the strategic nature of the world they wish to create. My work suggests that it is not quite the utopia they dream of.

Robert Jervis has written that "good theories do not spring full-blown from the minds of a few scholars." Surely, a good and complete theory of conventional deterrence will not spring from this investigation. There being no existing general theory of conventional deterrence, this book is a small first step down a long road and should be seen as a kind of "reconnaissance by fire," testing reasonable and logical suspicions in a preliminary fashion. It is also but a modest start toward a history of Israeli deterrence. Envisioned is an iterative inquiry: A preliminary framework for analysis is deduced by considering the strategic characteristics of nonnuclear force. The framework is then applied to historical case study. The experience of historical exploration should help sharpen, clarify, and test the initial concepts and propositions and suggest ways to improve theory and, where possible, policy.

There are two possible approaches for developing a way to think about conventional deterrence: One is to start with a tabula rasa and develop propositions from basic principles. The other is to test and

[3]

modify the existing paradigm of nuclear deterrence theory. I have chosen to compromise, to develop logical-deductive propositions about conventional deterrence *and* try to understand them relative to nuclear deterrence. I have chosen to use nuclear deterrence as a benchmark because it is just that. The readers of this study presumably share the assumptions, paradigms, and language of nuclear deterrence. As a common foundation it is a good starting point for comparison and change.

The book proceeds in the following manner: Chapter 1 develops a framework for analysis of conventional deterrence that can be applied to historical study. A brief presentation of the general deterrence model precedes an exposition of the logic and language of mutual nuclear deterrence. The strategic characteristics of nonnuclear forces are then described along with the logic and language of conventional deterrence deriving from them. Development of this logic generates operational questions for analysis of the historical cases. The chapter ends by explaining the choice of cases and why the Arab-Israeli conflict is relevant to the study of conventional deterrence.

Chapter 2 provides a short introduction to the first two cases and then studies Fedayeen infiltration from Jordan in the years 1953–54. Chapter 3 examines Fedayeen infiltration from Egypt and direct harassment by the Egyptian state between 1953 and 1956. Chapter 4, the third case, covers the Egyptian-Israeli War of Attrition, 1967–70. A concluding chapter draws on all three cases to assess the prospects for parsimonious and predictive theory and to make some specific propositions about conventional deterrence theory and policy.

[4]

[1]

From Nuclear to Conventional Deterrence: A Framework for Analysis

DETERRENCE: A GENERAL MODEL

Deterrence is a form of coercion, the latter defined by Klaus Knorr as follows: "When power is used coercively, an actor (B) is influenced if he adapts his behavior in compliance with, or anticipation of, another actor's (A) demands, wishes, or proposals. B's conduct is then affected by something A does, or by something he expects A to do. In consequence, B will modify his behavior (if he would not have done so otherwise), or he will not modify his behavior (if he would have altered it in the absence of external influence)."[1] But not all influence is coercive. Knorr continues: "It is *coercive* when B's conduct is affected by his fear of sanctions of one kind or another, that is some threat, actual or expected, to his goal achievement. B's choice of behavior is consequently restricted by A's influence."[2] Deterrence is a specific coercive phenomenon: a defender's dissuasion—through the use of implied, explicit, stated, or demonstrated threats—of an opponent's intention to undertake or expand violent action.

With slight modification, the most satisfying formulation of the general deterrence model is Glenn Snyder's. Focusing on the potential challenger's decision rule, Snyder describes a four-argument calculus:

1. Valuation of his war objectives (vs. the status quo);
2. the costs he expects to suffer from various responses (by the defender);

---

1. Klaus Knorr, *The Power of Nations* (New York, 1975), p. 4.
2. Ibid.

3. the probability of various responses, including "no response"; and

4. the probability of winning the objectives with each possible response.[3]

Deterrent threats are the responses Snyder refers to. These are normally conditional, of the form "If you do . . . then I will. . . ." Various kinds (or aspects) of threat emerge from Snyder's formulation. The reference to costs (in the second argument) is normally associated with the threat of *punishment*. The prospect of not winning the objective (in the fourth argument) is the threat of successful defense, or *object-denial*.

The central problem of deterrent threats is credibility, and Snyder's model directs our attention to two of its dimensions. First, from the perspective of the challenger, *can* the defender deny the object or inflict unacceptable costs? Second, on the issue of probability, *will* the defender execute his threats? On neither count is the problem of credibility trivial. There is no reason to assume a priori that a defender really has either the ability or the will to make an appropriate response. But even if he does, convincing his challenger of this is another matter. Credible will is especially problematic when, from the defender's perspective, execution of a threat is not desirable ex-post even when the threat may be desirable to make ex-ante. Just as the challenger has a decision rule that takes into account costs and object attainment, so a defender may incur tremendous and unacceptable costs in executing a threat.[4] The challenger knows this, of course, a fact that places downward pressure on his assessment of the probability of various responses. The defender may somehow have to make the irrational rational, either by irrevocably committing himself to a certain response or by in fact becoming irrational.[5]

I have been depicting deterrence as an exercise in communication, the defender striving to convince the challenger of both his will and skill. More broadly, deterrence depends on the creation of a minimum of shared or common knowledge. Before a defender communicates threats he must devise them, and to do this appropriately he must understand his challenger's available strategies and valuation of war objectives and costs. In order to devise appropriate threats and communicate them he needs to understand something about the challenger's

3. Glenn Snyder, *Deterrence and Defense*, p. 12.
4. On the defender's calculus, see ibid., p. 13.
5. The best discussion of commitment is Thomas Schelling's in *Arms and Influence* (New Haven, Conn., 1966), chap. 2.

rationality.[6] Thus the problems of credibility and rationality are subsumed within the more general problem of common knowledge.

Ideas of threat, commitment, and communication suggest that we step back for a broader perspective of deterrence in the context of strategic interaction. Strategic moves such as threat and commitment are relevant in what game theory refers to as "non–zero-sum games." The relationships of the actors are not solely or completely competitive, and they share interests to some degree.[7] This kind of relationship is most probably the norm in life, even when violent military confrontation threatens. The most obvious example is the mutual U.S.-Soviet interest in avoiding nuclear war.

Deterrent threats are not always sufficient to dissuade a potential challenger. Depending on the particular relationship—available strategies and different valuations—successful dissuasion may require both a deterrent threat and a conciliatory promise. In some situations in fact, the main relevant dissuasive instrument is conciliation or constructive appeasement.[8]

Since Munich many people view the term *constructive appeasement* as a logical or moral nonsequitur. Indeed, appeasement of Hitler's Germany was misplaced, conciliation having been pursued where deterrent threats were relevant and appropriate. But during the past decade deterrence scholarship has begun to explore the alternative error: the pursuit of deterrence where conciliation is appropriate. If the first error might lead to encouragement of an aggressor, the second can cause a spiral, a gratuitous cycle of escalatory moves fed and fired by self-fulfilling pessimistic images held by opponents, each of the other.[9] The

6. "Rationality" is used here, broadly defined, to refer to the ordering and transitivity of values, the learning and decision processes, and the control of execution. On notions and definitions of rationality and rational (and irrational) behavior, see Edward J. Rhodes, "Nuclear Weapons, Irrational Behavior and Extended Deterrence" (Ph.D. diss., Princeton University, 1985); Thomas Schelling, *The Strategy of Conflict* (Cambridge, Mass., 1980), pp. 13–16; Morton D. Davis, *Game Theory: A Nontechnical Introduction* (New York, 1973), chap. 4.

7. On cooperativeness and strategic moves, see Schelling, *Strategy of Conflict*, chap. 5. See also Davis, *Game Theory*, chap. 5.

8. For some theoretical development of the need to mix threats and promises, see Schelling, *Strategy of Conflict*, chap. 5; Davis, *Game Theory*, chap. 5. For discussions of appeasement, see Yohanan Cohen, *Umot be-Mivhan* [Small nations in times of crisis and confrontation] (Tel-Aviv, 1985), pp. 19–28; Robert Gilpin, *War and Change in World Politics* (New York, 1981), pp. 193–94, 206–7.

9. Prominent work on this question includes Alexander George and Richard Smoke, *Deterrence in American Foreign Policy: Theory and Practice* (New York, 1974); Robert Jervis, *Perception and Misperception in International Politics* (Princeton, N.J., 1976), esp. chap. 3; Richard Ned Lebow, "The Deterrence Deadlock: Is There a Way Out?" *Political Psychology* 4, no. 2 (1983); David A. Baldwin, "The Power of Positive Sanctions," *World Politics* 24

idea of a spiral is important, for it serves as an operational and visible indication of the bounds or limits of deterrence theory, an indication of where deterrence is not the relevant phenomenon or appropriate strategy.

Mutual Nuclear Deterrence

The logic of mutual nuclear deterrence results from special characteristics of nuclear weapons. Most prominent is the ability of merely a few successfully delivered devices to inflict unambiguously unacceptable costs. Also significant is the inability of nuclear forces to neutralize each other. The states involved in such a relationship can be seen as living in a game of "Chicken," in which the payoff of mutual defection is enormously negative, so much so that the Chicken relationship is clear and inescapable and dominates all aspects of their interaction.

In terms of the general deterrence model presented earlier, nuclear deterrence operates on the second argument—the expected costs or punishment. These are usually perceived to be so catastrophic that they completely overshadow any possible valuation of war objectives (argument one), so that avoidance of nuclear war is a central concern of nuclear states. Because the relative size of nuclear forces is not critical to relative power except at extreme disparities, the relationship is essentially *symmetrical*. By similar reasoning, relative power is little influenced by the addition of other nuclear states in alliances, so that the deterrence relationship is inherently *bilateral*.

Nuclear statesmen are not only careful to avoid nuclear war or high conflict but go to great pains to avoid any direct conflict with each other. The fear of nuclear exchange is inescapable and ubiquitous; it provides downward pressure on all conflict and sanctifies the status quo.[10]

What is required in the way of shared (or common) knowledge for a deterrence relationship to hold? A minimal level should suffice, and credibility may actually *depend* on less than perfect rationality. Mutual nuclear deterrence is an unambiguous game of Chicken regardless of

---

(October 1971); Robert Jervis, "Cooperation under the Security Dilemma," *World Politics* 30 (January 1978).

10. Robert Art, "To What Ends Military Power," *International Security* 4 (Spring 1980): 16. See also Phillip Green, *Deadly Logic: The Theory of Nuclear Deterrence* (Columbus, Ohio, 1966), p. 155; Watkins, "Deterrence Theory," p. 486. For discussions of the disutility of nuclear weapons except as deterrent instruments, see Jonathan Shimshoni, "Conventional Deterrence: Lessons from the Middle East" (Ph.D. diss., Princeton University, 1986), pp. 18–22; Ian Clark, *Limited Nuclear War* (Princeton, N.J., 1982).

force sizes, specific technologies, doctrines, or alliance systems. As Shai Feldman put it, "Where both sides can inflict unacceptable punishment, the capability factor in each half of the deterrence equation may be considered identical and hence may be cancelled out."[11] What opposing states must know about each other, then, is rather simple: they are nuclear powers, and therefore something terrible will happen in the event of war.

What do the opponents make of the probability of a nuclear response to a challenge? Everything argued so far suggests that a rational defender should capitulate once challenged rather than risk nuclear annihilation. And because both actors know this, deterrence should be fragile. At this point, the minimal requirements of common knowledge are joined by somewhat strange ones of rationality.

Preservation of deterrence is made possible by a compromise between a certain irreducible rationality and an inescapable irrationality. Perfect rationality, in the sense of value transitivity and maximization, is not required of a decision maker in order for him to understand the implications of a nuclear exchange; minimal rationality should suffice. But despite the clearly irrational nature of nuclear retaliation, it might, as Robert Jervis suggests,[12] happen because of an irreducible irrationality inherent in the possession of such weapons. In a sense, the necessary minimal rationality is imposed on the players by the sheer magnitude of fear maintained by the combination of the effects of the weapons and the fact that, in Thomas Schelling's words, "it is hard for a government, even a responsible one, to *guarantee* its own moderation in every circumstance."[13] The knowledge about the other's rationality that each player must share is thus devoid of detail. What they must know about each other they can simply assume: that both are bound by this minimal rationality.

Although discussion so far may seem to suggest that nuclear states are locked in the status quo, we know that this is not so and that the superpowers engage in verbal, economic, political, and even some forceful bargaining. But the dominating game of Chicken greatly influences all interaction and bargaining.

If the question of relative skill is moot in nuclear power relations, then all the more attention is diverted to the question of relative will. In any given confrontational situation there is tremendous pressure on the protagonists to establish common knowledge on one question: in

---

11. Feldman, *Israeli Nuclear Deterrence*, p. 31.
12. Jervis, "Deterrence Theory Revisited," p. 300.
13. Schelling, *Arms and Influence*, p. 41.

whose favor is relative will, or in other words, whose resolve is stronger? Where this is clear, nuclear powers leave each other alone. The United States was allowed to pursue its war in Vietnam, the Soviets to invade Czechoslovakia in 1968 and Afghanistan in 1979. Where relative will is not clear, we expect either rapid clarification, as in the Cuban Missile Crisis, or that the status quo prevail.

What is the nature of forceful bargaining when it occurs? The model as described so far would see it as a contest in risk taking. We expect bargaining to take place at a low level but to be dominated by the risk of inadvertent escalation. A defender, for example, can initiate intentionally low-level violent activity that may—unintentionally—escalate out of control. If he is more willing than the challenger to accept the risk of escalation, then he should prevail in the contest of wills, and deterrence holds.[14] Because the risk introduced is independent of both parties and fear dominates, we expect such challenges to be infrequent. This test of wills is recognized as brinkmanship. Writes Schelling: "If brinkmanship means anything, it means *manipulating the shared risk of war*. It means exploiting the danger that somebody may inadvertently go over the brink, dragging the other with him."[15]

Two complementary implications of this discussion capture the logic of mutual nuclear deterrence. First, because of the fear of upward escalation, limited war can serve as a bargaining tool between nuclear powers. It is, in a sense, inescapably strategic. Second, the very pursuit and outcome of low-level conflict are directly affected by the high-level relationship, again because of the fear of escalation.[16] In nuclear life, then, deterrence at the highest strategic level is convertible to deterrence of tactical violence.

A Conceptual Digression: Defining Deterrence and Success

Key terms and their definitions should be chosen with care, for these greatly influence the interpretation of events. I briefly address here two key terms, *deterrence* and *success*, in the nuclear context, and I do so again later, in the context of conventional deterrence, to see whether the same understanding persists.

Deterrence. Nuclear forces are not perceived as "useful"; thus the idea of deterrence is different in kind from that of defense or offense accomplished by the actual engagement of forces. Glenn Snyder dichotomizes deterrence and defense, arguing that the requirements of

14. Feldman, *Israeli Nuclear Deterrence*, p. 31.
15. Schelling, *Arms and Influence*, p. 99.
16. Bernard Brodie, *War and Politics* (New York, 1973), p. 403.

deterrence (through the threat of punishing retaliation) and defense (cost reduction once deterrence fails) are drastically different and mutually exclusive, possibly necessitating a choice between them. Because nuclear weapons are useful only for deterrence and conventional weapons only for defense, resources have to be allocated to one or the other. In another distinction Snyder writes that "perhaps the crucial difference between deterrence and defense is that deterrence is a peacetime objective, while defense is a wartime value. Deterrent value and defense value are directly enjoyed in different time periods."[17]

Schelling distinguishes deterrence from compellence. In his scheme, deterrence is passive, a reactive use of force, while compellence is active, the initiative with the compeller.[18] There appears to be a consensus that deterrence is easier than compellence. Given the logic of mutual nuclear deterrence and the inherent clarity and stability of the status quo, a conscious decision to upset it is unlikely. As Paul Kecskemeti put it, there is an "aggressor's handicap."[19]

Success. The outcome of a deterrence crisis is normally conceived of as binary. In a given confrontation either deterrence succeeds and the status quo prevails or else the status quo is challenged and deterrence fails. This notion flows from the disutility of nuclear force except for threat, the catastrophic implications of any exchange of blows between nuclear states, and the distinction between deterrence-for-peace, defense-for-war. Robert Art provides an appropriate summary: "Deterrence therefore employs force peacefully. It is the threat to resort to force that is the essence of deterrence. If the threat has to be carried out, deterrence by definition has failed."[20]

THE NATURE OF CONVENTIONAL FORCES

We all know what conventional weapons are, and many probably have even seen them used. But if we are to understand their implica-

17. Glenn Snyder, *Deterrence and Defense*, p. 3. For his general discussion of this issue, see pp. 3–9. For a similar distinction, see Kenneth N. Waltz, "Toward Nuclear Peace," in Robert Art and Kenneth N. Waltz, eds., *The Use of Force*, 2d ed. (Washington, D.C., 1983). See also the distinctions made by Yaniv, "Harta'ah ve-Haganah ba-Estrategiya ha-Yisraelit," and Barry Posen, *The Sources of Military Doctrine: France, Britain, and Germany between the World Wars* (Ithaca, N.Y., 1984), pp. 14–15.

18. Schelling, *Arms and Influence*, pp. 69–71. For a similar differentiation, of "peaceful" versus "physical" uses of force, see Art, "To What Ends Military Power," p. 5. For the insistence on deterrence as reactive, see Patrick Morgan, *Deterrence: A Conceptual Analysis* (Beverly Hills, Calif., 1977), p. 35.

19. Cited in Jervis, "Deterrence Theory Revisited," p. 297.

20. Art, "To What Ends Military Power," p. 6.

tions for deterrence, we need to think explicitly about the characteristics of conventional forces and weapons that influence the nature and extent of their strategic utility. I have identified eight. Generally, conventional forces

1. can inflict relatively small direct punishment, and indirect punishment only with great difficulty;
2. are competitive in their application;
3. are sensitive in quality and size to objective facts—to a country's ability to create, sustain, and mobilize them;
4. are sensitive in quality, size, and successful application to political decisions and executive skill, in both the long and short run;
5. are sensitive to time and timing;
6. allow for discriminatory use;
7. are critically additive; and
8. know no steady state, are constantly changing.

Let us look at each of these, if only briefly.

Small Punishment. It would be absurd to assert that conventional ordnance delivers no pain, but the strategic hurt is greatly proscribed by two factors. One, direct punishment, like that delivered by missiles or strategic bombing, has not proved horrible or quick enough to be politically useful. Extensive local punishment is possible with conventional weapons. But it is just that: local, and thus not overwhelmingly shocking to the receiving nation. Two, because it requires tremendous effort to inflict even local pain, punishment does not carry a convincing promise of more, of engulfing the entire receiving nation in unbearable pain.[21] Since Giulio Douhet's writing of the early 1920s we have learned, in our collective experience, that the fear of punishment that so affected British behavior and thinking in the late 1920s was misguided.[22] Strategic bombing in World War II and twenty years later in Vietnam have instructed us in the strategic limits of nonnuclear punishment.[23]

Infliction of real pain requires victory, which is not necessarily possi-

---

21. Schelling, *Arms and Influence*, pp. 17–18.

22. For an extensive discussion of pre–World War II British strategic thinking on deterrence, see George H. Quester, *Deterrence before Hiroshima* (New York, 1966).

23. On the efficacy of strategic bombing in World War II, see Bernard Brodie, *Strategy in the Missile Age* (Princeton, N.J., 1959), pp. 131–43. For a discussion of the limited effects of the bombing campaign of North Vietnam (Rolling Thunder), see Guenter Lewy, *America in Vietnam* (New York, 1978), pp. 391–92.

ble or even desirable in all circumstances. But even for a victor, inflicting pain may be difficult, expensive, or distasteful. The requirement of victory introduces a major asymmetry into conventional confrontations. In the nuclear world the capacity to punish is equally distributed between victor and loser—whatever these words mean—but not so in conventional conflict.[24]

Competitive in Application. The ideas of victory and defeat introduce two features of the application of conventional forces: one, to prevail requires skill, or capability, in addition to will; and two, this skill is meaningful only relative to the skill of one's opponent. The minimal requirement of simply possessing forces, which is sufficient for nuclear powers, is not enough in conventional contexts.

Objective Facts. A state must create military power from various resources, over which it may have no control, at least in the short run. These resources have been identified by Knorr as the sources of "putative power" and include population, national income, natural resources, and geographic providence.[25] A state has even less control over its opponents' putative power. Various sources of might on both sides of a conflict may interact to render the underlying power relationship completely asymmetric.

Politics and Craftsmanship. Creation of significant conventional military power, its mobilization, and its manipulation involve large political and social decisions to divert and harness existing national resources. These decisions are difficult because they involve large opportunity costs.[26] Once the decision to expend resources is made, success depends on the skill with which this is done. Moreover, as military strength is relative, the correct mobilization of resources requires an accurate perception of the opponent's skills and prescience about how he is developing. Correct decisions on general force development do not guarantee its correct expression in a confrontational crisis with another state. The skill of knowing when to mobilize and how to overcome political obstacles to action is not trivial and may be crucial to the strategic utility of power.

Time and Timing. Specific activation of forces is an inherently lengthy process because of both political constraints and the physically slow and

24. Schelling, *Arms and Influence*, pp. 17–23.
25. Knorr, *Power of Nations*, chap. 3.
26. For a discussion of some of the difficulties inherent in these decisions (in periods of decline), see Gilpin, *War and Change*, pp. 158, 167.

labor-intensive nature of mobilization. Yet given the competitive nature of conventional confrontation, timing may be decisive.

Discrimination. In applying conventional forces, a state may discriminate in timing, place, size of forces, extent of damage, and length of engagement. There is operational meaning to ideas like *demonstration, counterforce*, and *limited war* which is absent in nuclear contexts. Obstacles to significant punishment combine with discrimination to make conventional force useful at various levels and for many purposes.

Additivity. An important component of capability is the quantity of forces available, relative, of course, to the opponent's. Nuclear power may also be sensitive to force size, but in a manner markedly different from conventional power. Above a fairly low number, the addition of nuclear devices does not make destruction more assured; the basic symmetry is hard to upset. The outcomes of conventional conflict are highly sensitive to relative force sizes, and only at high levels of armament does the marginal utility of additional force degenerate.

This fact further amplifies considerations of resource allocation and timely mobilization. It also externalizes—internationalizes—relative power, making it sensitive to alliances. In an important sense, any conventional bilateral confrontation is inherently multilateral, whereas its nuclear parallel is essentially bilateral.[27] Additivity thus introduces another critical potential asymmetry in relative power, which in turn invokes new dimensions of relative skill and will: sensitivity to alliances and skill in systemic manipulation.[28]

Constant Change. Conventional forces are constantly changing, especially in relative capabilities. We can analyze change in various time frames: immediate battlefield innovations in tactics; medium-term, two- to fifteen-year, doctrinal, technological, and political changes and innovations; long-run changes in military science, technology, and sources of putative power, normally exogenous to the immediate decision-making unit.[29] Confining ourselves to the medium term we see change, both exogenous and endogenous, that may have tremendous effects on relative power. Change highlights the problem and importance of pre-science: some innovations require considerable time and resources, and mistakes may lead unavoidably to periods of relative inferiority.[30]

27. Glenn Snyder, *Deterrence and Defense*, pp. 44–45.
28. For the effects of alliance politics, see Posen, *Sources of Military Doctrine*, pp. 17, 61–64.
29. Gilpin, *War and Change*, pp. 59–66.
30. On the sources and explanations of innovations, see Posen, *Sources of Military Doctrine*, pp. 29–33, 54–57.

Conventional Deterrence

The strategic characteristics of conventional forces impose a logic on conventional deterrence very different from the rationale of its nuclear relative. The key difference is the lack of a simple, self-evident organizing device; there is no conventional counterpart to the ubiquitous game of Chicken. Because to punish is difficult and the application of force can be laborious and onerous yet discriminatory, the fear of mutual defection—war—may not be so overwhelming. Furthermore, because conventional weapons are competitive and additive, power relations are not necessarily symmetrical; and because force is additive, power relations between two conventional states are heavily influenced by other actors, so that the relationship is not essentially bilateral.

With the specter of Armageddon missing, conventional force is, very simply, useful. As Bernard Brodie described war in the Renaissance, so it remains for conventional powers today: "War was something that had to be risked not only occasionally, and strictly for matters of great moment but constantly, on all sorts of issues."[31] Deterrence cannot hope to be a robust phenomenon in such an environment. There should be (as we know there are) many situations in which, regardless of a defender's threats, his challenger benefits by resorting to violence.

The problems of punishment nudge conventional deterrence toward object denial, but not exclusively. The expectation of a costless failure is hardly deterrent, so that conventional deterrent threats must include aspects of both denial and punishment. A defender must establish his credibility, that is, his relative ability to deny objects and cause pain and his will to do so in the event of a challenge. The defender's skills must appear relevant to the specific set of possible challenges; a general possession of power (sufficient for nuclear states) is not enough to render skill credible.

Threats, as I mentioned earlier, may lose credibility of will by being clearly undesirable to execute though reasonable to issue. In nuclear contexts this obstacle is overcome by the fear of inadvertant execution; but the ponderous, onerous, discriminatory, and reversible characteristics of conventional force application render inadvertence highly unlikely. In sum, then, conventional deterrent threats face inherent obstacles to credibility on both flanks: skill and will.

A clarification is in order here. In a consideration of the issue of will, it is necessary to depart from the narrow kind of confrontation depicted by Glenn Snyder and John Mearsheimer. These scholars consider situations in which the challenger places the defender's vital territory or very

---

31. Brodie, *War and Politics*, p. 225.

independence at risk. Mearsheimer correctly argues that the issue of credible will is irrelevant in these situations: "My concern with situations in which two large armies directly face each other moots the question of whether or not the defender should respond when attacked. I assume that both forces immediately become entangled, and the defender's type or level of response seems plain: he will certainly—automatically, in a sense—employ all of his available resources (nonnuclear) to thwart the enemy."[32] Our concern is with a much wider range of possible situations—a natural orientation in light of the utility of force for both large and small purposes.

Recall that for deterrent threats to work at all, to be credible, requires the sharing of knowledge between defender and challenger. The mutual possession of nuclear weapons greatly simplifies these requirements, obviating the need for detailed mutual understanding of each other's capabilities, desires, and rationalities. But our consideration of conventional weapons and deterrence suggests an acute problem for common knowledge. The nonnuclear world is messy and detail intensive; yet sharing the knowledge of this detail of the tangible and intangible, physical and political, constant and dynamic aspects of relative will and skill is critical for both generation and comprehension of relevant and credible deterrent threats.

For the practitioner-statesman and for the analyst who would explain or predict the outcomes of deterrence situations, this is a dismaying state of affairs. It is all the more discouraging if he takes into account the numerous psychological and social barriers to common knowledge and rational decision making, these surely amplified by the wealth of detail involved.[33]

And so the analyst and practitioner seek devices to organize this detail and simplify the requirements of sharing. In constructing such a framework, I purposefully, in the interest of parsimony, avoid a level of analysis that takes into account the psychological barriers to perception and communication just mentioned. Even so, it should be clear at the outset that there is little hope for the homogeneous simplicity of mutual nuclear deterrence.

As a basis for analysis of deterrence relationships, I adopt a structural

32. Mearsheimer, *Conventional Deterrence*, pp. 18–19.

33. For discussions of these, see John D. Steinbrunner, *The Cybernetic Theory of Decision* (Princeton, N.J., 1974); Klaus Knorr, "Threat Perception," in Klaus Knorr, ed., *Historical Dimensions of National Security Problems* (Lawrence, Kans., 1975); Irving L. Janis and Leon Mann, *Decision Making* (New York, 1977); Jervis, *Perception and Misperception*; Robert Jervis, Richard Ned Lebow, and Janice Gross Stein, eds., *Psychology and Deterrence* (Baltimore, Md., 1985).

approach, analyzing the basic elements that determine the relative will and skill to apply force. These elements include relative will (or interests) in the dispute, the influences of internal politics and alliance relationships, and the possibilities and capabilities of mobilizing and applying power.[34] Aside from this basic structure of a relationship, over which the defender has little control in the short run (*during* a crisis), there are a number of instruments that can clarify or simplify the relationship, create the necessary common knowledge, or else rapidly alter the relationship's strategic implications and improve the defender's bargaining position. These include escalation, brinkmanship, and the substitution of a general reputation for detailed knowledge.

The Structural Elements of Deterrence Relationships

RELATIVE INTERESTS

The relative strength of interests in the disputed object has been advanced by a number of scholars as a critical factor determining deterrence outcomes. The protagonist with stronger interests (or will) in any bargaining situation (including deterrence) should prevail. Glenn Snyder developed the language of interests, differentiating intrinsic from power interests, or values: "Intrinsic values are 'end values;' they are valued for their own sake rather than for what they contribute to the power relations between the protagonists. . . . Power values are 'instrumental values,' not end values. That is they are valued not for their own sake but for what they contribute to the security of intrinsic values."[35] These interests are ordered, with intrinsic values stronger than power, or instrumental, ones.

Unfortunately, this ordering does not completely remove possible ambiguity from the relative strength-of-interest calculus. For example, two states may dispute the rights to a tract of territory. State A may have no intrinsic claim on the land in question and desire it only as a strategic buffer—a clear power interest—whereas for state B the territory is part of the historic motherland and of great intrinsic concern. In the balance

34. The reader may identify the influence of systemic or balance-of-power theories on my approach. See Kenneth N. Waltz, *Theory of International Politics* (Reading, Mass., 1979). For a general discussion of systems theories with many examples, see Robert Jervis, "Systems Theories and Diplomatic History," in Paul Gordon Lauren, ed., *Diplomacy: New Approaches in History, Theory, and Policy* (New York, 1979).

35. Glenn Snyder, *Deterrence and Defense*, pp. 30–31. See also Jervis, "Deterrence Theory Revisited," pp. 314–15.

of interests the value may nonetheless be more vital to A, in which case A would be expected to prevail in bargaining. Unfortunately, vital interests may also be ambiguous, subjective, and changeable, and in any event debatable, so that weighing vitalness of interests will not always yield a neat result.[36]

This problem is not exclusively one of conventional deterrence, but it is greatly exacerbated in a nonnuclear context. We observed earlier that in nuclear confrontations the fear of upward escalation and the risk inherent in low-level conflict put tremendous pressure on the protagonists to clarify their relative interests either by simply accepting the status quo, or else with careful, minimal, and rapid probing. In conventional situations, the problems of time, political and economic costs of force mobilization and application, together with the discriminatory and reversible strategic characteristics of conventional force, make experimentation, or "probing," a reasonable policy for a challenger to adopt in trying to ascertain the balance of wills. A challenger may use *some* force in an attempt to decide whether to use *more*.[37]

POWER AND POLITICS

The physical power of two states is difficult to compare, relative strength depending as it does on intangibles like doctrine, tactics, and the quality of execution, including timing. Furthermore, the logic of a conventional confrontation makes this knowledge problem inescapable, for both challenger and defender are under great pressure to deceive one another. The potential challenger is constantly busy developing points of superiority he is not about to divulge. The defender is in a real dilemma: To deter, he must *appear* to be ex post superior, capable of executing his deterrent threats. But to really *be* ex post superior, he must keep most of his capabilities secret. Completing the circle, if his critical capabilities are indeed secret, why should his potential challenger decide not to attack? Given the dynamic nature of conventional forces, both challenger and defender are apt constantly to change their force structures, doctrines, and tactics in response to inaccurately perceived conditions on the other side. The inaccuracy is inevitable because of deception compounded by the need for prescience. Sooner or later the challenger is likely to perceive a window of opportunity, real or not.

Often confronting states must mobilize their forces to challenge, react, or both. The need to mobilize adds to the fragility of deterrence by introducing additional ambiguous abilities and allowing the intrusion

36. Bernard Brodie, *War and Politics*, chap. 8.
37. The idea of "probing" is developed by George and Smoke, *Deterrence in American Foreign Policy*, pp. 540–43.

of political-social factors and constraints. For example, if both sides require mobilization, the challenger to achieve his object and the defender to deny it, then timing and speed become critical. He who can mobilize faster will prevail. The slow nature of mobilization combines with its high costs to place a premium on the clarity and precision of a defender's threat perception as well as on his speed. Communicating one's possession of these abilities can be a difficult task indeed. Furthermore, there is a strong inducement for a challenger to manipulate the defender's perception of threat, even by resorting to repeated mobilizations. The relative skill in speedy mobilization and the relative economic and political ability to sustain the costs of repeated mobilizations greatly influence the long-term outcome of deterrence. As it takes only one successful deception to foil deterrence, its long-term prospects under such conditions seem unpromising. Moreover, the idea that costs can be cumulative suggests a challenger's policy akin to "controlled pressure," as described by George and Smoke.[38] It may be possible through a series of mobilizations to impose such costs on the defender that his valuation of the object decreases compared with his valuation of peace. Again, success depends on relative political-economic ability to sustain costs.

Because conventional power is expensive and additive, having allies may be critical to a defender's ability both to build and to field forces capable of executing his deterrent threats. Though it seems clear that, all things being equal, the side with more alliance assistance should prevail, use of alliances is not so simple. The basic ways to use allies are as sources of economic and material assistance in creating one's forces and for actual political and military support during a crisis. Mobilizing allies for general assistance gives a defender an image-projection problem. While he needs to impress his opponent with his strong relative capability and his willingness to absorb the costs of mobilization and conflict, he needs to convince allies, and especially patrons, of his relative weakness and need for assistance. Even in approaching an ally there may be contradictory requirements, for appearing too weak may convince an ally that he is not worth supporting. So it is again that structural factors intervene directly to impede clear, consistent common knowledge.

When allies are required or desired for assistance in combat or crisis, a number of interesting dynamics occur. A challenger's need for allies may provide the defender with excellent political and military opportunities to divide and conquer, such as bribing one or more of the

38. Ibid., pp. 543–47.

challenger's allies. The natural desire in alliance systems to transfer costs to other members makes this possible.[39]

A defender who needs allies for combat faces a formidable deterrence task. First, he should expect allies to attempt buck-passing, especially when, in a given confrontation, he is at direct risk but not they. This makes the credible projection of capability difficult. Second, his allies may be sufficiently engaged at one level of threat but not at others. This exacerbates the knowledge problem as allies bicker over the magnitude of threat. Because timing may be everything, a cunning challenger may be able to manipulate this argument until effective intervention is impossible. Third, a defender's ally may perceive the threat as benign, believing that mobilization of forces by the defender would only serve to actuate a spiral, causing gratuitous escalation. Pressure by such an ally may not only retard his own involvement in the confrontation but critically influence the defender's decisions as well, opening windows of opportunity for the challenger and undermining deterrence.

If a defender's deterrent threat is preemptive attack, then alliances again intrude to undermine credibility. Allies are reluctant to support, much less to participate in, a preemptive attack. To make matters worse, attacking the challenger may enable him to manipulate and activate his own alliances, turning a short-term loss to his long-run benefit. If both players share this understanding of the systemic constraints, a defender will suffer serious obstacles to establishing his credibility of will.

Instruments of Bargaining and Communication

One choice instrument of deterrence is escalation, for which a defender may have three possible purposes when challenged. The first is to demonstrate superiority or the ability to execute deterrent threats. The second is to engage his challenger's interests and perhaps to change them while signaling or explaining his own. The third is to introduce an independent risk of inadvertent escalation all the way to a mutually undesirable outcome—to deter through brinkmanship.

Escalation for demonstration has limited use, for it cannot completely escape the innate obstacles to the proper sharing of knowledge of relative power. A limited escalation may be too small, and hence not convincing, or it may reveal too much. A persuasive demonstration may *teach* as much as it frightens. These are limits to the upward convertibility of deterrence.

39. Posen, *Sources of Military Doctrine*, pp. 61–64.

The second potential purpose of escalation derives from two facts: that conventional force may be used for many purposes and a variety of objects, and that a conventional deterrence relationship is not inherently bilateral. For example, a challenger may engage a defender in violence to alter either relations between the challenger and a third country or his own internal politics. The defender faces a disconcerting deterrence problem because he has no direct access to the sources or objects of violence.[40] Unable to engage in object-denial, he must devise a punishment, a difficult task with conventional weapons, especially if the level of violence is low to begin with.

Under these circumstances, the defender can escalate to make the bilateral relationship central, or at least more important to the challenger. By escalating and engaging interests central to the challenger, and by demonstrating the strength of his own interests, the defender may change the challenger's calculus sufficiently to make him desist. Unfortunately, such escalation can be a double-edged sword, for there is no guarantee that the resulting balance of interests will be in the defender's favor. Also, depending on structural features, escalation may merely enable the challenger to mobilize allies or create support and order at home, further undermining deterrence.[41] An interesting possibility is that in such circumstances a defender's best option may be to drop deterrence by escalation and decide either to live with some violence or simply go to war.

The complex relationships I have been describing can be simplified through the instrument of brinkmanship. If an independent risk of inadvertent and uncontrollable escalation to something terrible can be created, then a symmetrical game of Chicken can be said to prevail, and there is some hope for deterrence. But the devices of probing, controlled pressure, and demonstration are all antithetical to loss of control. We are at the crux of the logic of conventional deterrence. Brinkmanship is a problematic instrument of conventional deterrence, for regardless of where the balance of interests lies, convincing an opponent that things may get out of hand can be difficult or impossible for two reasons. First, inadvertent escalation usually seems unlikely given the nature and reversibility of decisions about the mobilization and application of forces together with the time and labor implementation requires. Second, even where inadvertent escalation might be a convincing prospect, it may not appear headed for Armageddon. Thus, both the process and destination of inadvertent conventional escalation pose serious obstacles to successful brinkmanship.

40. A similar idea may be found in Lebow, "Deterrence Deadlock."
41. For a discussion of possible consequences of escalation, see Fred Charles Ikle, *Every War Must End* (New York, 1971), pp. 38–58.

I am not trying to argue that brinkmanship with conventional forces is impossible. Surely there are situations in which losing control of escalation to an exchange of lethal proportions is possible. A good example is the process of the outbreak of World War I. But note that this escalation occurred under special conditions: very large armies were mobilized, all of the participants believed in an offensive advantage, and few anticipated that the outcome would be as horrendous as it turned out to be.

Finally, if upward pressure of risk does not provide downward pressure on conflict, the implication is that deterrence convertibility from a high-level relationship to low-level conflict is inoperable. It also means that low-level conflict can stand on its own, with its own agendas, bargaining or substantive. Limited war may be just limited war and not necessarily a competition in risk taking.

A third instrument, a reputation for successful and highly damaging war fighting whenever challenged, would appear to be an alternative organizing and simplifying principle in a conventional world. Economic game theory argues that in situations of uncertainty, reputation may be an extremely efficacious deterrent. Scholars have suggested, for example, that in attempts by market incumbents to deter entry of new firms, inducing uncertainty and confusion can even enhance deterrence by reputation.[42] Schelling explores the idea of reputation in his discussion of the interconnectedness of commitments,[43] as does Glenn Snyder in *Deterrence and Defense.* For both writers, reputation, or "future deterrence," is an interest in itself in any present confrontation. Thus, reputation appears to have several sources of utility in a given crisis. Past behavior indicates a defender's level of interests and capabilities, compensating for the lack of detailed knowledge. At the same time, the very need to project reputation forward to the next crisis is itself an interest, and both sides expect it to be protected.

A number of deterrence theorists have questioned the practical utility of reputation. Jervis argues that, from a cognitive perspective, we simply do not know how reputations are made or decay.[44] If reputation is an interest, it must compete with other interests, attended by all the usual ambiguities and room for experimentation. Stephen Maxwell hits on the central problem of reputation when he argues that it is applicable only under conditions similar to those that produced it. In terms of

---

42. David M. Kreps and Robert Wilson, "Reputation and Imperfect Information," *Journal of Economic Theory* 27 (August 1982). A very accessible piece is Carl Shapiro and Steve Salop, "A Guide to Test Market Predation" (Princeton University, n.d.).

43. Schelling, *Arms and Influence,* pp. 55–59.

44. Jervis, "Deterrence and Perception."

game theory, Maxwell is saying that reputation in a repeated game depends precisely on its repetition. If the game changes from play to play, reputation for interest or ability in one variant is useless in others.[45] Yet my earlier discussion of conventional forces and structural asymmetries indicates that the game is indeed constantly changing, as technology and internal and external politics create and destroy pressures and opportunities.

Not only does the structure of a relationship undergo constant natural change, but the very engagements that produce reputation actually accelerate such dynamics. To establish a reputation for capability requires that relative superiority be established, in technological and doctrinal details. The very act of establishing such superiority—violent engagement—is also the first step in its own undermining. Every engagement is a lesson, instructing the challenger in his own and in the defender's relative strengths and weaknesses, suggesting ways to get around them in the next round.

A reputation for will is similarly difficult to maintain because of fatigue. The social, political, economic, and physical costs of applying force once may make it impossible or difficult to apply it again, at least soon. In the economic analogy an incumbent may be able to afford only one price war, so that having engaged in one successfully he is powerless to deter further entry in ensuing rounds.

To summarize, it is possible that reputation has value in overcoming barriers to common knowledge by allowing for some generalization, but only under proscribed conditions. It is not a panacea and does not constitute a conventional counterpart to the ubiquitous fear of total destruction in nuclear confrontations.

Spiraling and De-escalation

The general deterrence model suggested that not all confrontational situations are deterrent in nature and that there may be misplaced attempts to dissuade by threats, where reconciliation is relevant, leading to unnecessary spirals. This section explores the implications of conventional forces and deterrence for a strategy of de-escalation, the ability to identify situations where constructive appeasement is relevant, and the probability of pursuing such a policy.

The strategic relationship between any two states in the international system has been depicted as a Prisoners' Dilemma, in which the lack of confidence of each in the other's propensity to cooperate induces *both* to

45. Stephen Maxwell, *Rationality in Deterrence*, Adelphi Paper no. 50 (London, 1968).

adopt antagonistic postures. Both, as a result, are worse off than had they cooperated. Economic game theory provides a solution. It has been demonstrated that if identical confrontations between two adversaries are repeated a number of times, then even if knowledge is poorly shared, one party can induce cooperation by adopting a tit-for-tat strategy—appeasing when appeased, confronting when confronted.[46] In a sense this calls for development of a kind of reputation, which immediately suggests the limited applicability of this approach.

A possible escape from unnecessary and gratuitous spiraling is to engage in purely object denial or defensive threats. Surely this is a reasonable suggestion, but it faces a number of obstacles. A state's geostrategic situation may preclude a credible defensive threat. Also, it is not ostensibly clear what defensive forces look like. In the world of modern weaponry the greatest differentiation between offense and defense is in doctrine, not hardware, so how does one credibly project the possession of an exclusively defensive capability? This is not to say that it is absolutely impossible. Obviously Switzerland and Yugoslavia have devised unequivocally nonoffensive forces. But their forces are also *nondefensive*, rather, purely deterrent. The Swiss and Yugoslavs can neither deny entry to their countries nor threaten meaningful punishment. But they can (and do) threaten to make entry and especially occupation unbearable. Not all states can pursue such a policy, for its relevance depends on geography and topography, the relative sizes of the defender's population and the challenger's military, and the nature of the challenger and his interests.

Just as in some cases deterrent threats may be useless (e.g., when the challenger is an imperialist with superior forces or when the object of violence is not directly contested by both players) so may conciliation. Facing a hungry imperialist, a defender may not be capable of conceding enough. Where the defender simply does not possess the object of violence, there may be no meaningful concessions he can make.[47] There is an interesting, if perverse, implication to all this: escalation of conflict may raise the stakes for both players to the point where they are engaged in either a Prisoners' Dilemma, with some hope of cooperation, or perhaps even a symmetrical game of Chicken, where cooperation can be self-enforcing.

In a nuclear context a decision maker would prefer to err on the side of conciliation because the cost of misplaced deterrence could be glob-

46. David Kreps et al., "Rational Cooperation in the Finitely Repeated Prisoners' Dilemma Game," *Journal of Economic Theory* 27 (August 1982).

47. For a similar (if not identical) argument by a social psychologist, see Morton Deutsch, *The Resolution of Conflict: Constructive and Destructive Processes* (New Haven, Conn., 1977), p. 133.

icide. This calculus is not self-evident, however, in a conventional context. The difficulty of inflicting punishment, the reversibility of political decisions, and discrimination in applying forces may combine to suggest that the costs of unintended war could be less than the costs of unintended concessions, for example, loss of independence or the ability to protect it. In a world of poorly shared and uncertain information, a rational decision maker may prefer to err on the side of deterrent threats even should they lead to undesirable escalation or spiraling.

Earlier I suggested that in some circumstances neither deterrence nor despiraling are workable.[48] It is also possible for both to be relevant simultaneously, at different levels of a single bilateral relationship. Because levels of conventional violence can exist independently of each other, it may be possible to induce cooperation on one front without altering the overall relationship. Alternatively, it may be possible to deter at a low level of confrontation while pursuing detente or cooperation at a higher strategic plane.

A Conceptual Digression—Round Two: Redefining Deterrence and Success

Deterrence. In the nuclear environment, recall that deterrence was, conceptually, starkly different and separate from defense (or offense). In the conventional world of useful force, these distinctions blur. If in nuclear contexts different kinds of forces accomplish deterrence and defense, in conventional arenas these are the same forces exactly. A conventionally armed state does not have one army for engagements and another for threats. Furthermore, the deterrent instruments— escalation, brinkmanship, and reputation—are wielded through engagement. Feldman has called this creation of deterrence through engagement "active deterrence," breaking Snyder's barrier between deterrence for peacetime and defense for war.[49]

Distinguishing deterrence from compellence may be problematic if one is deterring a challenger from continuing or expanding something he is already doing. Schelling recognizes this ambiguity but offers no clear distinction.[50] There is none, I believe, especially if we allow for *active* deterrence. Also, because force is useful for many purposes and at different levels, at times simultaneously, a bilateral relationship may be

---

48. Jack Snyder argues that in some dilemmas neither works; see his "Perception and the Security Dilemma in 1914," in Robert Jervis, Richard Ned Lebow, and Janice Gross Stein, eds., *Psychology and Deterrence* (Baltimore, 1985).

49. Feldman, *Israeli Nuclear Deterrence*, p. 26.

50. Schelling, *Arms and Influence*, p. 77.

characterized simultaneously as compellent and deterrent. Schelling uses the example of the American blockade of Cuba, which set up a "tactical 'status quo'" and so made the American blockade an act of tactical deterrence within a context of strategic compellence.[51]

More important, in conventional settings it is not at all clear that deterrence is easier than compellence. If relationships are not necessarily dominated by the game of Chicken, then an aggressor's handicap should not hold. The status quo may be unclear, not agreed upon, and not strongly binding. Depending on relative interests and other structural features, one side may prevail in bargaining, but not necessarily the defender.

Success. In a world where probing and pressure are expected, in which reputations may have to be established physically and repeatedly, and where it may be possible to deter "actively," we lose interest in a binary success/failure concept, for all its simplicity. What appears to be a failure in the short run may sufficiently change the challenger's calculus in the long run to create long-standing successful deterrence. If limited war has meaning and not all violence is automatically escalatory and strategic, then challenge at a tactical level may reflect successful deterrence at a higher level, more important to the defender. Is this success or failure? Not every silence—if we assume aggressive designs—signifies success; it may simply camouflage active preparation for future aggression. Alternatively, extensive silence may *cause* interests to change, as the challenger becomes frustrated by the passage of time.[52]

Deterrence success (or failure) is thus a relative notion. Observing an apparent failure one should immediately seek accompanying successes. The critical questions to ask before assessing a deterrence outcome must be In what time frame? At what level? Before we turn to the operational questions on which to base a historical study of Israeli deterrence, table 1 summarizes the essential differences I have drawn between nuclear and conventional deterrence in the discussion to this point.

GUIDING QUESTIONS

The logic of conventional deterrence developed so far yields seven sets of questions or categories of analysis. The first three, each relating

---

51. Ibid.
52. On possible effects and uses of time provided by deterrence, see George and Smoke, *Deterrence in American Foreign Policy,* p. 5.

Table 1. Comparison of conventional and nuclear deterrence

Characteristic	Nuclear deterrence	Conventional deterrence
Mode of threat	Punishment (costs)	Object denial (and punishment)
Dimensions of threat credibility	Will	Will and skill
Structure of relationship	Symmetrical Bilateral Static Inescapably strategic Game of Chicken	Can be asymmetric Very susceptible to outside involvement Dynamic Can be nonstrategic May be any structure
Requirements of shared knowledge and importance of detail	Minimal, detail not important; desire to share critical knowledge	Maximal; detail critical; ambivalent desire to share critical knowledge
Convertibility and brinkmanship	Highly convertible between levels; brinkmanship effective	Convertibility and brinkmanship difficult; depend on specific structural characteristics
Deterrence-compellence (d-c)	Status quo clear; d-c easy to differentiate; compellence more difficult	Status quo not clear; d-c difficult to differentiate; compellence not clearly more difficult
Relevance of deterrence	Mutual fear of punishment dominates; deterrence always relevant	May or may not be, depending on structure of relationship
Success/failure	Clear, dichotomous	Not clear; dependent on time frame and level of analysis

to a different aspect of the structure of a relationship, concern the relative interests of defender and challenger, the constraints and possibilities that result from alliance and domestic politics, and the relative sources and expression of physical power. The analysis has suggested that structure may directly hinder deterrence or create ambiguities that undermine it and that to overcome these problems a defender can resort to escalation (for demonstration, manipulation, or brinkmanship) and reputation. This yields the two categories: brinkmanship and escalation, and reputation and knowledge. Analysis also suggested that deterrence is not applicable in all situations. The alternative is explored through the category of conciliation. Finally, the dependent variable, success, allows the exploration of the effects and implications of relativistic analysis. In applying these categories of questions to the case studies, I depart from this strict and logical ordering at one point to ensure continuity of discussion. The question of conciliation and de-escalation appears immediately after escalation and brinkmanship, and only then do I consider reputation and knowledge.

Here are the guiding questions in some detail:

1. *Relative interests.* This category is a natural starting point, for it asks the question What is the conflict about? More specifically of concern are these questions:
   a. Where and what is the challenger's object of violence?
   b. Are this object and its value to the challenger created outside his bilateral relationship with the defender? If so, what are the implications for deterrence?
   c. Is there any meaningful comparison of stakes? What insight is gained by ordering intrinsic versus power interests or by considering the relative vitalness of stakes? How does the deterrence-compellence ordering fare in explaining deterrence outcomes?

2. *Political asymmetries.* Once we have established the source and nature of the desire for violence and the relative stakes (or interest), with this category we consider the structural effects on real and perceived possibilities for, and proscriptions of, violent or other strategic action on both sides.
   a. The international system
      (1) What are the effects of each actor's alliance systems on his (and his opponent's) ability to mobilize and use force? How do these affect the acceptable level and nature of force application (e.g., for punishment, preemption)?
      (2) Are the players capable of manipulating each other's alliances? To what effect on deterrence?

[28]

       (3) What are the implications of the nature of the alliance systems and the dependence on them for the ability to project and perceive accurately?
   b. Domestic or internal factors
       (1) How do differences in domestic politics, society, and culture influence the ability and freedom to use force and sustain costs?
       (2) What effects on deterrence do differences in political-military culture, accountability, or attitudes to truth have?

3. *Power asymmetries.* This category encompasses questions of putative and actualized power and of the real and perceptual effects—simple, contradictory, or combining—of:
   a. Relative size
   b. Requirements of and for mobilization
   c. Economic constraints on frequency and length of mobilization
   d. Dependence on specific strategies: defense, offense, preemption
   e. Relative physical ability to inflict punishment
   f. Geographic dispositions[53]

4. *Escalation and brinkmanship*
   a. Is the manipulation of shared risk attempted by the defender, and to what effect? What are the limits to downward convertibility?
   b. Does the defender attempt to engage his challenger's central interests by escalating? Does he escalate to demonstrate will or skill? To what effect? What are the limits to upward convertibility?

5. *Conciliation and deterrence*
   a. Is despiraling or appeasement attempted? What limits to its relevance are imposed by the structural characteristics uncovered above?
   b. Is there simultaneous deterrence and despiraling at different levels?

6. *Reputation and knowledge*
   a. Where deterrence succeeds, how detailed is the shared knowledge? Where it fails, would improvement of detailed knowledge have improved deterrence?

---

53. Physical and political asymmetries are not mutually independent and may have contradictory and compounding effects on deterrence. In the extreme, the compounding may be highly injurious to deterrence, for example, when the physical constraints dictate preemption, whereas alliance building requires appeasement.

    b. How successful are attempts to create credibility through repu-
       tation? What are the obstacles to creation of "generalized"
       knowledge?
7. *Success or failure.* Naturally, for each crisis we consider the question
   Was deterrence successful? and we try out relative notions:
    a. Can actively created deterrence be considered success-through-
       failure?
    b. What is the effect on the assessment of success or failure of
       looking at different possible levels of challenge and of consider-
       ing different time frames?

CHOICE OF CASES IN THE MIDDLE EAST

Before we proceed, it is necessary to anticipate one important question: Is the Middle East really a nonnuclear environment? I argue that it
is "essentially conventional," that the intrusion of nuclear weapons has
not upset the conventional nature of the prevailing deterrence logic.
Certainly until the early 1960s neither the Arab countries nor Israel had
nuclear weapons. Since then Israel has become "ambiguously nuclear,"
either possessing an option to become nuclear or else having a "bomb in
the basement." But Yigal Allon's statement in 1965 still reflects Israel's
declared nuclear policy: "Israel will not be the first to introduce nuclear
weapons into the Middle East. May I add that Israel will not permit any
of its neighbours to start this destructive race."[54] Israel's neighbors have
remained unambiguously nonnuclear. Let us, then, first examine the
basic reasoning of deterrence between nuclear and nonnuclear states
and then observe this logic at work in the Middle East before I present
my cases and the rationale for their selection.

Deterrence of a conventional challenger by a nuclear state is surely
influenced by fear of escalation to the point where nuclear weapons
might be used. But the relationship is not necessarily Chicken dominated, for it lacks much of the inescapable upward pressure of mutual
nuclear escalation that so dampens *any* violence. The nuclear state has
no fear of sustaining a nuclear first strike and so is under no pressure to

---

54. Quoted in Fuad Jabber, *Israel and Nuclear Weapons: Present Options and Future Strategies* (London, 1971), p. 122. For other studies of Israeli nuclear development and policy,
see Alan Dowty, "Israel and Nuclear Weapons," *Midstream* 22 (November 1976); Feldman, *Israeli Nuclear Deterrence;* Yair Evron, "Israel and the Atom: The Uses and Misuses of
Ambiguity," *Orbis* 17 (Winter 1974); idem, "The Relevance and Irrelevance of Nuclear
Options in Conventional Wars: The 1973 October War," *Jerusalem Journal of International
Relations* 7, nos. 1–2 (1984).

deliver one itself. This in turn frees the conventional state to act, so long as the action does not endanger the defender's existence, and possibly even if it does, by using "salami tactics."

In such a one-sided confrontation, an important determinant of escalating pressure to use nuclear weapons is the conventional security margin of the nuclear state. As long as neither its survival nor its nuclear force are endangered, it has every incentive not to escalate into nuclear threats or action. Historically, conventional states confronting nuclear ones have appeared to understand this. Both the Soviet Union and the People's Republic of China basically ignored, or at least belittled, the role of nuclear weapons in their relations with the United States in the years before they themselves became nuclear powers.[55]

In the Middle East, Israel has tried to do everything possible to keep the conflict within the realm of conventional warfare through a highly ambiguous declaratory policy and by trying to maintain wide conventional security margins. Israel's refusal to admit to the possession of nuclear weapons, to make explicit threats, or to develop a doctrine can be seen as an attempt to widen the apparent margins. Israel is thereby saying, in effect, that it does not depend on nuclear weapons for its security. The result may be a severe credibility problem for her covert nuclear threats. To the natural uncertainty as to whether she would actually ever *use* nuclear weapons is added the uncertainty as to whether she even *has* them, as Feldman has noted.[56]

So much for words. In action Israel has created extremely wide conventional security margins. The way in which she has done this should (a) create a wide area in which conventional logic dominates and (b) further undermine the credibility of nuclear threats, feeding back to (a). Israel's visible strategic doctrine is entirely conventional in nature. Its idiom is dominated by phrases such as "quantitative balance," "preemptive counterattack," "speed of mobilization," and "secure borders."

Perhaps the most extreme manifestation of this orientation is the insistence on a quantitative conventional balance. Israel has devoted about one-third of GNP to the pursuit of size, despite the tremendous

55. On the apparent lack of concern among Soviet leaders around the end of World War II, see John Lewis Gaddis, *The United States and the Origins of the Cold War, 1941–1947* (New York, 1972), pp. 244–46. For the early Chinese response to American nuclear power, see Lawrence Freedman, *The Evolution of Nuclear Strategy* (New York, 1983), pp. 274–82.

56. Feldman, *Israeli Nuclear Deterrence*, p. 10. On the problem of covert or ambiguous threats, see also Shlomo Aronson, "The Nuclear Dimension of the Arab-Israeli Conflict: The Case of the Yom Kippur War," *Jerusalem Journal of International Relations* 7, nos. 1–2 (1984): 110–11.

political, social, and economic costs of doing so. The willingness to do so must mean one or more of the following: (a) Israel has no nuclear weapons, (b) Israel does not believe in their deterrent power, or (c) Israel is deliberately widening the margin for conventional action.

Israeli and Egyptian behavior and reasoning surrounding the Yom Kippur War are most telling in this respect.[57] Declaratory policy on both sides between 1967 and 1973 was completely devoid of references to Israeli nuclear weapons. Israeli reasoning before October 1973 follows conventional logic. The Israeli estimate that the probability of an Egyptian attack was essentially zero rested on factors like the Suez Canal barrier, the Sinai buffer, and Israel's conventional reputation of 1967. Most important, Israeli Defense Forces (IDF) Intelligence *did* predict a general Egyptian attack in 1975–76, when Egypt was expected to have acquired medium-range bombers.

Reasoning on the Egyptian side was apparently just as "conventional." Yair Evron writes that if nuclear weapons were "present" in the Egyptian calculus, they were marginal and essentially irrelevant. Despite the ten-division army at their disposal, the Egyptian military elite was pessimistic about achieving even minimal objectives. In convincing the army of the possibility of a successful attack, Sadat had to fire his minister of war and replace him with Ahmad Isma'il Ali. As far as we can tell, the Egyptian fears were rooted in the conventional balance. Their final war plan reflected the belief that all they could really hope to accomplish was a canal crossing and acquisition of a narrow strip on the east bank.

In considering how to overcome Israeli capabilities—the relevant details of her deterrent threats—the Egyptians concentrated on the specifics of her conventional security doctrine: air superiority, mobile warfare, technological superiority. In the various Egyptian accounts there is not a word about Israel's nuclear capability and how to overcome it, despite the fact that the Egyptians considered their challenge to be strategic, if not a threat to Israel's existence.

Since 1973 Israel has continued to do everything in her power to keep the Middle East conventional. With her major current opponent, Syria, Israel maintains wide conventional margins in both territory and force size. Israel has also made clear that she still means the second part of Allon's statement—by destroying the Osiraq nuclear reactor in 1981.

I have singled out three cases of conflict and crisis in which Israel felt it necessary to deter further aggression:

57. The following discussion of the Yom Kippur War is based on these sources: Evron, "Relevance and Irrelevance"; Haim Herzog, *The War of Atonement: October 1973* (Boston, 1975), chaps. 1, 3, 4.

1. Fedayeen infiltration from Jordan, 1953–54;
2. Harassment from Egypt, 1953–56, including:
   a. Fedayeen infiltration from the Gaza Strip, and
   b. direct Egyptian harassment in the form of military violence, 1954–56, and commercial blockade of sea (and then air) traffic between Israel's southern port and Africa and Asia; and
3. The Egyptian-Israeli War of Attrition, 1967–70.

These cases may strike the reader as obscure, my reasons for choosing such low-level and protracted violence less than evident. One reason is precisely that they *are* obscure. Because one of my purposes is to contribute to the history of Israeli deterrence, the events of these periods are important yet understudied. As an integral part of Israel's defense experience, they need to be brought into the Israeli security debate.

A second reason is my interest in relativistic notions of deterrence success; the study of protracted conflict allows experimentation with varying time frames of analysis, and the fluctuating intensity of violence within each period permits consideration of the effects of level of violence. Also, by following the unfolding of protracted conflict and crisis, one hopes to observe processes of escalation, brinkmanship, and demonstration as well as the effects of structural changes.

These periods of protracted low-level violence naturally sat between Israel's more widely recognized large engagements, making it possible to examine the effects of large wars on subsequent low-level conflict, and vice versa. Effects of the 1948 War of Independence will be important to the analysis of events of the early 1950s, which in turn have a role in explaining the 1956 Sinai Campaign. Similarly, the War of Attrition is inseparable from the Six Day War before it and the Yom Kippur War that followed. And so my approach, rather than ignoring the larger wars, views them in a nontraditional perspective. Now, the historical analysis.

[2]

Infiltration from
Jordan, 1953–1954

Israel's War of Independence ended without an ending, with a truce instead of peace, along armistice demarcation lines in place of borders (map 1). Some five hundred thousand refugees fled to the Jordanian side of the frontier, leaving communities split and farmers separated from their land and property. In Gaza there were some two hundred thousand refugees; but wherever they were, the Palestinian people felt betrayed. Five Arab armies had been defeated in "The Catastrophe," a defeat to be avenged. Despite fading hopes for a real peace, Israel launched into nation building, massive immigrant absorption, and settlement. She needed both recognized borders that would assure territorial integrity and the freedom to pursue commercial maritime traffic to Asia and Africa through the Red Sea. Achieving these was to prove, alas, no mean feat.

Immediately after the armistice agreements in 1949, there began a period of so-called innocent infiltration, in which refugees or villagers in the West Bank would cross the frontiers into Israel for family reunions, smuggling, or theft. By 1953 infiltration from Jordan had grown in volume, changed in character, and become more politically motivated. It aimed at murder, terror, and sabotage. In mid-1954, as the Jordanian frontier fell silent, infiltration on the Egyptian front, mostly from Gaza, also became political in motivation, but with a critical difference: first questionably, by 1955 without doubt, the activities from Egypt were directed by the Egyptian army, which also added army regulars to the Fedayeen (as the marauders were then called) and small-scale military incidents to the infiltration.

Throughout this period, Israel had to contend with the ever-tightening Egyptian blockade of her maritime access to Africa and Asia through

1. The State of Israel, 1949–1967

the Red Sea. At first it was limited to passage through the Suez Canal. In late 1953 the Egyptians expanded it to include passage from Eilat through the Straits of Tiran, and in 1955 to include air passage as well. The saga of harassment and blockade ended with the Sinai Campaign of 1956.

Statistics may convey a sense of the problem as felt by the Israelis at the time. For example, table 2 contains the figures on civilian casualties Ben-Gurion presented to the Knesset in 1956. The magnitude and trend of the challenge, the predominant importance of these two frontiers, and the changing weight between them are all clear from these figures. Not shown in this table is the large resurgence of activity from Jordan in 1956. Counting incidents (rather than casualties), the Israelis claim 11,650 related to infiltration between 1949 and the Sinai Campaign.[1]

To most countries, perhaps, such low-level harassment would not have seemed the strategic challenge Israelis took it to be. Yigal Allon revealed Israelis' fears of both personal and national consequences when he listed the perpetrators' goals:

1. Prevent the freezing of the status quo, keeping the Palestine question open,
2. maintain perpetual warfare between the 1948 War and the war of revenge, which would surely come,
3. discourage foreign investment and tourism in Israel,
4. undermine the endurance of frontier settlements, especially those settled by new immigrants,[2]
5. force Israel to allocate scarce resources to "current security" instead of to "basic security,"[3] and
6. inflict immediate costs, pain and damage.[4]

Because of its small size and long, meandering border, Israel could not consider infiltration to be merely frontier warfare or an isolated problem of frontier security. In 1955, Moshe Dayan described the problem as follows:

1. Walter Eytan, *The First Ten Years: A Diplomatic History of Israel* (New York, 1958), pp. 108–9.

2. A description of Ben-Gurion's reaction to an attack on such a village, Patish, may be found in Michael Bar-Zohar, *Ben-Gurion* (in Hebrew) (Tel-Aviv, 1977), pt. 3, pp. 1139–40.

3. For a discussion of the distinction, see Shimon Peres, *Hashlav haba* [The next phase] (Tel-Aviv, 1965), pp. 9–15. The Israeli term *current security* refers to the realm of everyday security problems such as terrorism or state belligerence that do not pose a general threat to the state or to its existence.

4. My translation of Yigal Allon, *Massakh shel Khol* [Curtain of sand] (Tel-Aviv, 1959), pp. 17–18. All translations from the Hebrew are mine unless otherwise noted.

Table 2. Israeli civilian casualties caused by infiltrators, 1951–1955

Year	Country or origin		All fronts
	Jordan	Egypt	
1951	111	—	137
1952	111	—	147
1953	124	26	162
1954	117	50	180
1955	37	192	258

Seven years after its War of Independence the State of Israel still faces a security problem of unusual complexity. The area of the country is only 8,100 square miles. But owing to the configuration of its territory there are 400 miles of frontier. Three-quarters of the population of Israel lives in the coastal plain, running from north of Haifa to south of Tel-Aviv, with a slender salient branching off to Jerusalem. This densely settled area has an average width of no more than twelve miles between the Mediterranean and the Jordanian border. From the Israel Parliament buildings in Jersualem the armed sentries of the Jordanian Arab Legion can be seen a few hundred yards away. The headquarters of the Israel General Staff in the coastal plain are within clear view of the hills which mark the Jordan frontier. The country's main roads are exposed to swift and easy incursion. Scarcely anywhere in Israel can a man live or work beyond the easy range of enemy fire. Indeed, except in the Negev, no settlement is at a distance of more than 20 miles from an Arab frontier.

Thus the term "frontier security" has little meaning in the context of Israel's geography. The entire country is a frontier, and the whole rhythm of national life is affected by any hostile activity from the territory of neighboring states.[5]

The raiding and sabotage created or enforced an existential crisis, for they appeared to be proof of the Arab intent to destroy the state. Speaking to the Knesset in 1956, Ben-Gurion stated, "I have discussed in detail the 'small war' of our neighbors not only because of its own seriousness, but because it is an organic part of the systematic and unceasing program of violence directed by the Arab rulers, aimed at destroying Israel and undermining her very existence, without having to risk (yet) a frontal attack."[6] Harassment, then, was the continuation

5. Moshe Dayan, "Israel's Border and Security Problems," Foreign Affairs 33 (January 1955): 250.

6. Quoted in David Ben-Gurion, Yechud ve-Ye'ud [Uniqueness and destiny] (Tel-Aviv, 1972), pp. 232–33. Also, Nadav Safran, From War to War: The Arab-Israeli Confrontation, 1948–1967 (New York, 1969), p. 43; Michael Brecher, Decisions in Israel's Foreign Policy (New Haven, Conn., 1975), p. 261; Earl Berger, The Covenant and the Sword: Arab-Israeli

of war by other means, and it was imperative for Israel to dissuade her opponents from expanding or escalating—indeed continuing—their warlike acts.

The main instrument Israel used to deter further harassment on and through her frontiers was the military reprisal (table 3), which Barry Blechman defines in the context of Israeli policy as "the use of force by a nation, without the intent of occupying territory other than as required to complete the immediate application of force, in response to acts or omissions on the part of another state, with a view toward causing the cessation of such acts or omissions in an indirect manner."[7] Reprisal is a classic form of active deterrence aimed at bringing ongoing challenges to a stop through the *creation* of deterrence within a crisis. Reprisals may be used to demonstrate overall strategic superiority, to actuate a brink-manship relationship, or simply to inflict pain and costs on the challenger.

Actually, in the early years—mostly before 1953—Israeli reprisals were also intended to coerce directly the infiltrators and the villagers who harbored them, as much as the host states themselves. In 1954–56, chiefly in Gaza, the purpose was to deter Egypt from sending Fedayeen and from instigating direct military clashes with Israeli forces.

Why, we ask, did Israel choose this approach? Why not defense? Why not war? For all the strategic problems posed by infiltration and harassment, Israeli leaders did not see the challenge as a direct or immediate threat to Israel's existence that could take precedence over all domestic development goals or justify ignoring foreign policy con-straints imposed by outside powers. Even Ben-Gurion, looking back, had to admit that "frontier skirmishes are not war."[8] But if they were not war, and Israel had to prepare vigilantly for the real "second round," then she could not afford to turn her army into a police force. Dayan and Shimon Peres both strongly believed that, especially given the configuration of the frontier, to try to police it would be both futile and a strategic error.[9] Israel therefore devised the reprisal, to operate, according to Dayan, on the following principles:

Relations, 1948–56 (London, 1965), p. 207; Eedson L. M. Burns, *Between Arab and Israeli* (New York, 1963), p. 61.

7. Barry M. Blechman, "The Consequences of the Israeli Reprisals: An Assessment" (Ph.D. diss., Georgetown University, 1971), p. 54.

8. David Ben-Gurion, *Israel: Years of Challenge* (New York, 1963), p. 90. See also his statement to the Knesset, in *Divrei ha-Knesset* [Proceedings of the Knesset], 15 October 1956.

9. Peres, *Hashlav haba*, p. 10; Moshe Dayan, "Pe'ulot Tsva'iyot bi-Ymei Shalom" [Military actions in times of peace], *Maarachot* 118–19 (May 1959). *Maarachot* is an IDF journal that serves, inter alia, as a forum for the exchange of ideas among officers on questions of policy, doctrine, and technology.

Table 3. Israeli reprisals in Jordan and Egypt, 1953–1956

In Egypt			In Jordan		
Date	Location	Arab casualties (killed/total)	Date	Location	Arab casualties (killed/total)
			1/1/53	Budrus	*
			1/25/53	Falameh	3/15
			1/28/53	Rantiss	*
			2/21/53	Kh. el Deir	0/1
			3/9/53	Nazlet Issa	0/3
			5/17/53	Beit Serra	1/4
			5/18–5/21/53	Several locations	*
			5/28/53	Dawayima	*
			6/12/53	Kh. Beit Evin	1/2
			7/20/53	Nahleen	2/2
			8/11/53	Idna	*
8/29/53	el-Bureij	20/82			
			10/15/53	Qibya	66/75
			11/2/53	Budrus	*
			12/18/53	Hebron	1/1
			12/21/53	Turqumiya	0/1
			3/29/54	Nahleen	9/28
4/3/54	Gaza	3/6			
			4/7/54	Hussan	*
			5/9/54	Kh. Ilin	*
			5/27/54	Kh. Jinba	4/4
			6/28/54	Azzoun	4/7
			8/1/54	Jenin	1/3
			8/14/54	Sh. Madhkur	1/2
8/15/54	Bir es Safa	1/1			
			8/30/54	Kh. Sikka	1/4
			9/2/54	Beit Liqya	2/10
2/28/55	Gaza	39/71			
5/19/55	Gaza Strip	—			
5/21/55	Gaza Strip	1/8			
9/1/55	Khan Yunis	25/54			
10/28/55	Kuntilla	12/46			
11/2/55	Sabha	50/?/50 prisoners			
4/5/56	Gaza	59/152			
8/17/56	Gaza Strip	1/10			
8/31/56	Gaza Strip	13/16			
			9/11/56	Rahwa	20/23
9/12/56	Sinai	5/6			
			9/13/56	Gharandal	11/17
			9/26/56	Hussan	39/50
			10/11/56	Qalqilya	48/71

Source: Mainly Barry M. Blechman, "The Consequences of the Israeli Reprisals: An Assessment" (Ph.D. diss., Georgetown University, 1971), tables 4, 7; also Zeev Schiff and Eitan Haber, eds., *Lexikon le-Bitahon Yisrael* (Tel-Aviv, 1976); Moshe Dayan, *Avnei Derekh* (Tel-Aviv, 1976), pp. 111–15.
*No casualties reported.

We cannot guard every water pipeline from explosion and every tree from uprooting. We cannot prevent every murder of a worker in an orchard or a family in their beds.

But it is in our power to set a high price on our blood, a price too high for the Arab community, the Arab army, or the Arab government to think it worth paying.

We can see to it that the Arab villages oppose the raiding bands that pass through them, rather than give them assistance. It is in our power to see that Arab military commanders prefer a strict performance of their obligation to police the frontiers rather than suffer defeat in clashes with our units.[10]

When infiltration or violence was supported or instigated by Arab states, reprisals were to operate as follows:

We can cause the Arab governments to renounce a "policy of strength" towards Israel by turning it into a demonstration of weakness.

The decision not to get into quarrels with Israel will come only if the Arabs have reason to suppose that otherwise they will have to reckon with sharp reactions from our side and be dragged into a conflict in which they would be the losers.[11]

This last statement reveals a number of important ideas that motivated Israel's reprisal policy. Latent force together with the prospect of being "dragged" evoke the idea of brinkmanship. Giving the Arabs "reason to suppose" suggests using reprisals for demonstration. Thus, the policy could introduce a fear of escalation and, at the same time, indicate the nature of the destination: "a conflict in which they would be the losers." Ben-Gurion's biographer Michael Bar-Zohar describes the former's approach to reprisal as desiring just enough escalation to dissuade the Egyptians from undertaking violence at any level: classic escalation for de-escalation.[12] Finally, to the message of latent force was added its conditional use. Reprisals were basically applied in a tit-for-tat manner, demonstrating that the challenger could control his own punishment and incorporating the promise of exchanging "no pain" for "no harassment."[13]

10. From a lecture by Dayan to a group of officers. The translation is from "Why Israel Strikes Back," in Donald Robinson, ed., *Under Fire: Israel's Twenty Year Struggle for Survival* (New York, 1968), pp. 122–23. See also Burns, *Between Arab and Israeli*, p. 58.

11. Dayan, "Why Israel Strikes Back," p. 123.

12. Bar-Zohar, *Ben-Gurion*, pt. 3, p. 1137; Michael I. Handel, *Israel's Political-Military Doctrine*, Occasional Papers in International Affairs No. 30 (Cambridge, Mass., 1973), p. 23; Dayan, "Pe'ulot Tsva'iyot bi-Ymei Shalom"; Horowitz, *Hatfisa ha-Yisraelit shel Bitachon Leumi*, pp. 14–22.

13. Shlomo Aronson and Dan Horowitz, "Ha-Estrategiya shel Tagmul Mevukar: Ha-Dugmah ha-Yisraelit" [The strategy of controlled reprisal: The Israeli example], *Medinah, Memshal ve-Yakhasim Bein-Leumim* 1 (1971): 78–79.

Although this entire period of infiltration could be viewed as one major crisis, it serves my purpose to analyze the events as two exercises in deterrence, as two separate cases, the Jordan experience here, the deterrence relationship with Egypt in the next chapter. Because the crises were complex and extended in time, a reconstruction of the history of events precedes analysis of those events in terms of the framework developed in Chapter 1.

A History

In the course of the 1948 war the Hashemite Kingdom tripled its population, adding to four hundred thousand East Bankers some one million Palestinians on the West Bank, half of them refugees and the other half villagers and townspeople, all of dubious loyalty to Amman. The first years of nation building were to prove a difficult balancing act. The young monarch Hussein had simultaneously to integrate and control the West Bank, in a polity susceptible to pressure and undermining by Egypt and Syria. Jordan was small, weak, and poor compared with her neighbor, Israel, and throughout the first decade of her independent existence she held on obstinately to the one straw that could pull her through these troubled waters: Great Britain.[14]

Throughout 1952, Jordanian policy toward pacification of the Israeli frontier was ambivalent. Officially Amman opposed infiltration, but neither Jordan nor Israel seemed to treat the situation as one of high conflict, and Jordan did little enforcement. Israel resorted to small-scale retaliatory raids that inflicted but minor damage, and Jordan insisted that border supervision be treated as a local, "police" affair.[15] The Jordan-Israel Mixed Armistice Commission (MAC) was the source of much attempted cooperation on border problems, for example, the successful decentralization and coordination of border supervision by the establishment of Local Commanders' Agreements (LCAs).[16] Such cooperation was often vetoed by Amman.

14. P. J. Vatikiotis, *Politics and the Military in Jordan: A Study of the Arab Legion 1921–1957* (London, 1967), pp. 9, 80. For a discussion of the difficulties of integration and foreign intrusion, see Shaul Mishal, "Conflictual Pressures and Cooperative Interests: Observations on West Bank-Amman Relations, 1949–1967," in Joel S. Migdal, ed., *Palestinian Society and Politics* (Princeton, N.J., 1980); John Baggot Glubb, *A Soldier with the Arabs* (London, 1957), pp. 216–17. For a general overview of the problems of integration, see Aqil Hyder Hasan Abidi, *Jordan: A Political Study, 1948–1957* (New York, 1965), chaps. 3–6.

15. Berger, *Covenant and the Sword*, p. 86.

16. For the success of the early LCAs, see Elmo H. Hutchison, *Violent Truce: A Military Observer Looks at the Arab-Israeli Conflict, 1951–1955* (New York, 1956), pp. 18, 102. Hutchison was observer and then chief of the Israel-Jordan MAC from summer 1953 until November 1954.

[41]

Toward the end of 1952, as "innocent" infiltration decreased and politically organized or motivated infiltration began in earnest, the Jordanian government publicly renounced any responsibility for "civilian" activities from across its frontiers and stated that these would no longer serve as legitimate issues for consideration by the MAC.[17] Israel withdrew from the LCAs in January of 1953, where this case study begins.

January–October 1953

By January 1953 serious infiltration was in full swing, as a glance at table 4 will confirm. Incidents included derailment of a train, slaying of Israeli soldiers and policemen, murder of villagers and farmers, and attacks on homes, all in the coastal plain and often quite near Tel-Aviv. There were also a small number of direct clashes between Israeli and Jordanian forces, most notably a shoot-out in Jerusalem in April.[18]

Israel simultaneously pursued three different policies aimed at reducing or stopping harassment from across the border. One was a direct appeal to the Western powers and Turkey to try and influence the Jordanian government.[19] At the same time United Nations Truce Supervisory Organization (UNTSO) Chief of Staff Riley appealed through the Security Council in an attempt to involve the powers.[20] Neither appeal elicited a meaningful response.

The second policy tool—applied twice—was a vague threat of invasion of all or part of the West Bank. In February the Israeli government was pressured domestically to undertake military action. In June, despite renewal of the LCAs, a rise in infiltration and attacks on Israeli villages caused Israel to reconsider partial invasion and occupation. This Israeli threat again coincided with attempts by Riley to convene high-level talks between Israel and Jordan. The latter flatly refused.

Jordan's response to Israel's intimations of invasion was to invoke the Anglo-Jordanian defense treaty, which she did both in February and June.[21] British response rendered this Israeli policy at least partially successful. Having no interest in getting involved in a Middle East war,

17. On the changing mixture of economic and political infiltration, see Glubb, *Soldier with the Arabs*, p. 316; Berger, *Covenant and the Sword*, p. 89; Ehud Ya'ari, *Mitsrayim veha-Fedayeen, 1953–1956* [Egypt and the Fedayeen, 1953–1956] (Givat Haviva, 1975), pp. 9–11.

18. For descriptions of some incidents, see *New York Times*, 2, 3 February, 11 March, 9, 10 April, 19 May, 10, 14 June, 19 September 1953. Also, Glubb, *Soldier with the Arabs*, p. 304; Berger, *Covenant and the Sword*, p. 93.

19. *New York Times*, 10 April 1953; Berger, *Covenant and the Sword*, pp. 92–93.

20. Rosalyn Higgins, *United Nations Peace-Keeping 1946–1967: Documents and Commentary: The Middle East* (London, 1969), pp. 167–68; *New York Times*, 12 May 1953.

21. *New York Times*, 5, 6 February 1953; Berger, *Covenant and the Sword*, p. 94.

Table 4. Infiltration incidents originating from Jordan and Egypt, 1949–1956

		Number of incidents	
Time period		Originating from Jordan	Originating from Egypt
July–December	1949	1	0
January–June	1950	3	1
July–December	1950	0	0
January–June	1951	5	2
July–December	1951	2	1
January–June	1952	5	2
July–December	1952	1	2
January–June	1953	37	1
July–December	1953	29	2
January–June	1954	45	17
July–December	1954	7	100
January–March	1955	8	62
April–June	1955	6	13
July–September	1955	4	25
October–December	1955	12	5
January–March	1956	9	18
April–June	1956	24	76
July–September	1956	19	17
October–December	1956	52	16

Source: Barry M. Blechman, "The Consequences of the Israeli Reprisals: An Assessment" (Ph.D. diss., Georgetown University, 1971), tables 3 and 5.

London promised to uphold the treaty and, at the same time, urged Jordan to find ways to ease tensions.[22] On 30 June, Jordan formally agreed to high-level talks and to clamp down on infiltration.[23] July witnessed a decline in the number of incidents, which then rose again steeply in August, September, and October.

The third, and central, deterrent instrument was the reprisal raid. Over the nine-month period, Israel carried out some ten raids against Jordanian hamlets or villages. The Israelis did not respond immediately to incidents of infiltration but waited instead for accumulations of infringements. Then they would raid villages close to the points of crossing, on the assumption that they had harbored infiltrators and their equipment.[24] The actual perpetrators were virtually never punished

22. *New York Times*, 6 February 1953.
23. See a report by Riley's successor, Bennike, S/3047 of 30 June 1953, in Higgins, *United Nations Peace-Keeping*, p. 168.
24. Moshe Brilliant, "Israel's Policy of Reprisals," *Harper's Magazine* 210 (March 1955); Blechman, "Consequences of the Israeli Reprisals," pp. 76, 137–38; Handel, *Israel's Political-Military Doctrine*, pp. 21–22.

because politically motivated infiltration normally originated in the refugee camps (away from the frontier) and was financed and organized
abroad. For the particular hamlet or village suffering a retaliatory raid,
the experience was a discrete offensive and belligerent act because
almost no village was attacked more than once. Israeli reprisals at the
time were small and generally unsuccessful in military terms. Executing
units were normally squads; these, though at times reaching company
size, managed to inflict only a small number of casualties. In at least four
instances the raiding unit failed to achieve its mission, being outfought
by small numbers of local National Guard militiamen.[25]

In one failure, during the night of 25 January, a company led by a
batallion commander on a mission to destroy houses in Falameh (map
2) was turned back by a small number of local riflemen. The same
happened at Rantiss on 28 January. During the nights of 18 through
21 May, paratroopers were to penetrate the villages of Hussan and
Midyah. In Hussan they were kept out of the village by a few local
fighters. At Midyah they succeeded in entering the village but could not
complete the mission and so fired at the local herd instead![26] Signifi-
cantly, these and other Israeli failures did not go unnoticed by the
Jordanian Arab Legion, as its British commander John Baggot Glubb
points out.[27] They greatly worried the IDF and led to the formation of
the "101" commando unit, whose mission became the execution of
more professional reprisals by larger squads.

Despite Jordan's official agreement in June to arrest infiltration, a
drop in July was followed by serious resurgence between August and
October. Except for one minor and one unsuccessful raid in August,
Israel did nothing, diplomatic or by force, during the period. There is no
record of appeals to outside powers, maneuvers at the MAC, or reprisals of any kind. Why? Unfortunately, there is no discussion of this
"fact" on record. It may have been an experiment in despiraling. We
know that Prime Minister Moshe Sharett in general supported the idea
of giving the Jordanians an opportunity to learn to control their side of
the border.[28] An alternative explanation is that when the IDF decided to
establish Unit 101, after another failure on 11 August at Idna, they also

---

25. The feeling of frustration in the general staff was apparently quite acute, as described to me by Gen. (Res.) Elad Peled, then operations officer of the Southern Command. (Interviewed in Jerusalem, 18 November 1984.)

26. These examples are from Moshe Dayan, *Avnei Derekh* [The story of my life] (Tel-
Aviv, 1976), pp. 111–15.

27. Glubb, *Soldier with the Arabs*, p. 302.

28. For example, Moshe Sharett, *Yoman Ishi* [Personal diary], vol. 1 (Tel-Aviv, 1978),
p. 250.

2. Central Israel and the West Bank, 1949–1967

decided to defer reprisals until the unit was ready for action. Six weeks to organize a new unit may be reasonable.

On the Jordanian side we note that Glubb identified the summer of 1953 as the real turning point in the nature of infiltration. By his analysis:

> In the summer of 1953, however, appeared a new feature—infiltrators who went only to kill. The new pattern gradually became apparent. Infiltration for stealing had been greatly reduced by the activities of the Jordanian police and troops. Now, at occasional intervals, two or three Arabs would appear in Israel and shoot one or two people at night, or throw a hand grenade into a window. These parties were all armed with new Sten guns and hand grenades. The tactics they used were always the same. A new factor had obviously appeared.
>
> Investigation soon revealed the identity of the new movement. It originated with a group of refugees in Damascus, all of them former terrorists employed by the Mufti in Palestine. The Saudian Arabian government was arming and subsidizing these men to infiltrate through Jordan into Israel and kill Jews.[29]

There is obviously room for argument about the timing, and other sources have claimed that the real change took place in January. But it is clearly possible that the foreign-directed and foreign-based operations improved and increased, reaching a certain scale and proficiency by the summer. If Glubb is more or less correct, then the events of the summer may be attributable not to Jordanian policy but rather to the fact that the nature of the problem had changed. While the legion may have had a reasonably easy time learning to control the more innocent species of infiltration and the behavior of local villagers in the National Guard, a political operation financed and operated from abroad would clearly have presented a greater challenge. Israel, moreover, was providing little incentive to the Jordanian government to increase its efforts to stop infiltration, nor would the prospect of renewed reprisals of the nature described have appeared especially formidable.

October 1953–July 1954

During the night of 12 October, infiltrators—activated from Syria according to Glubb—killed a mother and two of her children in the village of Yahud near Petah-Tikva.[30] The Israeli response, the Qibya raid of 15 October, began a process that altered the nature of the Israeli-

29. Glubb, *Soldier with the Arabs*, pp. 305–6.
30. Sharett, *Yoman Ishi* 1:34–36; Glubb, *Soldier with the Arabs*, p. 313.

Jordanian relationship. Examination of the raid and its aftermath should shed much light on the process of reprisal-as-deterrence.

Immediately after the Yahud murder the Jordanians indicated they would do everything possible to apprehend the perpetrators and condemned the incident in the MAC. Glubb flew to Jerusalem and, through UNTSO, asked for cooperation, even offering to allow an Israeli tracking police dog to cross the border in search of the infiltrators. Prime Minister Sherett believed that the Jordanian reaction was exactly what Israel should hope for. Glubb ought to be aided, he thought, and Israel should honor his request not to retaliate. In his view, reprisal would only justify the Arab Legion in sitting back and not intervening in the future.[31]

The factors converging in support of reprisal were too many and too strong; Sharett was overruled. Ben-Gurion, who was officially on leave from the government at the time but still politically powerful, seemed to give his support to Defense Minister Pinkhas Lavon, Dayan, and the general staff of the army, who advocated not just reprisal but, rather, a "meaningful" and "effective" operation. A desire to engage the Western powers; revenge for Yahud; the IDF's need to prove itself after the numerous failures that year; the eagerness of Arik Sharon, who had just established the 101; and, of course, deterrence all contributed to the demand for an action that would show the Jordanians that Israel meant business. The operational intent was to cause ten to twelve Jordanian casualties and destroy several scores of houses in Qibya, a large village of 1500 people and one the IDF believed had been housing infiltrators and storing their equipment.[32]

During the raid Israeli paratroopers dynamited some forty-five houses while their inhabitants hid inside. The Israelis believed that the houses were empty. In one instance, an Israeli officer heard crying in a house after lighting the fuse; he managed to run in, save a child, and escape with seconds to spare. On the other hand, the operational orders as rewritten by the Central Command's operations department called explicitly for hurting inhabitants.[33] The results were horrendous. Tallies vary, but there appear to have been over fifty civilian deaths.[34]

What were the strategic results of Qibya? As Israel had hoped, the

31. Sharett, *Yoman Ishi* 1:35–37; Hutchison, *Violent Truce*, p. 43.
32. Bar-Zohar, *Ben-Gurion*, pt. 2, pp. 974–77; Dayan, *Avnei Derekh*, p. 115; Berger, *Covenant and the Sword*, p. 96; *New York Times*, 16 October 1953; Safran, *From War to War*, p. 45.
33. Bar-Zohar, *Ben-Gurion*, pt. 2, p. 976.
34. Blechman, "Consequences of the Israeli Reprisals," p. 80; Hutchison, *Violent Truce*, p. 44.

Western powers did become engaged, but not quite in the manner intended. For the first time since 1950 the Security Council considered a reprisal and condemned Israel for its breach of the armistice. Among the Western powers the British were naturally the most upset and made some noises about possible intervention. The United States held off at the United Nations but decided not to transfer a promised grant of $75 million to Israel. France remained basically uninvolved.[35] Because of their strong interests in Egypt and Jordan, the United States and Britain aborted Israeli efforts at the United Nations to expand the Qibya deliberations into a general discussion of Israeli-Jordanian relations and problems. Israel's U.N. representative Abba Eban therefore invoked Article 12 of the General Armistice Agreement, which legally obligated Jordan to attend a special conference with Israel to reconsider the armistice provisions.[36]

The reactions to Qibya within Jordan underscored the constraints on the king's freedom of action. The rift between the West and East Banks was highlighted as Palestinian nationalist politicians and Egyptian provocateurs incited crowds against the monarchy for failing to protect them against the brutal Israelis. The image of the legion as a British tool rather than a Jordanian or Arab force was strengthened, which fueled the fires of nationalist opposition.[37] Hussein, in his youthful wisdom, trod a near perfect line. Publicly he turned militantly anti-Israel, promising revenge in speeches to parliament and in a visit to Qibya.[38] But, although the raid made active suppression of infiltration politically more difficult, the Arab Legion further improved its anti-infiltration measures. These less conspicuous measures were cleverly balanced by enhancing the defensive capabilities of the local National Guard units. Despite her apparent willingness to take part in the general conference Israel had asked for, Jordan was "persuaded" not to attend by other Arab states and by the need to appease rising domestic nationalist opposition.[39]

The Qibya raid and its repercussions induced serious soul-searching among Israelis. Within Israel there was strong public and private revulsion on moral grounds. The government was at a loss to explain the tragedy and tried to maintain the dubious fiction that the raid had been a private affair by citizens angry over Yahud. The reaction of the West-

35. *New York Times*, 17, 19 October, 12 November 1953; Blechman, "Consequences of Israeli Reprisals," pp. 199–200.
36. Berger, *Covenant and the Sword*, pp. 97–100.
37. Vatikiotis, *Politics and the Military*, pp. 119–20; *New York Times*, 23 October 1953; Glubb, *Soldier with the Arabs*, pp. 313–16.
38. *New York Times*, 2, 10 November 1953.
39. Berger, *Covenant and the Sword*, pp. 99–100.

ern powers in and out of the United Nations and of world Jewry deeply affected Israeli decision makers. Dayan wrote, "Israel learned that even when the Arabs hit peaceful citizens, we must direct our reactions to military objectives. What is 'allowable' to the Arabs—and to other peoples—will not be forgiven to Jews and Israelis. Not only foreigners, but Israeli citizens and world Jewry expect from us a 'purity of arms' greater than that normally found in any army."[40] Israel did continue to target civilian objectives, like villages, but with strict orders to preserve the lives, if not the property, of noncombatants.[41] One noteworthy change in policy was to post more border police, a decision to enhance pure defense, possibly reflecting a desire to avoid "having" to retaliate in the future.

What of deterrence? After a short-term drop in infiltration, November and December saw a resurgence of the old pattern: murderous infiltration in one direction and small-scale reprisals in the other. But at this point the Jordanian authorities apparently became fearful of another Qibya. Comdr. Elmo Hutchison, head of the Jordan-Israel MAC, describes Jordanian efforts as he saw them at the time:

> Along with other Military Observers, I investigated the Jordan claims of cooperation even though many of the measures taken to fight infiltration were well known by those of us working along the border. We were able to verify that Jordan had increased the number of border police and border patrols by over 30 percent. Three village Mukhtars and thirteen area commanders had been moved from their sectors because of laxness of border control. The jails at Nablus, Hebron and Amman were loaded with prisoners, many of whom were being held on nothing more than suspicion of infiltration. I personally read the order that was sent from Arab Legion Headquarters to area commanders to prevent illegal cultivation. New powers were granted to local judges to enable them to take firmer measures against those who grazed their flocks too close to the border or cultivated beyond the UN line of demarcation. Bedouin tribes living east of the Wadi Araba in the southern part of Jordan were warned to stay back from the frontier area. Many of us knew Jordan's efforts to curb infiltration reached the total capabilities of the country. We were aware that many needed improvements were being by-passed to afford this vigilance. Jordan was not a rich country.[42]

Despite these efforts and a low incidence of infiltration in February, Israel was shaken in March by two serious incidents and an apparent

40. Dayan, *Avnei Derekh*, p. 115.

41. Bar-Zohar, *Ben-Gurion*, pt. 2, p. 981. See also Glubb's account of the subsequent Nahleen raid in *Soldier with the Arabs*, p. 322.

42. Hutchison, *Violent Truce*, pp. 105–6. See also the report in February by the UNTSO chief of staff to the Security Council, quoted in ibid., pp. 104–5.

all-time high in "serious infiltration." On 17 March a bus in the Negev was ambushed at the Scorpion Pass near the Jordanian border. Eleven were killed and two wounded. Israel's attempts to involve the powers failed. Although the identity or origin of the killers has never been established, this incident combined with the killing of a guard at Kissalon on 26 March to provoke a second large reprisal: the Nahleen raid of 28 March. On a smaller scale than Qibya, Nahleen inflicted thirty-seven casualties, among them nine deaths.[43]

In its strategic effects, the Nahleen raid appears to have been of just the right dimensions. The case reached the UN Security Council, but discussions there merely petered out. The Jordan-Anglo treaty was reaffirmed—by then surely a predictable and harmless exercise from Israel's perspective. In Jordan, the crown and the legion again took considerable heat for their failure to protect the villages, but less than after Qibya. At the time Arab nationalist and Palestinian unrest were, in any case, bringing Jordan to the brink of an internal crisis (the government was to fall in May). It is thus difficult to analyze the contribution of Nahleen to internal unrest. Aqil Abidi's political history of the period suggests that Nahleen was useful as additional fuel for an already burning fire.[44]

After Nahleen we see a steady decline in infiltration, and explicit positive steps by the Jordanian authorities to apprehend and jail infiltrators who succeeded in the more violent missions.[45] In light of Jordan's internal problems, the decline in infiltration after Nahleen is actually quite remarkable. Apparently, the crown was strong enough to deal forcefully with radical elements, vetoing the formation of two extreme political parties and using the legion to quash riots during the elections in October 1954.[46]

During July and August there was virtually no infiltration from Jordan. Nevertheless, the IDF executed four small raids, which appeared to have nothing to do with deterrence, their purpose being to amass a stash of hostages. These were deemed necessary for Israel to bargain for the release of a soldier captured in a raid at Azzoun in June.[47] The last of

---

43. Sharett, *Yoman Ishi* 2:403–8, 410–17, 420; Hutchison, *Violent Truce*, chaps. 6 and 9; Brilliant, "Israel's Policy of Reprisal," p. 71; Glubb, *Soldier with the Arabs*, pp. 321–22.

44. Sharett, *Yoman Ishi* 2:419–21, 426, 429; Blechman, "Consequences of Israeli Reprisals," p. 199; Berger, *Covenant and the Sword*, pp. 102–3; *New York Times*, 31 March 1953; Vatikiotis, *Politics and the Military*, pp. 119–20; Glubb, *Soldier with the Arabs*, pp. 337–39; Abidi, *Jordan*, chap. 5.

45. For one example, see Sharett, *Yoman Ishi* 2:549–50.

46. On the elections see Abidi, *Jordan*, pp. 115–18; Glubb, *Soldier with the Arabs*, chap. 21.

47. Burns, *Between Arab and Israeli*, pp. 35–38.

this series, at Beit Liqya, caused a number of casualties among Arab legionnaires ambushed on their way to reinforce the village under attack. Although Glubb described the raid as misdirected and uncalled for, the legion appears to have entertained no thoughts of escalation or revenge.

Despite a subsequent trickle of serious infiltration, Beit Liqya was virtually the last Israeli reprisal against Jordan until the summer of 1956. By then the Israelis probably realized that Jordan was doing all she could. Prime Minister Sharett was in any case convinced that further reprisals would achieve no positive results and could only cause more direct IDF-legion clashes with counterproductive results.[48] After mid-1954 infiltration decreased dramatically, with serious incidents reduced to about one per month and practically no murders recorded. This situation held—more or less—until 1956.

AN ANALYSIS

Having described the events of 1953–54 I move on to a more formal analysis of the deterrence problem by applying the framework developed in Chapter 1. Considering these events (together with other "facts" as required) in terms of the seven theoretical categories should elucidate this apparently successful exercise in active deterrence.

Relative Interests

As we begin the analysis we are confronted by a serious problem: First, whose interests are we to compare? The defender in this case is easy to identify, but not the challenger. Infiltration was at no point an act of the Jordanian state or its army. Rather, the challengers were local villagers (who were Palestinians) and, later, Palestinian refugees, organized, financed, and at times coming from outside, and despite, the Jordanian state.

Regarding the heart of the conflict—the competition for Palestine— one might reasonably conclude that the intrinsic interests of Israel and the Palestinians were equal in intensity. Even so, Israel's opponents enjoyed a bargaining advantage. Politically motivated Palestinians had as their immediate object violence and maintenance of a fluid status quo. Opposing this was an Israeli interest in pacification. The bargain-

---

48. See Sharett's lengthy letter (26 October 1954) to Eban at the United Nations quoted in Sharett, *Yoman Ishi* 2:591–96.

ing advantage held by the Palestinians at this level did not result from their interest in violence being stronger than Israel's in pacification. Rather, it resulted from the special nature of the object. It is most difficult to devise an appropriate strategy for dealing with an opponent bent on violence per se. How does one deny it? Or even appease it?

Further exacerbating these difficulties was the fact that Israel had no access to the infiltrators and so could not punish them directly. Because the infiltrators derived positive satisfaction from the consequences of Israeli reprisals, indirect deterrent threats were also inefficacious. Israel could only direct its attention to the Jordanian state; yet Israel and Jordan were not opponents, in the traditional sense, over the issue of infiltration or at that level. There was no identifiable contested object between them. In fact they were collaborators, both desiring a pacified frontier, for different reasons and at different intensities. Israel's deterrence thus depended on indirect manipulation of Jordanian interests so that the challenge posed by infiltrating Israel became, as a result of Israel's response, a challenge to Jordan's integrity. This created a convergence of Israeli and Jordanian interests in the status quo. The critical question of interests, then, is centered around Israel and Jordan; the direct challengers are important—and are considered—for their effects on this central balance of interests.

Comparing interests before Qibya (October 1953) reveals that Israel saw the problem of infiltration as strategic, of serious national consequences, especially as it became ugly in 1953. Jordan's interest in the status quo differed from Israel's. She was at an early and troublesome stage of national integration and had to appease West Bank Palestinian and Arab Nationalist positions, among them an anti-Zionist, anti–status quo posture. She also needed to coexist with her neighbor, Israel. Thus, Jordan was ambivalent over whether the armistice demarcation line should become an international border. As long as some infiltration occurred but the Israeli response was minimal, Jordanian interests seemed to be satisfied.[49]

Though probably inadvertently, before Qibya the Israelis did manage to manipulate some of Jordan's concerns, but not through retaliatory raids. Early Israeli threats of invasion forced Jordan to realize that her ally Great Britain did not wish to be forced to intervene on her behalf. Hussein then understood that he had a strategic interest in preserving the status quo.

Later, the series of large raids—Qibya, Nahleen, and Beit Liqya—was a violent manipulation of Jordan's relative interest in the status

---

49. See "Domestic Factors" below.

quo, for it strengthened the radical opposition within Jordan, creating animosity and alienation between Hashemites and Palestinians, East and West Bankers. For reasons that should become clear as the analysis proceeds, there was only one way to deal effectively with disintegration yet maintain a conservative and pro-British posture: avoid such disruptive reprisals by preventing the provocative infiltration.

Reprisals, then, were effective not because they somehow centralized the Israeli-Jordanian conflict or because they proved Israel's greater interest in the status quo. Quite the opposite. The large raids had a disrupting effect on Hussein's main object, national integration, which had little to do with Israel; and instead of demonstrating Israel's superior valuation of the status quo, they established Hussein's stake in it.

General lessons emerge regarding the comparability and the stability of relative interests. Ranking the relative interests of protagonists, it appears, may be quite complex. Most important, the comparison critical to deterrence may not always be between the interests of the two immediate protagonists; in this case it was between those of the defender and a third party—Jordan. The second lesson is that in an extended low-level crisis it is possible for the defender actively and dramatically to alter other actors' interests, so that the structure of the relationship changes as we examine it. This change is, in a sense, akin to that resulting from "controlled pressure" as described by Alexander George and Richard Smoke, but here the *defender* exerts the pressure instead of the challenger.[50] Neither analysts nor policy makers should be satisfied to compare interests as fixed values but rather should be aware that they are changeable. Effecting change in interests may be a policy goal and must be an important "activity" of active deterrence.

Political Asymmetries

What were the political-systemic effects that proscribed both sides' freedom of action and hence the efficacy and credibility of their moves?

THE INTERNATIONAL SYSTEM

Israel's external relations were generally miserable during 1953–54, this period falling within what Nadav Safran has called Israel's "Four Lean Years" (1953–56).[51] In 1950 the three Western powers had promised to maintain the status quo between Israel and her Arab neighbors

---

50. George and Smoke, *Deterrence in American Foreign Policy*, pp. 543–47.

51. For a general and concise description of Israel's foreign relations at the time, see Nadav Safran, *Israel: The Embattled Ally* (Cambridge, Mass., 1981), pp. 347–53.

through the Tripartite Declaration.[52] Until 1953 they appeared to be keeping their promise. The Soviet Union was not a major actor in the Middle East (and would not become one before 1955), and at first, at least, Israel's policy of neutrality seemed to keep her in reasonable relations with both East and West.

By 1953–54, Israel's relations with the Soviet Union had degenerated considerably. Soviet policy assumed the form it would maintain for decades: anti-Semitic in flavor, anti-Zionist in ideology, and explicitly supportive of the Arab cause at the United Nations.[53] Upon assuming office in 1953 the Eisenhower administration dragged the Cold War into the Middle East by trying to enlist Arab states—especially Egypt and Iraq, but also Jordan—in an anticommunist alliance. Secretary of State John Foster Dulles hoped to establish a "northern tier" (of Turkey, Pakistan, and Iraq) and then to enlist other Arab states in a general pact to prevent the southward spread of international communism. Israel played no part in these plans.

Concurrently, Israel "discovered" her Western orientation, supporting the United States over Korea and denying recognition to the People's Republic of China. The West did not reciprocate. In accordance with the provisions of the Tripartite Declaration, the United States, Britain, and France refused to provide Israel with economic assistance or military aid. But the United States was willing to supply arms to Iraq, for example, to help cement the Northern Tier or the Baghdad Pact. These arms supplied by the West to thwart the Russians could easily, in Israel's view, be used in other directions.

As for the Arab-Israeli conflict, the United States and Britain could only hope that it remain dormant, as they were guarantors of the status quo. Flare-ups would demand intervention and taking sides, which could only cause alienation and deflection from the pursuit of more critical policies. The Arab-Israeli conflict was to be kept off the agenda. The West's attitude is clear from its failure to take action after the Egyptian blockade of the Suez Canal or, even worse from Israel's perspective, after Egypt's arbitrary disruption of commercial traffic in the Gulf of Eilat (Aqaba) in 1954. When Israel tried to force the issue by sending a ship (the Bat Galim) through the Suez Canal in September of 1954, the United States and Britain were only embarrassed and angered

---

52. Michael Brecher, *The Foreign Policy System of Israel: Setting, Images, Process* (New Haven, Conn., 1972), pp. 41, 59.

53. On Israel's shift westward and deteriorating relations with the USSR, see ibid., chap. 4; Safran, *Israel*, pp. 338–47. For the first Soviet pro-Arab vetoes at the United Nations, see Ya'akov Ro'i, *From Encroachment to Involvement: A Documentary Study of Soviet Policy in the Middle East, 1945–1973* (Jerusalem, 1974), pp. 115–24, 127–31.

by the provocation and acquiesced in Egypt's impounding of the ship.[54] Israel's failure to obtain justice or at least a just hearing (in her view) at the Security Council, led Sharett to despair of the United Nations as a forum for pursuing Israeli interests.[55]

As the West's relations with surrounding Arab states improved, Israel tried to gain entry into NATO or to convince the United States to sign a mutual defense treaty with Israel. Both bids were abortive.[56] But most complicated were Israel's relations with Great Britain. Although her position in the Middle East had declined considerably after World War II, when the United States began to take over as the primary external actor, Britain was still a major factor in Israel's foreign policy until the Sinai Campaign. The legacy of the mandate and the War of Independence was adversarial. Throughout the latter part of the mandate and during the war itself Britain had pursued a holding action to preserve her imperial position by siding explicitly with, and threatening intervention for, the Arabs of Palestine, Jordan, and Egypt.[57] In 1953 she was maneuvering to maintain minimal rights to the Suez Canal and to extract Egyptian agreement on Anglo-Sudanese relations. This further enforced her pro-Arab position and indifference to Israeli claims of injury. By 1954, having agreed to evacuate her Suez Canal bases and having lost hope of incorporating the Sudan in the Commonwealth, Britain's last physical presence and strong alliance in the Middle Eastern heartland was in and with Jordan.[58] To maintain this last foothold, Britain guaranteed Jordan's defense, pitting Britain in potential physical conflict against Israel.

These interests in the Arab world created an alliance-perception problem between Israel and the Western powers. Because taking sides would potentially have hurt their positions, the United States and Britain adopted a benign view of the implications for Israel of violent infiltration. Most telling was Prime Minister Sharett's failure to elicit an

54. For a general discussion of the politics of the blockade, see Berger, *Covenant of the Sword*, chap. 11. On the Western reaction to Bat Galim, see Safran, *Israel*, p. 351.

55. Sharett, *Yoman Ishi* 2:421.

56. Nadav Safran, *The United States and Israel* (Cambridge, Mass., 1963), pp. 232, 234; Ernest Stock, *Israel on the Road to Sinai, 1949–1956* (Ithaca, N.Y., 1967), chap. 5. IDF Chief of Staff Dayan, on a military visit to the United States in 1954, wrote home of extensive American attempts to portray his visit to the U.S. military as a "private" affair; see letter quoted in *Avnei Derekh*, p. 128.

57. For the early record of Jewish-British relations in Palestine and the War of Independence, see Safran, *Israel*, pp. 54, 60; Brecher, *Foreign Policy System of Israel*, p. 246; Safran, *From War to War*, pp. 65, 93. The fear of British intervention remained through 1956; see Aronson, *Conflict and Bargaining*, pp. 6, 16.

58. Robert Stephens, *Nasser: A Political Biography* (London, 1971), pp. 129–35.

American response to the Scorpion Pass bus incident of March 1954.[59] Although the extreme international reaction to Israel's raid on Qibya established the upper bounds of allowable violence against Jordan, no one was willing to establish such bounds on violence against Israel.[60]

Israel's two threats in 1953 to invade Jordan were clearly empty. Neither Sharett nor Ben-Gurion were willing to confront the British directly on an issue that was important but not critical to survival, especially as Israel depended on England to help guarantee her survival through the mechanism of the Tripartite Declaration.[61]

Jordan's principle alliance at the time was with Great Britain. In this relationship the Hashemite regime was highly dependent, for Britain completely financed Jordan's defense expenditures, amounting to more than half of Jordan's national budget. This support went primarily to maintain the Arab Legion, the highly professional and loyal army that sustained the Hashemite crown against both internal and external enemies.[62]

As a result, Amman enjoyed a certain security, rendering hollow Israel's threat of invasion. At the same time, Britain's interest in not getting involved in local conflict and her desire that the area remain pacific forced Jordan to pursue policies that would not lead to a general war. Of this condition Glubb wrote:

> In view of this situation, to encourage infiltrators to murder an occasional Jew was ridiculous. Such pinpricks could do Israel no serious harm, but might give her a pretext to attack Jordan in overwhelming strength. Were that to happen, only Britain could save Jordan from destruction. But if Jordan had deliberately encouraged pin-prick raids, then British support might not be forthcoming. The only reasonable policy to follow, therefore, was to work for a quiet border, to rely on British help if Israel should attack, and to hope for better days.[63]

Given the buck-passing tendencies of allies, the Jordanians could probably never be quite sure that, in case of a conflagration, their interpretation of "who provoked whom" would coincide with Britain's.

59. Sharett, *Yoman Ishi* 2:415–17.

60. For Ben-Gurion's analysis that the West's reaction to Qibya reflected their interests in the Arab world, see ibid. 5:1314.

61. Aronson, *Conflict and Bargaining*, pp. 22–23. Zeev Schiff, the noted Israeli military correspondent, expressed the opinion that the Great Britain-Jordanian alliance prevented Israeli consideration of "serious" violence against Jordan. (Interviewed in Washington, 2 October 1984.)

62. For the extent of British financial support, see Vatikiotis, *Politics and the Military*, pp. 10–11, 105n. For the legion's role in sustaining the regime, see ibid., chap. 4.

63. Glubb, *Soldier with the Arabs*, p. 340.

Glubb's assertion that "only Britain could save Jordan" raises eyebrows and the question What about the rest of the Arab world? Not a reliable source of salvation, as we shall see. With the historical and traditional enmity of the Saudi and Hashemite families ever present, Jordan had to contend with a number of isolating Arab coalitions. In the 1940s, Jordan's king, Abdullah, faced a Syrian-Egyptian-Saudi coalition formed to oppose his imperial plans for unification and domination of the Fertile Crecent.[64] In 1949–50, Jordan remained isolated from other Arab states but now in the context of the Palestine question. First there was the Egyptian and Syrian sponsorship of the All-Palestine Government in Gaza, a direct challenge to Abdullah's authority and rule in the West Bank. Then came the nearly successful elimination of Jordan from the Arab League because of her annexation of the West Bank, with only Iraq supporting her. It is telling that Jordan became the very last state to sign the Arab Mutual Defense Treaty of the Arab League, three years after its general acceptance.[65]

In the Palestine War of 1948–49, Jordan learned one important lesson, which she also taught: pursuit of the war and participation in it by the Arab states reflected inter-Arab competition at least as strongly as Arab-Israeli rivalry. The various states entered the war to pursue their own goals, fought in ways to maximize them, and quit the fighting similarly. Among the Arabs, fighting and armistice were both uncoordinated and competitive.[66]

Not being able to rely on Arab assistance in case of a threat from Israel, Jordan's interest in the status quo was further enhanced. Jordan would not have been much better off if she *had* been able to rely on military assistance, for another Arab army on her soil would have complicated her situation. Hussein would never have been certain whether this foreign army was really after him or the Israelis. Also, Israel had long considered the presence of a foreign army in Jordan as a *casus belli*.[67] Could Jordan afford to convert the fear of possible Israeli attack to an event of higher probability? And again, how would the British react?

In 1953–54, Nasser began to blend the Palestinian question, Arab

---

64. Abidi, *Jordan*, pp. 21–23; Safran, *From War to War*, pp. 62–68; Avraham Sela, *Achdut betoch Perud ba-Maarekhet habein-Aravit* [Unity within conflict in the inter-Arab system] (Jerusalem, 1983), p. 3; Vatikiotis, *Politics and the Military*, p. 137.

65. Abidi, *Jordan*, pp. 49–60, 75–78; Sela, *Achdut*, Introduction.

66. For Dayan's analysis of Abdullah's "bind" in the Arab system during the 1948 war and in its aftermath, see his articles in the Tel-Aviv daily *Yediot Aharonot*, 11, 19 June 1959. For a description of the lack of Arab coordination in the war, see Trevor N. Dupuy, *Elusive Victory: The Arab-Israeli Wars, 1947–1974* (New York, 1978), pp. 93, 95, 100, 114.

67. Brecher, *Foreign Policy System of Israel*, p. 67.

nationalism, and anti-imperialism—all extremely salient issues in Jordan. Beginning to develop the techniques of direct penetration of foreign polities, mainly through radio, Nasser was able to mobilize and amplify antimonarchist forces in Jordan, creating disorder and imposing severe constraints on Hussein's policies. Among the constrained policies was the king's ability to accommodate Israel. Thus, the same system on whose help he could not rely in case of war, would also not permit him freedom to seek ways to avoid it.

DOMESTIC FACTORS

Critical differences that greatly influenced bargaining between the protagonists were the strength or extent of the sense of community, of national integration, and of central control and responsibility. Israel's high degree of national integration and community had somewhat contradictory implications. On the one hand, any injury to a citizen was a violation of "the state," creating a sensitivity to low-level violence and a substantial national stake in preservation or restoration of the status quo. On the other hand, having a strong and responsible central government meant that reprisal was a "national" affair, decided on and executed by the government or, at the very least, the chief of staff. Every decision on action became a substantial one, interdependent with previous decisions. The result was downward pressure on the reflex of reprisal; Israel tended to accumulate grievances before retaliating.[68]

The Jordan of 1953–54 as yet only aspired to a sense of community and national integration and control.[69] The effect was a lengthy, complex, and indirect bargaining process ending in success for Israel because of one clinching factor: the Arab Legion. Small-scale and intermittent Israeli raids could hardly influence infiltration. The infiltrators were either from refugee camps, far removed by then from the frontier, or else from abroad, and they surely felt no sense of community with the villagers who suffered from Israeli wrath. On the contrary, because the major immediate object of infiltration was to upset the status quo and provoke Israeli-Jordanian violence, Israeli retaliation probably suited the infiltrators and their organizers just fine. And to a nation as unintegrated as Jordan was at the time, the early, small reprisals seem not to have evoked a sense of national or communal responsibility that went beyond the demand for better defense. Thus the response to the chal-

68. For the idea of small anti-Israeli infiltration as "salami tactics," see Handel, *Israel's Political-Military Doctrine*, p. 21.

69. J. Doriel discusses the impossibility of Israeli coercion via reprisals when the feeling of community is absent; see his *Habitakhon ha-Leumi shel Yisrael: Mavo le-Gisha Hadashah* [The national security of the Jewish people] (Tel-Aviv, 1974), chap. 7.

lenge of Israeli raids was to enhance the defensive capabilities of the local National Guard.[70]

We can surmise that the situation on the frontier suited Hussein's internal needs and constraints perfectly. Hussein's program of national integration required that he balance the need to protect the state from without—avoid war with Israel, remain allied to Britain—with the Palestinian demand that, in principle at least, the status quo should not be recognized and solidified. Given the minimal nature of Israel's responses before the Qibya raid, infiltration and reprisal seem to have been a solution that met everyone's requirements.

Because of these realities of Jordanian political life, Hussein's interest in the status quo had to be created by (Israeli) actions that threatened the state's integrity. The large raid on Qibya and especially the downgraded attacks on Nahleen and Beit Liqya did not engage the external international system but did throw the internal system off balance. These large raids worked not by evoking the sense of community but rather by creating in Hussein the fear of losing it, releasing tremendous antiregime sentiment, and creating fertile ground for opposition activism from within and abroad. As Hussein could not meet the villagers' demand for protection against Israel, he resorted to the one avenue open to him: preempt Israeli reprisals by avoiding their provocation.

In the end, success of this rather indirect Israeli policy depended on the existence of the Arab Legion. A highly professional force constituted mainly of East Bank Bedouins loyal to the Hashemites, the legion was not to any debilitating extent caught in the currents of Palestinian or Arab nationalism. It also seemed to have no qualms about enforcing Amman's policy by policing, jailing, or removing village mukhtars.

If we step for a moment out of the time limits of our case and into 1956, we may learn something about deterrence in 1953–54. By 1956, Pan-Arab and anti-imperialist ideology had overtaken Jordanian domestic politics to the point where Hussein started to lose control. To maintain a modicum of nationhood he agreed to fire Glubb and the other British officers in the legion and canceled plans to join the Baghdad Pact. At the time, not only was Nasser exercising political penetration to the hilt, but he was using Jordan's territory as launching ground for Fedayeen operations. Israel did not retaliate until the summer, understanding, apparently, that violence against Jordan could only

70. Having the National Guard allowed the regime to enhance defense and integration without incorporating Palestinians (in large numbers) into the (praetorian guard) legion. See Vatikiotis, *Politics and the Military*, pp. 28, 79, 80; Glubb, *Soldier with the Arabs*, p. 289; Safran, *From War to War*, p. 233.

undermine the regime. Israel could no longer coerce Jordon into controlling infiltration and discovered that it was easier to bargain with a strong state than a weak one.[71]

Power Asymmetries

By 1953–54, Jordan looked across the frontier at a neighbor far superior in both putative and actualized power. With populations of roughly equal size—about 1.5 million in 1954—Israel enjoyed a GNP roughly seventeen times that of Jordan. The Israeli army, when mobilized, was some ten times larger than the Arab Legion; so was Israel's defense bill, even though Jordan's was completely financed by Britain.

In actualizing power, Jordan's most binding constraint was internal-political. The only large pool of unexploited manpower was the West Bank Palestinian population, whose dubious loyalty made them only trustworthy enough to defend themselves. Therefore they were organized into the local militia, the National Guard.[72] In the mid-1950s the Arab Legion had a ceiling of about 17,000–20,000, and the National Guard some 30,000 members. In comparison, in 1949–50, Israel had already produced, from a population of only 750,000, a standing army of 70,000. By middecade, from a population equal to Jordan's, Israel had developed a standing force of 50,000 and about 200,000 mobilizable reserves. In hardware the comparison is similar. By 1954, before the influx of French arms in 1955–56, Israel had acquired about two hundred tanks and two hundred aircraft, including fifty jets. Jordan had a force of about forty tanks and no air force to speak of at all before 1956.[73]

The requirements of mobilization, normally so critical for the Israeli calculus, appear to have played no major role in the deterrence problem under consideration. At the strategic level the Israeli advantage was so pronounced that her standing army alone could have dealt Jordan a rapid deathblow, or at least conquered the West Bank. For Jordan,

71. A. I. Dawisha, *Egypt in the Arab World: The Elements of Foreign Policy* (New York, 1976), chap. 2; Vatikiotis, *Politics and the Military*, pp. 112, 118; Ya'ari, *Mitsrayim veha-Fedayeen*, 1953–1956, p. 21; Dayan, *Avnei Derekh*, p. 229; Glubb, *Soldier with the Arabs*, chap. 26. Dan Scheuftan argues that at this time Hussein was afraid that should he fight infiltration too vigilantly, Nasser would topple his regime. See his "Harta'ah Yisraelit be-Sikhsukh Yisrael-Arav: Haperspektiva ha-Aravit" [Israeli deterrence in the Israeli-Arab conflict: The Arab perspective] (December 1982), p. 17. For the dilemma facing the Israelis, see idem, *Optsiah Yardenit: Yisrael, Yarden veha-Palestina'im* [A Jordanian option: The "Yishuv" and the State of Israel vis-à-vis the Hashemite regime and the Palestinian national movement] (Tel-Aviv, 1986), pp. 259–61.

72. See n. 70, above.

73. For the figures used above see Safran, *From War to War*, pp. 156–61, 180, 223. For development of the legion after 1948 see Vatikiotis, *Politics and the Military*, chap. 5 and p. 121.

living in the shadow of the IDF was unpleasant, whatever the political constraints on Israel's behavior. In dealing with the problem of infiltration, Israel's policy of reprisal was particularly elegant. Not only did it not require mobilization of forces, but it actually imposed no costs whatsoever on Israel, either immediate or cumulative, in the relevant period. Therefore the Israeli threat to "continue reprisals if the infiltration continues" should have been credible.

The geographic arrangement interacted with political and power asymmetries to place Jordan at a considerable bargaining disadvantage. Ostensibly, Jordan held greater Israeli values at risk than vice-versa, the West Bank topographically dominating and geographically surrounding the Tel-Aviv-Haifa coastal plain and the Jerusalem corridor, whereas Israel dominated neither the Jordan valley food basket nor Amman the capital. But Jordan was in no position to put Israel's central values at risk, for the Israeli army's sheer superiority imposed a purely defensive general strategy on the legion. In a highly controversial internal Jordanian plan, Glubb held most of the legion on the East Bank, far away from the frontier, hoping at best to salvage by counterattack potential Israeli conquests.[74] As late as 1956, Israel had not yet developed, in hardware or doctrine, the blitzkrieg offensive orientation she was to enjoy in later years. Given the proximity of the West Bank to Israel, its heartland quality, mountainous terrain, and the shortness of distances within it, the question of an Israeli blitzkrieg was moot and would probably have been so even had the forces been more equal in size.

Again, the elegance of the Israeli reprisal strategy was its independence of the strategic threat to invade the West Bank, a threat that existed but had only limited credibility. Just as Israel could not prevent Jordanian infiltration, Jordan could not defend the long, winding border against Israeli reprisals. The political problems of Jordanian integration gave high strategic value to Israel's retaliatory actions, which indirectly threatened the existence of the Jordanian state, a kind of threat never imposed on Israel by infiltration from Jordan. Because Jordan could not threaten Israel with escalation, Hussein adopted the only course available to him: to prevent the provocation of Israeli reprisals.

Escalation and Brinkmanship

Israeli escalation was a pedagogic tool, serving to clarify certain facts about the structure of the prevailing relationship. Escalation also ac-

---

74. Glubb, *Soldier with the Arabs*, chap. 22; Vatikiotis, *Politics and the Military*, pp. 115–17.

tively altered the nature of the relationship. In both functions, escalation enhanced deterrence. In the first capacity, escalation demonstrated the strength of Israel's interest in a pacified border. Escalation also clarified for Jordan the nature of her alliance with Great Britain and the severe limits on London's propensity to actually get involved. As a constructive instrument escalation made the relationship between Israel and Jordan strategic where it had not been before. Escalation engaged central Jordanian interests and gave her a major stake in the border war.

Escalation was also an instrument of brinkmanship. Recall that early in 1953 (before Qibya) Israel twice threatened to invade in force. Israeli superiority was so overwhelming, and a decisive campaign would have been so short and final for Jordan, that, despite the apparent constraints on Israeli behavior, even the small possibility that Israel would act against her own interests and invade Jordan was enough to coerce the latter. In this context, the large raids would have made the probability of even more massive Israeli action appear real—and degeneration to war possible—despite the constraints.

Deterrence, Spiraling, and De-escalation

Israeli pursuit of "escalation for de-escalation" raises the questions Did spiraling result? and Did Israel also pursue de-escalation, or appeasement? The question of spiraling arises because two escalations on the Jordanian side did occur, creating a need to evaluate Israel's contribution to them. The initial escalation, in the volume and nature of infiltration, took place in 1953. The second—outside our time-frame—was the resurgence of serious infiltration in late 1955 and 1956. The evidence available would deny a spiraling interpretation, for both escalations were due to forces beyond Jordan's control and not related to specific Israeli activities on the Jordanian front. The first was the fruit of initiative and control by Palestinian organizations in Damascus, the Husseini family, and Saudi money. The second was promoted and executed by the Egyptian authorities.

As for her relations with the Jordanian army, there is no evidence that at any point Glubb's legion considered counterreprisals. It appears more than coincidence that, except at Beit Liqya (and even there indirectly), the legion was never a target of Israeli aggression. Israel never directly engaged the organization, whose cooperation she sought, and avoided involving the legion's prestige or morale in a confrontation with the IDF.

Did Israel actively de-escalate? What were the results? At one level, interpretation is quite tricky. By not retaliating in a tit-for-tat manner (a reprisal per infiltration), could Israel have been signaling, if inadvertently, an attempt to induce cooperation? Possibly, but given the mutual independence of the infiltrators and the targets of reprisal, such despiraling could have had no direct effect on the perpetrators, just as escalation could not.

In 1951 and again in 1952—in the days of "innocent infiltration"—Israel attempted classic despiraling. She did this by suggesting to the Jordanians that the economic sources of infiltration (like the separation of farmers from their lands by the new frontiers) be removed by appropriate territorial exchanges between the two countries. The Jordanians refused, apparently fearing the political consequences of such a de jure acceptance of the status quo. Israeli suggestions to mark the border, physically and clearly, and her offers to allow passage of refugees through Israel between Gaza and Jordan for family reunifications met the same fate.[75] Recall that at the time neither side saw the situation as critical. This Jordanian reaction in 1951–52 gives at least some support to the notion presented in Chapter 1 that, for meaningful de-escalation, one may need first to engage in escalation.

In the period immediately after the Qibya raid, Israeli and Jordanian policies aimed explicitly at de-escalation generated a dynamic of escalation. The Arab Legion increased its presence along the border to stop infiltration. The IDF did the same to enhance pure defense. As a result of their proximity, a number of fire engagements developed. Fortunately, decision makers on both sides understood what was happening, and the escalatory process did not get out of control.[76]

After mid-1954, Israel pursued de-escalation by not responding to sporadic infiltration. Her leadership apparently understood that increased pressure could only have deleterious effects. In early 1956, when serious infiltration surged, Jordan was a weak and disintegrated polity, much influenced from abroad, and therefore not much of a partner for negotiation or bargaining. These conditions rendered both escalation and de-escalation futile policies.

Reputation and Knowledge

Israel's sheer superiority greatly simplified the shared knowledge required for the creation of relevant and credible deterrent threats at the

75. Berger, *Covenant and the Sword*, pp. 86–89. The centrality of nonrecognition of the status quo to Hussein's relations with the West Bank is described by Mishal, "Conflictual Pressures and Cooperative Interests," pp. 183–84.

76. See Dayan's explanation to Sharett of unintended incidents, in Sharett, *Yoman Ishi* 2:496; regarding the consequences of one such unauthorized patrol, the Bakra incident, see ibid., pp. 540, 547. For the view of these from the other side, see Glubb, *Soldier with the Arabs*, pp. 317–18.

strategic level. Israel's relative skill did not depend on tactical or doctrinal intangibles, nor did she have to generate an unlikely "crazy state" image to convince Jordan of her will. In addition, Israel's reputation from the past and intracrisis use of reprisals should have served to settle any lingering doubts.

The main source of the general strategic reputation with which Israel entered the crisis in 1953 was the 1948 war. What were its lessons for Jordan? At the individual and unit level the Arab Legion could not have failed to discern its parity with, and at times superiority to, the Israeli forces. Throughout the war the legion acquited itself honorably in engagements with Israeli forces, as in the Etzion Block and the battles of Jerusalem, Latrun, and Beit Jubrin. In general, the legion was able to present King Abdullah with respectable territorial achievements, something the other Arab armies could not boast of.[77]

Despite these successes, even during the 1948 war the Jordanian military command took an extremely rational and strategic view of its capabilities relative to the IDF. At critical junctures Glubb opposed offensive actions and urged accommodation with the Israelis. The legion had no illusions as to the overall strategic balance or the probable results of full-scale Israeli aggression against Jordan.[78] Also, for all their microsuccesses in 1948–49, the fact must have been inescapable that the legion's freedom of action was due in large measure to the occupation of Samaria by the Iraqis, leaving the legion only half of the front to deal with. Also unavoidable was the fact that Israel had fought five armies and survived, a process that revolutionized the image of the Jews in Arab minds. Glubb himself said in explaining the defeat: "The Arab states thought the Jews of Palestine were the same as the Jews of the Baghdad Bazaar in Iraq or the inhabitants of Wadi An Jamil in Beirut."[79] This had clearly changed.

In 1953–54 the legion was basically the same organization it had been in 1949, commanded by the same senior officers, driven by the same ethos, and true to the same rational-strategic professionalism. As the IDF mushroomed in size next to the relatively static legion, Glubb entertained no illusions about the outcome of an Israeli invasion. The controversial defense plan of 1955 is testimony to his unemotional professionalism. In sum, Glubb and the legion clearly derived satisfaction and esprit de corps from their successes in the 1948 war but did not allow this to color their military-strategic analyses and assessments.

The existing power asymmetries also greatly simplified the credibility

---

77. Dupuy, *Elusive Victory*, pp. 39, 40, 52–54, chap. 6, pp. 99–100.
78. Glubb, *Soldier with the Arabs*, p. 152, chaps. 7, 8, esp. p. 165.
79. Quoted in Yehoshafat Harkabi, *Arab Attitudes to Israel* (Jerusalem, 1972), p. 369. For the general "shock of defeat" see pp. 369–76; Safran, *From War to War*, p. 40.

requirements for the will to attack in a major way. There was something of a nuclear logic at work: Even though Britain's threat to intervene greatly reduced the probability of an Israeli invasion, the Jordanians could never be absolutely certain that she would. And because the damage to Jordan could be lethal, Israel did not have to make a specific, credible threat or to develop a crazy-state reputation. She merely had to be incapable of promising to be completely rational. In sum, the knowledge requirements regarding both skill and will were quite general, minimal, and easy to share.

As the earlier discussion of brinkmanship and escalation suggested, the probability of inadvertent escalation was increased by the execution of reprisals, which also served as an intracrisis tool of instruction about both Israel's interest in pacification and the nature of Jordan's British ally. But the threat of retaliation also operated at its own level, independently of the strategic relationship. In the 1953–54 period neither Israelis nor Jordanians understood or knew very much about the technique, implications, and efficacy of retaliatory raids, so that the threat was not very potent. Indeed, the Israelis did not have much of a reputation at the small-unit level, either from the 1948–49 war or the 1950–53 period.

The extended and low-level nature of interaction allowed the Israelis to experiment, learn, and teach. In a process of "instrumental learning,"[80] Israel discovered first that tiny and unprofessional raids have no effect and then that "Qibyas" have detrimental collateral damage. Even if understanding of the mechanism by which the large raids worked had not been perfected by mid-1954, the "right size" had been identified. But there is some evidence that by 1954–55 the Israelis had developed a sophisticated knowledge of how these raids worked through Jordanian politics. Apparently they understood the constraints on Jordanian behavior well enough to desist from retaliation when Egyptian-directed infiltration from an internally weak Jordan surged in early 1956.

The elegance of low-level violence as a device for establishing common knowledge in this case is that it was effective yet relatively unobtrusive, in the sense that it did not deleteriously alter the internal and external systems within which it operated and about which it was teaching.

Success or Failure

Throughout this chapter I have referred to the Israeli policy as successful; it is time to be more precise. In what sense was it successful?

80. Steinbruner, *Cybernetic Theory of Decision*, pp. 78–80.

Was it a failure as well? A purist of the nuclear deterrence mold would surely have cause to dispute the conclusion that deterrence held. The very fact that violence against the defender was undertaken and then lasted for years should be cause enough to declare failure. Also, the perpetrators themselves were never coerced or reached by Israel but, rather, stopped by Jordanian policing. But such a conclusion, though perhaps true in a sense, is too simple and uninteresting, whereas a relativistic approach can incorporate the idea of active deterrence and then evaluate (measure) the extent of success or failure.

In this low-level and extended case of infiltration, much insight may be gained by exploring the sensitivity of the conclusions to variations in time frames, beginning with the smallest, deterrence within the crisis period. Work by Dan Horowitz and the exhaustive statistical study of retaliation and violence by Blechman present evidence that during 1950–54, raids against Jordanian territory were followed by a decrease in infiltration.[81] Blechman's results suggest that the volume of infiltration decreased dramatically during the first ten days after a reprisal, this effect then dissipating substantially, but not completely, toward the end of thirty days.[82] Already the time frame question rears its head: Do we care about ten days, or a month? Looking at six-month intervals, however, but still using Blechman's data,[83] we see the following mean trend of infiltration incidents:

	Total incidents	Mean/month
January–June 1953	37	6.2
July–December 1953	29	4.8
January–June 1954	45	7.5

These data indicate no decline in the average thirty-day volume of violence by infiltration. Clearly, the short-term effects and the broader mean trend require reconciliation. Two interpretations suggest themselves.

One possible explanation consistent with both statistical facts is that the reprisals had a disrupting effect, after which the Jordanian authorities simply relaxed their vigilance. The other interpretation is that infiltration, an activity requiring organization, recruitment, bribing, and so forth, progressed in a naturally cyclical fashion. As one might expect, Israeli reprisals coincided with the peaks but may not directly have

81. Horowitz, *Hatfisa ha-Yisraelit shel Bitachon Leumi*, pp. 17–22; Blechman, "Consequences of the Israeli Reprisals," pp. 157–80.

82. Blechman, "Consequences of the Israeli Reprisals," pp. 157–80.

83. Based on data presented in ibid., pp. 71, 85.

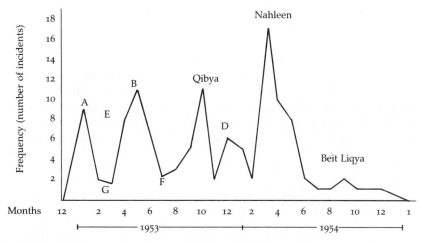

Figure 1. Frequency of serious infiltration from Jordan, 1953–54. From Barry Blechman, "The Consequences of the Israeli Reprisals: An Assessment" (Ph.D. diss., Georgetown University, 1971), p. 137.

caused the troughs. A careful examination of figure 1 should undermine the direct short-term causal explanation.

Despite the apparent significance of Israeli actions at points A, B, and D, these raids were really no different from those at F or G, or even E. Thus it is difficult to draw definite conclusions about the short-term effects of reprisals. But, looking at the same time series, we do see an almost monotonic descent after Nahleen, reinforced and made "final" after Beit Liqya. This suggests that the broader time frame, the one implicit throughout this chapter, may reflect greater success. In fact a sense of success is only possible if we define the relevant time frame as 1953–55. We may then view the first year and a half as the time when deterrence was "created," by the end of which "the Jordan government had nearly mastered infiltration."[84] In the second half of the period the fruits were enjoyed.

Israeli leaders, looking back in late 1954 and in 1955, took precisely this view of their accomplishments. In 1954 Peres said, "It is a fact that since Qibya (despite its definitely negative balance) and despite Nahleen the infiltration curve has plunged miraculously. The reason is that the Legion has decided to maintain order on the side of the frontier for which it is responsible."[85] And Hutchison, chairman of the Israel-

84. Glubb, *Soldier with the Arabs*, pp. 381–82.
85. Peres, *Hashlav haba*, p.10.

[67]

Jordan MAC, writes, "During my three years on the Jordan-Israel Mixed Armistice Commission, I watched Jordan's attitude towards border control change from one of mild interest to a keen determination to put a stop to infiltration."[86]

Finally, to place a limit on unduly optimistic conclusions, if we extend the period into the summer of 1956 we note that serious infiltration from Jordan rose to an average of seven incidents per month between April and September (table 4).[87] Thus, with its effect limited both in time and to circumstance, active deterrence-by-reprisal can be considered a relative success.

86. Hutchison, *Violent Truce*, p. 102.
87. Blechman, "Consequences of the Israeli Reprisals," p. 85.

[3]

Harassment from Egypt, 1953–1956

If the war of 1948 revolutionized the very nature of the Hashemite Kingdom of Jordan, thrusting it into the Palestinian problem and an intimate and inescapable relationship with Israel, this was not so of Egypt. Participation and defeat in the war may have inextricably tied Egypt to the Arab East and the question of Palestine, but the involvement was neither immediate nor crucial to Egypt's survival. Egypt had been late to enter yet the first to negotiate an armistice in the war, at the end of which the Egyptian army retreated back across the Sinai Peninsula and Egyptian politics continued on its prewar course toward revolution, an upheaval accelerated but not determined by "the disaster."

The Palestine War left in Egyptian hands the Gaza Strip, with some 250,000 people, of whom four-fifths were refugees. The Strip, separated from Egypt by the Sinai desert, was *not* incorporated into the country but maintained as an insignificant refugee camp—insignificant to the nation of some 20 million, which in July 1952 was busy consummating her revolution. On 22 July 1952 the Free Officers, led by Nasser, Sadat, Salah Salem, and Abdul Hakim Amer, overthrew the regime of King Farouk. At first Gen. Mohammed Neguib, a popular hero of the 1948 Palestine War, was made both president and premier. By March 1954 Nasser had overthrown Neguib, taken control, and become undisputed leader of the Revolutionary Command Council (RCC).

Speaking to the Knesset in August 1952 Prime Minister Ben-Gurion accepted the new Egyptian leadership warmly:

> The events that have taken place in Egypt during the past few weeks should be welcomed, and we are prepared to accept the testimony of Mohammed Naguib that he and most of his colleagues in the Egyptian army were opposed to the invasion of Israel. . . . The two countries are

separated by a broad and extensive desert, and there is no room for border disputes; there was not, nor is there now, any reason for political, economic, or territorial antagonism between the two neighbors. Israel wishes to see a free, independent, and progressive Egypt.[1]

By 1955, Egypt had become Israel's primary and immediate enemy, and in 1956, Ben-Gurion launched a war—the Sinai Campaign—against the Egyptian "dictator" and "tyrant," hoping (at least) to bring about his personal demise.[2]

As reflected in these end points, Israel's relations with Egypt between the Revolution and the Sinai Campaign changed from moderate to belligerent, from hopeful of accommodation to fearful, and from peripheral to central. Israel faced an ever-growing challenge from her southern neighbor, which she was wont to deter. The challenge took two basic forms: blockade of Israel's freedom of navigation through the Red Sea and low-level physical violations of her integrity. The blockade had been imposed on Israeli shipping in the Suez Canal since 1947. It was expanded in December 1953 to include Israel-bound shipping in the Straits of Tiran, and tightened again in September 1955, when air as well as sea transport was forbidden passage. Israel's commercial ties to Asia and Africa were choked off.

Egyptian policy on the ground evolved in four stages: Until mid-1954 there was a fairly clear policy to prevent infiltration across the Gaza armistice demarcation line (ADL) into Israel. From mid-1954 till February 1955, policy seems to have become "controlled omission." In other words, the Egyptian state selectively permitted and gave some assistance to Palestinian infiltration. The period between March 1955 and August of that year witnessed the advent of state-directed (Fedayeen) and state-performed (army) harassment across the frontier. Beginning in the fall of 1955 there was further organization and professionalization of the Fedayeen, direct Egyptian involvement in organizing Fedayeen activity from Jordanian territory, and increased direct participation of regular army units in violence across the border.

This trend leads quickly and seemingly surely to the conclusion that Israel's exercise of active deterrence failed to end Egyptian harassment. The result appears instead to have been escalation leading in the end to a general war. Whether and why this conclusion is correct is a major concern of this chapter. But first, the historical record:

1. Quoted in Ben-Gurion, *Israel*, pp. 64–65.
2. For a discussion of the attitude of Ben-Gurion and others by 1955–56, see Brecher, *Decisions in Israel's Foreign Policy*, pp. 244–45.

A HISTORY

1953–1954

Earl Berger has described the RCC's early policy toward Israel as a "rapprochement." In March 1953, Egypt actually presented specific demands as a basis for negotiating a settlement, including border adjustments, a land link to Jordan, and refugee compensation. These were acceptable to Israel.[3] Apparently, secret contacts were maintained on a regular basis through representatives in Paris, but by the spring of 1954 this rapprochement was winding down. By the end of the year the secret talks were terminated, despite Israeli efforts to conciliate by reaffirming her commitment to a cross-Negev land link and refugee compensation.[4]

This "winding down" occurred coincidentally with critical developments in Egyptian politics (which I explore later in some detail). Briefly, by mid-1954, Nasser had consolidated his control of the RCC and the latter's control of the Egyptian polity except for the Muslim Brotherhood opposition, which Nasser quashed later in the fall. By October, Egypt had secured British agreement to evacuate the Suez Canal Zone, thereby adding external independence to the internal control.

Until mid-1954 the fundamental orientation of politics and policy were internal, toward Egyptian problems and in an Egyptian idiom. But in the spring of that year one could see the first buds of externalization, as the regime turned to the Arab world as a major source of legitimacy. In a quest for leadership at home and abroad, and legitimacy at home, Nasser launched his "war" on the Baghdad Pact, imperialism, and Israel; let loose the appeal to Arab nationalism over the Voice of the Arabs (Sawt el-Arab); and used Israel as a proving ground for his credentials.

Egypt's blockade of Israel's opening to Asia and Africa was first imposed in the War of Independence, barring passage of all shipping to and from Israel through the Suez Canal. After a Security Council resolution in 1951 calling on Egypt to lift the blockade, Egypt promised to relax restrictions. But, in 1953 cargoes bound for Israel through the canal were one-tenth in volume of those of 1946–47, and in late December an

---

3. Berger, *Covenant and the Sword*, pp. 171–74.

4. Yair Evron, *The Middle East: Nations, Superpowers and Wars* (New York, 1973), p. 40; Berger, *Covenant and the Sword*, pp. 172–73. On the talks in Paris see Stock, *Israel*, p. 122; *Maariv*, 4 August 1961; *New York Times*, 27, 28 September 1954.

Italian ship en route to Eilat was fired on at the Straits of Tiran (map 3). The sea blockade was now complete.[5]

Naturally, in February 1954, Israel appealed to the Security Council for redress, where she received an unsympathetic hearing. The United States and Britain were reluctant to sponsor Israel's complaints because the British were in a difficult stage in their Suez Canal negotiations with Egypt. The debate at the Security Council ended with presentation of a New Zealand resolution that simply echoed the 1951 decision—and in the Soviet Union's first pro-Arab veto. Egypt made assurances that now—free of outside interference—Egypt would relax the blockade. And indeed, until October 1954 Israel-bound cargoes were allowed through the canal, but not through the Straits of Tiran.[6]

In September, as Egypt and Great Britain neared finalization of the canal evacuation accord, Israel executed a last-minute panic maneuver—trying to sail a commercial vessel, the Bat Galim, through the canal. The ship was impounded. The purpose seems to have been to force the Egyptians to declare their position on Israeli shipping in the canal before the British withdrawal. Thus, hoped the Israelis, if Egypt did not let the ship through, perhaps the British would not leave. Understanding this possibility, perhaps the Egyptians would let the Bat Galim through, establishing a precedent. Believing the seventy thousand–man British garrison to be a strategic buffer, the Israelis were unhappy with the prospect of the British departure and would have welcomed either outcome: freedom to sail or maintenance of a British presence. But Israeli attempts to force the Security Council to come to grips with the ship's impounding failed, and the exercise only resulted in the embarrassment and anger of the United States and Britain. Almost simultaneous with Bat Galim, and with the similar purpose of creating Western–Egyptian tensions, was the so-called Mishap—Essek ha-Bish—later known as the Lavon Affair: an attempt by a Jewish-Israeli spy ring in Egypt to sabotage American libraries and other objectives in Cairo and Alexandria. It was naïve in concept and, appropriately, failed.[7]

5. For a concise history of the blockade see Berger, *Covenant and the Sword*, chap. 11. For specific events in 1953 see *New York Times*, 13 September, 31 December 1953.

6. Richard N. Swift, "International Peace and Security," in Clyde Eagleton, Waldo Chamberlin, and Richard N. Swift, eds., *1954 Annual Review of United Nations Affairs* (New York, 1955), pp. 24–25; Ro'i, *From Encroachment to Involvement*, pp. 127–31; Berger, *Covenant and the Sword*, pp. 160–61.

7. On Bat Galim, see Safran, *Israel*, p. 351; for the Egyptian perspective see Stephens, *Nasser*, pp. 153–55; and for a detailed record of the Israeli decision-making process see Sharett, *Yoman Ishi*, the numerous entries under "Bat Galim" in the index, vol. 8. On Essek ha-Bish see Zeev Schiff and Eitan Haber, eds., *Lexikon le-Bitahon Yisrael* [Israel, army

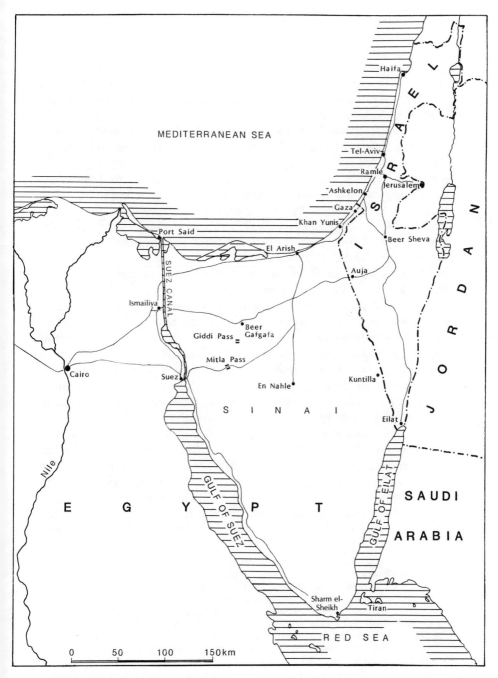

MEDITERRANEAN SEA

Haifa

Tel-Aviv

Ramle

Ashkelon
Jerusalem

Gaza

Khan Yunis

Port Said
El Arish

Beer Sheva

SUEZ CANAL

Auja

Ismailiya

Beer
Gafgafa
Giddi Pass

Mitla Pass

Cairo

Suez

Kuntilla

En Nahle

S I N A I

Nile

Eilat

EGYPT

GULF OF SUEZ

GULF OF EILAT

SAUDI

ARABIA

I S R A E L

J O R D A N

Sharm el-
Sheikh
Tiran

RED SEA

0   50   100   150km

3. Israel and Egypt, 1949–1956

In October, Egypt reimposed the prohibition on shipment of Israeli goods through the canal. The Bat Galim affair and its diplomatic aftermath represent Israel's last attempt to deal with the blockade either directly or indirectly. As we shall see, the idea of forcefully opening the Straits of Tiran would be considered a number of times in 1955—and dropped. As a practical matter, Israel appeared to acquiesce to the blockade, even as it was drawn tighter in 1955.

Meanwhile, through the early 1950s, infiltration from the Gaza Strip had been "innocent," carried out by dispossessed refugees who crossed the frontier for smuggling, theft, and even nostalgia. By 1953, as in Jordan, a certain politicization of infiltration had occurred, as extra-Gaza organizations began to contract local field operators to infiltrate. Involved in instigating infiltration were the Husseini family, the Saudis, and the "All Palestine Government" in Cairo; no local Gazan organization emerged before 1955 to pursue anti-Israeli terrorism.[8] In 1953 the volume of infiltration did increase, but unlike in Jordan at that time, did not become ugly. In all of 1953 we record three incidents of serious infiltration involving mining or sabotage (table 4), p. 43.

Through August of 1953 there is no evidence that either Israel or Egypt was unduly concerned with these events. Little interested in Gaza, Egypt maintained a weak military government in the Strip and enjoyed generally poor relations with the dominant local families. In all of the Gaza Strip the Egyptians deployed one infantry company. Official policy of the local Egyptian authorities was to prevent Palestinian infiltration, a policy they pursued without great vigilance but seriously enough to evoke complaints by Palestinians that "the Arab authorities are even stricter than the Israelis about Arabs crossing the lines."[9]

For her part, Israel seemed to accept the status quo, and between the July (1952) Revolution and August 1953 did not retaliate in any way.[10] Then, on the night of 31 August, two small squads of the unit then being formed as the 101 crossed the ADL into the Gaza Strip and entered the el-Bureij refugee camp, just south of the town of Gaza (map 4).[11] Once discovered, a fire fight with the local guards developed,

---

and defense: A dictionary] (Tel-Aviv, 1976), pp. 400–2; for the affair and its long-run intrusion to Israeli politics, see Aronson, *Conflict and Bargaining*, pp. 31–36.

8. Ya'ari, *Mitsrayim veha-Fedayeen, 1953–1956*, pp. 9–11.

9. Khalil Totah, *Dynamite in the Middle East* (New York, 1955), p. 42. For the Egyptian policy see Ya'ari, *Mitsrayin veha-Fedayeen, 1953–1956*, pp. 9–11.

10. See table 3. For Dayan's description of Israel's early policy as one of "patience," see his *Yoman Ma'arekhet Sinai* [Sinai Campaign diary] (Tel-Aviv, 1965), p. 9.

11. Unit 101 was an elite infantry commando unit established in 1953 by Chief of Staff Moshe Dayan and placed under the command of Maj. Ariel Sharon. It was established in response to the poor standards exhibited by regular units after the War of Independence

4. Southwestern Israel, Gaza, and Auja, 1949–1956

creating a general panic. Surrounded by hysterical refugees, the Israelis shot their way out and retreated back across the border. In the incident the refugees suffered some twenty deaths and sixty injuries.[12] What was the motivation for the raid, and what were its effects?

Perhaps the most striking discovery in a study of this raid is that for the Israelis it was a nonevent. There is almost no discussion of it in the literature, including the rather careful biographies of Ben-Gurion and Dayan, and the latter's autobiography. The explanation is, I believe, twofold. First, little importance was imputed to the Gaza problem at the time because most attention was focused on Jordan. The el-Bureij attack did not follow any serious change in the status quo by or from Egypt, nor did it reflect a new Israeli policy toward Egypt. In Uri Milstein's account of the operation a long list of prior "enemy" provocations is given,[13] almost none of them from Gaza! Inasmuch as the 101 was just in the process of formation, the raid may well have had more to do with unit building than with deterrence. The second reason for the raid's unimportance is that in the months following the raid, the situation on the Egyptian border did not change, for good or bad.

Within the Gaza Strip the effects of the raid were not benign. In el-Bureij rioters demanded that the authorities distribute weapons. The local police were incapable of restoring order and had to call in the army. The policy response echoes the Jordanian response to the Qibya raid: local Egyptian commanders concluded that the way to prevent such disruptions was to prevent Palestinian infiltration. But—and here is the difference from Qibya—just as it was local commanders who drew the conclusion, so it was local leaders who had to find a solution, for as far as I can tell, Cairo had no intention either of getting involved or investing more military or other resources in Gaza or of trying to enhance its rather poor relations with (and control of) the Strip. Lacking resources, the local solution was to form the Civil Guard, a unit of refugee camp residents, who were given the unlikely mission of preventing their bretheren from infiltrating Israel.[14]

Eight months later, in April or March 1954, the nature of relations across the frontier changed. Table 4 shows a general rise in serious

---

and in the hope that one active and successful unit would generate a general raising of standards throughout the IDF.

12. Uri Milstein, *Milhamot ha-Tsankhanim* [Wars of the paratroopers] (Tel-Aviv, 1968), pp. 19–20; Anthony Nutting, *Nasser* (London, 1972), p. 94; *Al-Ahram*, 30 August 1953, quoted in "Korot ha-Yamin" [Current events], *Hamizrah he-Hadash* [New East] 5, no. 1 (1953):34.

13. Milstein, *Milhamot ha-Tsankhanim*, pp. 19–20.

14. Ya'ari, *Mitsrayim veha-Fedayeen, 1953–1956*, pp. 12–13.

infiltration beginning in the spring. Some of it changed in character and seemed to reflect central, even Egyptian, organization. Israel began to capture infiltrators on so-called spying missions who admitted when interrogated that they were sent by Egyptian Army Intelligence. Israeli sources claim infiltrators on thirteen such missions were caught through February 1955.[15] As it increased in 1954 the infiltration became ugly, with sabotage, mining, and murder visited on Israeli settlements near the Strip and as far away as Tel-Aviv. There were also a small number of direct army-to-army confrontations, though of negligible proportions.

The Israelis concluded that this behavior reflected a discrete change of Egyptian policy, and in September the Israeli government issued a warning to the Egyptians, in which it claimed: "In our hands there is evidence that these operations are being performed directly by official bodies or by organized gangs, working in coordination with the Egyptian authorities in the Gaza Strip. There is reason to believe that the Egyptian authorities are interested in raising terrorism in Gaza since the accord [with Great Britain] on the [evacuation of] the Suez Canal Zone."[16] Was it a new policy? Despite incomplete evidence we can make out certain trends in Egyptian policy at the time.

The second half of 1954 witnessed a transformation of Egyptian involvement in the conflict with Israel. Until the spring of that year the interests of Nasser and the RCC were best served by a calm frontier with Israel. Nasser had not yet won the officers' loyalty and was reluctant to transfer resources to the army, an attitude strengthened by the requirements of the promised internal development.[17] But as Nasser solidified his position within the RCC and the army and as the competition with Iraq for pan-Arab leadership began, internal pressure for direct belligerence toward Israel grew.[18] Nasser answered these pressures by terminating the Paris peace talks, maintaining the blockade, and adopting a policy of directed and controlled omission across the Israel frontier.

The change in policy across the Gaza ADL was cleverly contrived, implemented so as not to require resource transfers, military redeployments, or diversion of attention. The local Civil Guard, henceforth

15. *Lamerhav,* an Israeli daily newspaper, quoted in Blechman, "Consequences of the Israeli Reprisals," pp. 82–83.

16. Quoted in Ya'ari, *Mitrayim veha-Fedayeen, 1953–1956,* p. 14. For Dayan's conviction that this represented a change in Egyptian policy, see *Yoman Ma'arekhet Sinai,* p. 9.

17. Keith Wheelock, *Nasser's New Egypt: A Critical Analysis* (New York, 1960), p. 222. See Nasser's remarks to Burns, in Burns, *Between Arab and Israeli,* p. 18. In the year after the Revolution military spending dropped some 20 percent, but police expenditures rose about 200 percent—Safran, *From War to War,* pp. 151–52.

18. Jean Lacouture, *Nasser* (New York, 1973), p. 275; Stephens, *Nasser,* pp. 142–43.

called the National Guard, was expanded and more closely integrated with the Egyptian army. In this way operations of the guard could be seen simultaneously as "Palestinian" and "military"—to everyone's delight. There was one problem: Giving this new responsibility to the military authorities in Gaza without giving the military governor the means either to control unauthorized infiltration or fend off Israeli responses put him in a tight spot. Despite a substantial effort on his part, he was incapable of tightly controlling infiltration. The result was more activity than initially intended.[19]

The Israelis did not support their September warning with physical activity. Between the el-Bureij attack in August 1953 and February 1955, Israel's retaliatory policy was most striking in its absence, despite the escalation in Egyptian violence. This is not to say there was absolutely no Israeli activity across the border. There was, but it was mostly small scale and not very violent, usually performed by tiny patrols of two or three 101 soldiers who would avenge theft with theft or sabotage with sabotage. The conflict at this level appears to have been unimportant to both Israeli and Cairene decision makers.[20]

In March and April 1954 there was a flurry of tit-for-tat activity, and for the first time the IDF and an Egyptian army unit (National Guard?) exchanged significant blows directly. The cycle apparently began when in late March an Egyptian unit kidnapped an Israeli soldier, in return for which the IDF on 4 April attacked an Egyptian army outpost in order to capture a hostage of their own. The cycle continued until Prime Minister Moshe Sharett decided to arrest it unilaterally, believing it could only spiral.[21]

Throughout that spring and into the fall Sharett found himself applying the brakes to the desires of Defense Minister Pinkhas Lavon and Chief of Staff Dayan, both of whom pushed for a more activist policy on the Egyptian frontier. In April we find Sharett trying to persuade Lavon that direct blows to the Egyptian army would not compel it to control infiltration but would rather push it to retaliate directly against the IDF.[22] In late September, after a period of enhanced infiltration activity that included a rather gruesome murder of two civilians at Beit Shikma, Dayan advocated a change in the scale of Israeli raids. He reasoned that

19. For a discussion of the military governor's (el-Agroudi's) efforts to control infiltration, see Ya'ari, *Mitsrayim veha-Fedayeen, 1953–1956*, pp. 13–16.

20. Milstein, in *Milhamot ha-Tsankhanim*, pp. 32–34, refers to these Israeli operations as "messimot." They appear to have been mostly macho-proving exercises and not part of a general security-enhancing strategy.

21. Sharett, *Yoman Ishi* 2:446, 451.

22. Ibid., pp. 462–63.

Cairo was not influenced by the small and sporadic garden-variety actions and that Israel should engage Cairo through large operations.[23] One cannot help noting that Dayan's demand was made in September 1954, just at the end of the Qibya-Nahleen-Beit Liqya series of raids in Jordan, which were proving so successful in eliminating infiltration by "engaging escalation." Sharett vetoed these pressures to escalate, and aside from a small raid for sabatage in August, Israel's policy remained conciliatory until February 1955.

January–August 1955

Between October 1954 and February 1955 the border was relatively quiet, almost no operations occurring in either direction, though there does appear to have been a slight increase in activity from Egypt in January and February.[24] On 26 February a team of infiltrators from Gaza penetrated as far as Ness Tsionah (near Tel-Aviv) for purposes of theft, espionage, and murder; they killed one civilian, and the evidence suggested they had been sent by Egyptian Army Intelligence.[25] On 28 February 1955 Israel carried out the notorious Gaza raid which, like Qibya in Jordan, heralded a new era in Israeli-Egyptian relations.

During the night two IDF paratroop companies crossed into the Strip and attacked the train station, water pumping station, and an army command post in the town of Gaza. A smaller group laid an ambush on the Gaza–Rafah road to interdict reinforcements. The results for the Egyptian forces were devastating. The Israelis reached their targets undetected and, despite some navigational errors and fierce Egyptian resistance, completed their missions and retreated with a small number of casualties. The Egyptians suffered some thirty-nine deaths and thirty-two injuries. More than half of the Egyptian deaths were inflicted when the interdicting ambush successfully intercepted a number of trucks carrying reinforcements to Gaza.[26]

The Gaza raid requires explanation, for it represented an extreme departure from Israeli policy toward Egypt in a number of respects. Most striking is that it was executed at all, given the relative tranquility

23. Ibid., pp. 591–92.

24. Barry M. Blechman, *Military Event Data Set* (1972). This data set Blechman compiled in support of his dissertation and is a detailed record of physical interactions between Israel and her neighbors, 1949–69; available on computer tape from Inter-university Consortium for Political and Social Research, as Tape 0489; Stock, *Israel*, p. 114; *Skirah Hodshit*, February 1955.

25. Sharett, *Yoman Ishi* 3:799.

26. For descriptions see Bar-Zohar, *Ben-Gurion*, pt. 3, pp. 1128–29; Milstein, *Milhamot ha-Tsankhanim*, pp. 35–46; Burns, *Between Arab and Israeli*, p. 17.

at the ADL during the preceding months. It was essentially unpro-
voked, unless the 26 February murder is considered provocation, in
which case the raid was relatively large, both in size of unit and in extent
of damage. Finally, it targeted the Egyptian army directly, going for a
central base. Why?

In trying to explain the policy departure we must be careful not to
read backward from results to intentions. It was not the policy departure it might seem to have been. What happened on the ground was not
what was intended by senior decision makers, and the large number of
Egyptian casualties was neither desired nor predicted, though the raid
was meant to be larger than, and different from, previous operations.
Reading the real-time account of the decision-making process in
Sharett's diary, most striking is the ease of decision and the lack of
serious debate, though having made the decision Sharett does seem
troubled by possible implications. Dayan and Ben-Gurion estimated
some ten to twelve casualties, and Sharett—normally opposed to reprisals—had no qualms.[27]

In part the extent of the raid's "success" is attributable to the size
and quality of the attacking unit. The departure in size was a function
of the nature of the target, and quality was the result of two years of
intensive training, mostly on the Jordanian front.[28] There was also
much luck involved in the results: had the Egyptian reinforcements not
approached as they did, with soldiers piled into trucks, the number of
casualties would have been much lower.[29]

But why a *military* target? One reason, clearly, was the lesson learned
in Jordan: that civilian targets were unacceptable. Another more basic
influence on the choice of target was the Israeli perception of the nature
of the challenge and the use of reprisal. We observed earlier that the
Israelis saw the infiltration as an increasingly state-directed policy of
commission. The murder at Ness Tsionah on 26 February seemed an
especially blunt manifestation of state espionage, theft, and now homi-
cide. Active deterrence of state actions would require the targeting of
state objects. But the Gaza raid was more than deterrence of infiltration;
it was also punishment for other acts of harassment by Egypt: the
impounding of the Bat Galim and the hanging in Cairo of two Jewish
spies, leaders of the Israeli-Jewish spy and sabotage ring that had
unsuccessfully tried to sabotage Western targets in Egypt during the

27. Sharett, *Yoman Ishi* 3:799–800.
28. Shabtai Teveth, *Moshe Dayan: Biographia* (Jerusalem and Tel-Aviv, 1971), p. 435.
29. According to Yehoshafat Harkabi, chief of military intelligence (1955–59), the
ambush was the critical event in the operation but was completely unforeseen. (Interviewed in Jerusalem on 29 October 1984).

previous summer.[30] Sharett wrote of his considerations during the cabinet meeting in which the Gaza raid decision was made: "When the two were hanged in Cairo we told ourselves: we will not retaliate (in a premeditated act) for the hanging, but if there is violence from the Strip we will retaliate in great force, to balance that account."[31]

As after the Qibya raid, Israel tried to fabricate an untenable account of the raid, claiming it was the spontaneous development of an engagement inside Israel between Israeli and Egyptian units, during which the IDF pursued the Egyptians into Gaza. This naïve attempt was ignored by the Western powers, whose reaction to the Gaza raid was extremely negative from Israel's perspective.[32] The Baghdad Pact had been signed just days before the raid and, fearful of losing Egypt, all three Western powers sponsored a Security Council resolution censuring Israel. John Foster Dulles was especially bitter in remarks to Sharett after the raid.[33]

Israel used the raid to try to convince Western audiences that there were serious dangers involved in the current state of relations. Sharett summoned the ambassadors of Britain and the United States and warned them that Gaza was proof of the costs and implications of their not undertaking to guarantee Israel's security, especially through armament. A weak state, implied Sharett, should be expected to panic and lash out.[34] Neither was especially moved.

Turning to the Eygptians in March, the IDF spokesman tried to mobilize the raid into a brinkmanship relationship. After Gaza he said, "It should be clear, that if the Egyptian authorities in Gaza continue in their games, and to the previous sin of failing to stop infiltration add the crime of instigating provocative operations, they will create a 'complication' that Israel does not desire. Responsibility for such developments will lie with them."[35] Egypt, too, remained unmoved.

After the Gaza raid relations across the frontier were revolutionized.

30. See n. 7, above.

31. Sharett, *Yoman Ishi* 3:800. See also Stock, *Israel*, p. 114; Bar-Zohar, *Ben-Gurion*, pt. 3, pp. 1127–28; Evron, *Middle East*, p. 36. One common explanation attributes the decision to Ben-Gurion's return from his year-long "vacation" at Sdeh-Boker—an announcement of a new activist policy. A related explanation refers to Sharett's fear of appearing too dovish; see Nutting, *Nasser*, p. 96; Stephens, *Nasser*, p. 155; Stock, *Israel*, p. 119; Evron, *Middle East*, p. 36; Bar-Zohar, *Ben Gurion*, pt. 3, p. 1127.

32. Sharett, *Yoman Ishi*, 3:805. This fabrication was even carried inward within the IDF; see *Skirah Hodshit*, February 1955.

33. Richard N. Swift, "Peace and Security in the United Nations," in Clyde Eagleton and Richard N. Swift, eds., *Annual Review of United Nations Affairs 1955–1956* (New York, 1956), pp. 8–9; "Korot ha-Yamim," *Hamizrah he-Hadash* 6, no. 3 (1955):219; Bar-Zohar, *Ben-Gurion*, pt. 3, p. 1130; Sharett, *Yoman Ishi* 3:854–55.

34. Sharett, *Yoman Ishi* 3:821, 837.

35. *Skirah Hodshit*, February 1955.

A series of anti-Egyptian demonstrations took place in the Strip similar to the disorder after el-Bureij. But instead of letting the problem die down as it had then, Egypt undertook a major policy change, signaled by Nasser's first visit to the Gaza Strip since the revolution.[36] The Egyptian army raised its force levels in Gaza and Sinai by a dramatic fifteen thousand soldiers, but it did not move in to *prevent* infiltration. It came to organize and support it and to add its own direct harassment.[37]

For the first time, official communications in Gaza and between Cairo and Gaza began referring to the infiltrators as "Fedayeen," a positively loaded term.[38] The National Guard, which had been established to help control infiltration, began to be activated by the Egyptian army to perform missions within Israel. It is not completely clear when the Fedayeen were established as a military unit, but the operations after March demonstrated improved training and organization and in some instances seemed to involve direct support of the infiltrators by military units. Some of the Egyptian National Guard units that had earlier harassed the British in the Canal Zone were brought to the Strip.[39] Dayan was convinced the Fedayeen were established in April: "But in April 1955 the Egyptian Staff decided to see in operations of terror and sabotage in Israel a manner of war, and established for this purpose a special unit."[40] The Egyptian army also began to harass the Israelis directly, by mining roads and firing on IDF patrols and civilian border settlements.[41]

On 24 March there was a traumatizing raid on a wedding party in the village of Patish, and in April infiltration activity crescendoed: Fedayeen raids resulted in twelve Israeli civilian deaths during the week of 5 April. In May, Egyptian artillery fire on Israeli villages degenerated into a number of all-out artillery duels across the border.[42] Israeli policy remained strikingly conciliatory. The IDF did fire when fired upon, and several times its patrols captured and released Egyptian outposts when the latter opened fire.[43] There were no reprisal operations.

In March, Ben-Gurion tried unsuccessfully to convince the cabinet

36. *Al-Ahram*, 31 March 1955, quoted in "Korot ha-Yamim," *Hamizrah he-Hadash* 6, no. 3 (1955):220. For pressure on the authorities see *Haaretz*, 3, 6 March 1955.

37. Sharett, *Yoman Ishi* 3:896. On the general deterioration see Higgins, *United Nations Peace-Keeping*, p. 151.

38. *Fedayeen* comes from the Arabic root meaning "sacrifice."

39. Sharett, *Yoman Ishi* 3:897.

40. Dayan, *Yoman Ma'arekhet Sinai*, p. 11.

41. Burns, *Between Arab and Israeli*, pp. 78–79.

42. For these and many other incidents, see *New York Times*, 30, 31 March, 1, 2, 3, 4, 6, 10, 17 April, 18, 22, 28, 31 May 1955.

43. Ibid., 8 April, 19 May, 8 June 1955.

not to undertake reprisals but to conquer the Gaza Strip instead and then hold it for bargaining. In the discussions, the maritime blockade emerged as an important motive for operating in Gaza—as it had the previous February.[44] In Ben Gurion's call for a major limited operation we can detect, as we do in Dayan's statement above, the harbingers of an undifferentiated strategic view of the Egyptian challenge in which *all* anti-Israeli activities were taken to be components of an aggressive and belligerent Egyptian policy with the ultimate aim of general and total war.

In April, Abba Eban tried to mobilize the Security Council to consider the state of relations between Israel and Egypt, but to no avail. After much procrastination the Security Council would only go so far as to appeal to both sides to avoid future clashes. Israeli disappointment is understandable in light of the report by UNTSO Chief of Staff Eedson Burns, laying blame for the escalation on Egypt.[45]

In May, Israel threatened Egypt with a major operation, which Nasser understood to mean capture of the Sinai Peninsula. According to Burns, Nasser took this threat quite seriously and allowed for the initiation of direct low-level military negotiations, which took place at the frontier.[46] The negotiations lasted through August, and while they were in progress the frontier was relatively quiet. They were a lively demonstration of the "Arab" limits to Egyptian conciliation. For example, the Egyptians could agree to mutual troop withdrawals but not to an Israeli suggestion that a physical barrier or fence be erected, for that would have represented too unambiguous an acceptance of the status quo.[47] Also, just as direct belligerence declined, the Egyptian export of infiltration from Jordan was stepped up. Thus Nasser pursued a policy belligerent enough to avoid excessive internal pressure and conciliatory enough to relax the Israelis.

44. Bar-Zohar points out that Sharett barely succeeded in blocking Ben-Gurion's initiative and had to rely on non-Mapai members of the cabinet to do so; see *Ben-Gurion*, pt. 3, pp. 1139–40. See also Sharett, *Yoman Ishi* 3:893–99; Dayan, *Avnei Derekh*, p. 143.

45. Stock, *Israel*, pp. 72–73; *New York Times*, 21 April 1955.

46. Burns, *Between Arab and Israeli*, pp. 79–83. See Nasser's warning to Burns that an Israeli attack on Gaza would lead to a general war: Cairo Radio, 5 June 1955, cited in "Korot ha-Yamim," *Hamizrah he-Hadash* 6, no. 4 (1955):302.

47. For descriptions of these negotiations, see Berger, *Covenant and the Sword*, pp. 186–87; Dayan, *Avnei Derekh*, p. 145; *New York Times*, 9 June, 14 July 1955; Burns, *Between Arab and Israeli*, pp. 79–83. In a strange maneuver before the start of negotiations, after agreeing tentatively (and temporarily) to Burns's suggestion of erecting a fence along the ADL, the Egyptians explained that it could not be erected *on* the ADL, but rather *within* the Strip, so that it would not be construed as Egyptian acceptance of a "border" with Israel; see Cairo Radio, 9 May 1955, cited in "Korot ha-Yamim," *Hamizrah he-Hadash* 6, no. 4 (1955):302.

In July the Egyptian-Czech arms deal was informally initialed, and on 22 August the Egyptians terminated the negotiations with Israel. This they accomplished by firing on an Israeli patrol, which returned fire, counterattacked, captured the offending outpost, and then retreated.[48] Apparently, the specter of new Egyptian power emasculated Israeli threats and at the same time raised internal pressure for action. In classic Middle Eastern (or Byzantine) style, Nasser created an incident that allowed him to break off negotiations and launch a major Fedayeen attack.

August–December 1955

During the ten days after the collapse of negotiations violent relations markedly intensified. Egypt launched a massive Fedayeen offensive all over the southern half of Israel. In twenty-three separate operations between 22 and 29 August, seventeen Israelis were killed. On 29 August an Egyptian fighter aircraft penetrated Negev airspace and was felled. Two Egyptian Vampires were shot down under similar circumstances on 1 September. Ehud Ya'ari claims that it is in *this* period that the Fedayeen really operated for the first time as units, though still organized into National Guard formations and becoming Fedayeen only when so ordered by the Egyptian army. Reflecting the centralized nature of the new policy was the media coverage of the Fedayeen operations. Departing from past policy, the Egyptian press and *Sawt el-Arab* provided excited, supportive, and exaggerated descriptions of their feats.[49]

After passively suffering this harassment for ten days Israeli forces dealt the Egyptians the greatest blow to their prestige yet. On the night of 30 August a force of about twelve half-tracks destroyed the old British Taggart-style police station in the town of Khan Yunis in the southern part of the Gaza Strip. The police station housed the regional command post of an Egyptian brigade with territorial responsibility. Egyptian casualties were high, numbering over forty dead, but most devastating was the style of the operation. The Israelis simply drove down the main road from the border to Khan Yunis, fought their way into the police station, blew it up, and drove home.[50] Egyptian chief of staff Amer

---

48. Sharett, *Yoman Ishi* 4:1143.

49. See the survey of the Egyptian press at the time in "Korot ha-Yamim," *Hamizrah he-Hadash* 7, no. 1 (1956):36. See also Berger, *Covenant and the Sword*, p. 188; Ya'ari, *Mitsrayim veha-Fedayeen, 1953–1956*, p. 19.

50. Milstein, *Milhamot ha-Tsankhanim*, pp. 47–54.

wanted to counterattack in Israeli territory in force but was denied permission by Nasser.[51]

The process leading to the Israeli decision to execute the raid suggests that the operation did not reflect a change in Israeli policy. Even after the difficult week of 22 August, Sharett was reluctant to approve any acts of reprisal but finally succumbed on 29 August, agreeing to a number of very small operations. These he canceled at the last moment, an act that prompted Dayan to submit his resignation. Unable to cope politically with this threat Sharett authorized the Khan Yunis raid.[52]

After Khan Yunis the Egyptians pacified the Gaza frontier for a while, but they did not decrease belligerent activity. They increased and displaced it. In September the Czech arms deal was made public, and in its wake Egypt tightened the blockade to prohibit air passage *over* the Red Sea as well as shipping in it. In late September the Egyptian army moved the arena of violent challenge to the demilitarized zone at Auja, south of the Gaza Strip. The area was considered a staging ground for major attacks by both sides and hence had been demilitarized in the General Armistice of 1949. In 1953, Israel had established there a paramilitary settlement—Ketsiot—a move Egypt had long disputed but never physically challenged. Beginning in late September the Egyptians tried to occupy portions of the area, waged small attacks on Israeli positions, and otherwise challenged Israel's rights in the DMZ. The Egyptian army also raised its presence west of the Ketsiot area to levels prohibited in the armistice.[53] The Israelis responded with two large raids.

The first operation took place against an Egyptian border police station in Kuntilla, south of Auja. In a daring operation the Israeli force traversed a large distance at night, continuing on foot after being stopped by the terrain, and surprised the Egyptian unit. Twelve Egyptian soldiers were killed, six wounded, and twenty-nine imprisoned. The Israelis also destroyed fifteen vehicles and took three with them.[54] Kuntilla was followed by the 2 November attack on the Egyptian positions at Sabha, just west of the frontier, near Ketsiot. This was the largest Israeli operation since 1949. The attacking force was of battalion strength and included both paratroopers and, for the first time, reservists and elements of the regular Golani infantry brigade. The defend-

51. Stephens, *Nasser*, p. 159.

52. Dayan, *Avnei Derekh*, pp. 150–51. Sharett has no entries in his diary for this period.

53. On the crisis at the Auja DMZ, see Burns, *Between Arab and Israeli*, pp. 92–103; Schiff and Haber, *Lexikon le-Bitahon Yisrael*, p. 368; Stock, *Israel*, pp. 74–75.

54. Schiff and Haber, *Lexikon le-Bitahon Yisrael*, p. 272; Bar-Zohar, *Ben-Gurion*, pt. 3, p. 1154.

ing Egyptian battalion was all but destroyed, suffering about fifty deaths and yielding some fifty prisoners. Egyptian attempts to use tanks failed.[55]

Quiet returned to the Auja area.

Unlike Qibya or Gaza, one could not argue—nor have I discovered any attempts to do so—that Khan Yunis, Kuntilla, or Sabha were unintentional successes. These raids were meant to be large and highly damaging. What was the reason for them, and what was the policy they implemented? In the summer and fall of 1955 the Israeli view of the Egyptian challenge changed dramatically, most notably in the eyes of Dayan and Ben-Gurion. Especially after the Czech arms deal, which had been privately agreed on by July, the Egyptian threat began to loom strategic, a perception only strengthened by the challenges at Auja and the further tightening of the blockade. In one blow the Czech arms deal revolutionized the Middle Eastern system by destroying the control of relative power so long enjoyed by the West. But the fact of Russia's entry did not seem to diminish the West's wooing of Nasser. These developments radically altered the Israeli national security debate—both public and private.[56]

In October the Egyptian announcement of the Czech deal was followed by Israeli failure to secure American or other arms. Defense Minister Ben-Gurion ordered Dayan to make plans and prepare the IDF to capture the Straits of Tiran and possibly also the Gaza Strip and northern Sinai.[57] This was a large conceptual leap from the plans in March to capture part or all of the Gaza Strip. It envisaged a large operation intended to solve the strategic problems rather than merely to end infiltration.

Dayan shared the view that Nasser was getting ready for a general war against Israel and was enthusiastic and hopeful as Ben-Gurion took control of the cabinet in November. But he was to be disappointed.[58] Just as the problem and the contemplated reaction were strategic, so too were the policy considerations. For all his purported activism, Ben-Gurion still shared Sharett's hope that Israel's basic integrity could be secured by American arms and security guarantees. He also feared British intervention on the Egyptian side and had serious misgivings about the long-run efficacy of preventive war.[59] The cabinet sharply

55. Milstein, *Milhamot ha-Tsankhanim*, pp. 55–60; Schiff and Haber, *Lexikon le-Bitahon Yisrael*, pp. 368–69.
56. On this progressively pessimistic view, see Bar-Zohar, *Ben-Gurion*, pt. 3, pp. 1156–58; Dayan, *Avnei Derekh*, chaps. 10, 11; idem, *Yoman Ma'arekhet Sinai*, p. 10; Sharett, *Yoman Ishi* 5:1315.
57. Bar-Zohar, *Ben-Gurion*, pt. 3, pp. 1153–54.
58. Dayan, *Avnei Derekh*, pp. 164–65, 174–75; Bar-Zohar, *Ben-Gurion*, pt. 3, p. 1156.
59. Bar-Zohar, *Ben-Gurion*, pt. 3, pp. 1156–57, 1159.

opposed both general preventive war *and* more limited action in the straits. Knesset debate (discussed later in detail) on preventive war and the Egyptian threat began in November and continued well into 1956, reflecting mounting national anxiety and growing pressure on the government to wage war. The cabinet was resolved to resist.

The relatively large IDF operations of August–November were not only active deterrence of harassment but attempts to deter the newly perceived growing strategic challenge. Ben-Gurion and Dayan believed in the upward convertibility of deterrence and that low-level demonstrations of prowess could deter general war. Symptomatic of his faith in the interchangeability of levels is Ben-Gurion's statement that Israel would know how "to quash any enemy or belligerent till he riseth not, as we did in the Yo'av Campiagn [in the War of Independence] and the Gaza Raid."[60] Dayan was more explicit; in August he said, "Our victories and failures in the small engagements on our frontier and beyond, have a very important influence on 'current security,' on the Arab assessment of Israel's power, and on Israel's self confidence.[61]

The Sabha and Kuntilla raids did restore quiet to the Auja area but were followed by Egyptian strategic and tactical escalations. Again belligerence was displaced, *back* to the Gaza frontier, where infiltration and mining picked up again to their pre-October levels. In December the Fedayeen underwent the final step in their legitimation. Egyptian Chief of Staff Amer ordered an increase in the number of Fedayeen and that they be given the status of an organizationally independent regular battalion with special missions.[62]

On 15 December 1955, Dayan reported that the Egyptians had two regular brigades inside the Gaza Strip, and by 28 February nine brigades in the Sinai Peninsula.[63] He must have recalled wistfully the days in 1953 when Egypt had all of one company in Gaza!

1956

Between late 1955 and April 1956, Israel's relations with Egypt continued to deteriorate, while relations with the three Western powers

---

60. *Haaretz*, 1 April 1956.

61. *Skirah Hodshit*, August 1955. There is some evidence that Dayan also had a contradictory concept in mind: hoping for degeneration of these skirmishes into a general war with Egypt. There is no evidence, however, that he waged private wars or deliberately tried to let events at the front take over. See Horowitz, *Hatfisa ha-Yisraelit shel Bitachon Leumi*, p. 16; Teveth, *Moshe Dayan*, p. 436; Sharett, *Yoman Ishi* 5:1319; Gen. Elad Peled and Zeev Schiff, also suggested this possibility in interviews (Jerusalem, 18 November 1984, and Washington, 2 October 1984, respectively).

62. Ya'ari, *Mitsrayim veha-Fedayeen, 1953–1956*, p. 23.

63. Dayan, *Avnei Derekh*, pp. 173, 180.

improved for the first time in many years. The enhancement of Israel's position was mostly a result of Egypt's deteriorating relations with the Western countries. Nasser's violent intervention in Jordanian politics, which led to the expulsion of the legion's British officers, combined with Nasser's support of the National Liberation Front (FLN) in Algeria to create an Anglo-French agreement to oppose Nasser. American commitment to Egypt had begun to wane in 1955, when the formation of the Northern Tier partially obviated the need for good relations with Egypt. As Nasser fought the Baghdad Pact, became a leader of the nonaligned bloc of nations, and then proceeded to recognize the People's Republic of China, Dulles's disaffection grew.

It was to take time, though, before this alienation would express itself in any pro-Israel policies. In August 1955, when the Czechoslovakian arms deal was not yet public yet undoubtedly known privately, Dulles told the Council on Foreign Relations that the United States was "a friend of both Israelis and Arabs" and called for minor border adjustments.[64] In November in his annual Guildhall speech, Anthony Eden suggested Israeli territorial concessions, and in January he told Parliament that the Tripartite Declaration made no guarantees of borders. And although immediately after the unveiling of the Czech arms deal Israel made abortive attempts to acquire weapons, Dulles told the Senate Foreign Affairs Committee in February, and repeated in a letter to members of the House, that Israel's security could not be achieved by arms.[65]

Yet only a few weeks later the United States lifted its prohibition on the sale of French (NATO) arms to Israel, and Israel began to purchase weapons in quantity and especially in quality on a level with Egypt's recent acquisitions. The flow of French arms did not, however, achieve meaningful proportions before the summer of 1956.[66]

The Egyptian challenge to Israel escalated during the early months of 1956. Between January and March the last attempt at negotiating an overall settlement was made by the United States through Eisenhower's envoy, Robert Anderson. His mission was terminated by Nasser in March, after he had made no progress and had no influence over concomitant military developments.[67] By spring the constantly rising

64. Saadia Touval, *The Peace Brokers: Mediators in the Arab-Israeli Conflict, 1948–1979* (Princeton, N.J., 1982), pp. 111–14.

65. Asher Goren, "Kavim u-Megamot" [Political summary], *Hamizrah he-Hadash* 7, no. 1 (1956), p. 30; Stock, *Israel*, pp. 169, 174–75.

66. On the efforts to acquire French arms, see Shimon Peres, *Kela David* [David's sling] (Jerusalem, 1970), chap. 3.

67. A detailed discussion of Anderson's mission can be found in Bar-Zohar, *Ben-Gurion*, pt. 3, pp. 1161–67. See also, Brecher, *Decisions in Israel's Foreign Policy*, pp. 259–60; Touval, *Peace Brokers*, chap. 5.

Egyptian force levels in Sinai had reached sixty thousand soldiers. Public Egyptian threats of their ability and intention to destroy Israel increased in frequency, and for the first time IDF Intelligence monitored Egyptian military exercises practicing offensive missions to capture such objectives as Beer Sheva.[68] Egyptian meddling in Jordanian politics was accompanied by a sharp rise in Fedayeen activity from Jordanian territory (Chapter 2), a development Israel felt helpless to deter.

On the Gaza frontier the level of Egyptian activity remained high. In March, Israel complained to the United Nations of 180 violent actions across the frontier during the preceding four months.[69] In April a series of incidents made the situation unbearable to the Israelis. It began on 3 April when an Egyptian ambush killed an Israeli soldier within Israeli territory. Egyptian artillery shelled the Israeli village of Kissufim on 4 April and then shelled other Israeli settlements on 5 April. After sustaining these attacks and other incidents that day, Israeli artillery retaliated by shelling the town of Gaza. This unfortunate Israeli action inflicted 152 mostly civilian casualties, among them 59 deaths. It is not completely clear who gave the order on the Israeli side. General Burns writes that it was a local commander's decision, while Sharett suggests that the response was a standard operating procedure. In any case, it appears that when Ben-Gurion heard of the incident (while it was in progress) he ordered the immediate cessation of Israeli artillery fire.[70]

The shelling of Gaza was followed by an unprecedented series of Fedayeen attacks on Israel that lasted about a week. In scores of operations inside Israel the Fedayeen caused over a dozen deaths,[71] among them four young boys killed in an attack on a group of religious school children near Ramle. United Nations Secretary General Dag Hammerskjold had just arrived in the Middle East, prompted by prior concern and rare interest on the part of the Western powers in returning calm to the frontier. Apparently, they believed that an Israeli-Egyptian war was imminent.[72] After tireless effort Hammerskjold secured a local cease-fire, which was promptly followed by further acts of infiltration,

68. Dayan, *Avnei Derekh*, p. 181; Bar-Zohar, *Ben-Gurion*, pt. 3, p. 1168.

69. Dayan, *Yoman Ma'arekhet Sinai*, p. 22.

70. Sharett, *Yoman Ishi* 5:1390; Burns, *Between Arab and Israeli*, p. 140.

71. For descriptions of that week see Ben-Gurion, *Israel*, pp. 96–97; Dayan, *Yoman Ma'arekhet Sinai*, pp. 13–14.

72. A reading of declassified U.S. Joint Chiefs of Staff (JCS) documents from the period shows that, beginning in December 1955, both U.S. and British intelligence services were convinced of imminent war. For example: JCS memo, subject: "US Objectives and Policies with Respect to the Near East" (NSC 5428), by the Joint Strategic Plans Group, dated 23 December 1955; JCS memo, subject: "Combined [with Britain] Planning Pursuant to the Tripartite Declaration of 1950," to Rear Admiral Curvie, from the Joint Strategic Plans Group, dated 4 April 1956. These and similar documents appear in the EMMEA files at the Modern Military Section, U.S. National Archives, Washington, D.C.

though not at the intensity of early April, an intensity never to be repeated.[73] As in August 1955 the Egyptians made no secret of their support for the Fedayeen. Cairo's *Al-Jumhuriyya* wrote that "the heroes are back from the battlefield . . . they have come back after they taught Israel a lesson she will never forget."[74]

On 3 April, Nasser tried to reassure the Israelis that he had absolutely no plans for a general war. In a newspaper interview he explained that while it was true that he had raised his force levels in Sinai, these were in defensive positions, and very small forces only were deployed in the very forward areas of Gaza.[75] It is possible that in Nasser's view attacks by Fedayeen were not as significant a challenge as attacks by Egyptian soldiers would have been and that he differentiated between the unambiguous *official* challenge of armies and the less clear one of proxies. Thus he may have been trying to have his cake and eat it too by demonstrating his belligerence to the appropriate Arab and Egyptian audiences yet diminishing the risk of Israeli response. Diverting Fedayeen activity from Gaza to Jordan may have had a similar purpose.

But to the Israeli leadership the situation seemed hopeless and war inevitable. Yitshak Navon spoke of Israel's feeling of insecurity at the time, conveying the perception that the Fedayeen raids had in themselves become a strategic threat. In explaining the background of the Sinai Campaign he said, "It couldn't go on forever. This [the Fedayeen] in itself provided the atmosphere, the mental preparation, the need to put an end to it. Government was being criticized. People were afraid to move at night [in] Nahal Oz, [due to] bombing [and] shooting. The *Feda'iun* danger was sufficient to lead to something drastic regarding Sinai and the Gaza Strip."[76] On 8 April, Sharett, the quintessential believer in negotiated settlement and peaceful outcome, wrote in his diary, "Night of horrors—are we on the brink of war? How will the Negev settlements survive?"[77]

Except for the shelling of Gaza, however, Israel's behavior throughout April was conciliatory. On 5 April, Ben-Gurion agreed to General Burns's request that patrols along the ADL be discontinued to allow Hammerskjold to try and work out an accord.[78] After Eisenhower

---

73. For a discussion of Hammerskjold's visit, see Burns, *Between Arab and Israeli*, pp. 141–47.

74. Quoted in ibid., p. 142. See also "Korot ha-Yamim," *Hamizrah he-Hadash* 7, no. 4 (1956):288–89.

75. *Haaretz*, 3 April 1956.

76. Quoted in Brecher, *Decisions in Israel's Foreign Policy*, p. 261.

77. Sharett, *Yoman Ishi* 5:1390.

78. Higgins, *United Nations Peace-Keeping*, p. 153; Dayan, *Avnei Derekh*, p. 188.

urged Israeli restraint Ben-Gurion presented the following letter to Hammerskjold on 17 April:

I write to confirm, on behalf of the Government of Israel, that in accordance with Article II (2) of the Egypt-Israel General Armistice Agreement, orders are in force, and have been repeated, for strict observance as from 6:00 P.M. Israel time tomorrow, April 18, 1956, prohibiting any firing by units of the Defence Army of Israel across the Demarcation Line by military or para-military forces, for any purpose whatsoever. This assurance is given on the understanding of full reciprocity on the part of Egypt.[79]

These promises were combined with appropriate threats of the consequences of Egypt's failure to restrain Fedayeen activity.[80] On the Gaza front the volume of Fedayeen activity dropped but did not cease, and at the same time the volume of activity from Jordan rose substantially. Israel did not retaliate, but after a daytime murder near Nahal Oz, Dayan ordered resumption of patrols along the ADL.[81]

In late summer Nasser apparently ordered the reduction both of infiltration from Gaza and of direct army-to-army harassment.[82] After nationalization of the Suez Canal, Egyptian attention again turned to problems closer to home, and Nasser felt obliged to transfer about half the Sinai garrison to the canal and delta regions. At the same time, especially in the early fall, Egyptian-induced activity from Jordan increased dramatically. Ben-Gurion clearly understood these developments, as he explained them to the Knesset on 15 October.[83] Nonetheless, Israel waged only a few minor operations against Egypt between April and the Sinai Campaign in late October.[84]

Nationalization of the Suez Canal pushed Britain, France, and Israel into an alliance for military action.[85] In August, Britain and France started exploring the possibility of Israeli participation in an action against Egypt, in which France and Britain would conquer the Suez Canal and Israel the Sinai. Dayan, Shimon Peres, and Ben-Gurion had

79. Quoted in Ben-Gurion, *Israel*, p. 100.
80. Berger, *Covenant and the Sword*, p. 199.
81. Dayan, *Avnei Derekh*, p. 190.
82. Stephens, *Nasser*, pp. 224–25; Ben-Gurion, *Israel*, p. 108.
83. *Divrei ha-Knesset*, 15 October 1956.
84. In September and October 1956, Israel did, however, execute four large raids against military objectives in Jordan: at Rahwa, Gharandal, Hussan, and Qalqilya. Neither the reasoning behind nor the purpose of these raids has ever been adequately explained. For possible explanations, see Stock, *Israel*, pp. 195–98.
85. On the Israeli decision and the process of tripartite negotiations, see Brecher, *Decisions in Israel's Foreign Policy*, chap. 6; Dupuy, *Elusive Victory*, pp. 176–93.

decided, independently of Nasser's takeover of the canal, that given an inevitable Egyptian offensive war, Israeli preventive war was the only viable solution to a mounting imbalance of power, blockade, and Fedayeen and military activity. The opportunity for tripartite action in the fall of 1956 seemed irresistible. Even so, Ben-Gurion was extremely reticent. Only on 25 October, four days before the attack, did he finally agree, and only after a formal alliance accord was signed at Sèvres, in which aerial coverage of Israel's territory was assured, as was a public stance of equally shared responsibility for the action.

On 29 October the IDF launched its second Sinai Campaign.[86] Organized into two division task forces and three independent brigades, the IDF executed a near classic blitzkrieg, capturing the entire peninsula and Gaza in less than a week. Israeli Defense Forces stopped some 15 kilometers east of the Suez Canal to allow the allies to execute Operation Musketeer, conquest of the canal.

As prearranged, the British and French did not start operations simultaneously with the IDF; only on 31 October did they bomb Egyptian airfields. The bombing provided substantial assistance to Israeli forces, for in its wake, Nasser ordered units from Sinai back to defend the canal against the foreseeable Anglo-French attack. As for Musketeer itself, it began only on 5 November with the successful assault on Port Said. But by 6 November, Britain had agreed to cease fire, aborting the attempt to capture the canal. The war was over.

An Analysis

Relative Interests

Analysis in this case demonstrates the importance of relative interests to the understanding of deterrence outcomes. The sources and distinct nature of Egyptian interests in violence help explain the successes and (mostly) failures of Israeli deterrence, although a full explanation based on ordering or comparing protagonists' interests—by any scheme—proves elusive.

The nature and intensity of Egyptian interests in the conflict with Israel evolved substantially between 1953 and 1956 and in ways that deeply altered the Israeli-Egyptian deterrence relationship. Egypt, having been central to the founding of the Arab League and a major

86. For details of the campaign, see Dayan, *Yoman Ma'arekhet Sinai*, passim; Dupuy, *Elusive Victory*, pp. 195–218; Haim Herzog, *The Arab-Israeli Wars: War and Peace in the Middle East* (New York, 1982), bk. 2.

participant in the war of 1948, was inextricably bound to the Arab East and the Palestine question. To this cause Nasser contributed the blockade against Israeli shipping. But before mid-1954, Gaza and Israel were only of marginal interest to Egypt. Adid Dawisha writes of Egyptian orientation through 1954: "Apart from the Sudanese involvement, the initial years after the revolution witnessed minimal Egyptian participation in Arab affairs. In fact, the period saw almost complete isolation of Egypt from the Arab world, as the new leaders chanelled their energies to Anglo-Egyptian relations and to the consolidation and legitimization of their political control within Egypt."[87] Israel and Gaza were both irrelevant to these concerns.

Violence across the ADL may therefore best be understood in terms of the local bilateral relationship between Israel and Gaza. In this context we have a trio of actors enjoying a relationship similar to the one in the Jordanian case: (a) Israel, with an interest in the status quo; (b) Palestinian refugees, with an interest in undermining it; and (c) the local (Egyptian) military government, with an interest in a modicum of order and control. As in Jordan, a large state (Israel) faced a weak entity (Gaza) whose local regime was endangered by the disruptive impact of reprisal, as demonstrated by the aftermath of the el-Bureij attack. The raid, and the threat of more, helped the local authorities develop a serious interest in preserving the status quo. The Gaza authorities created the Civil Guard and entrusted it with curbing Palestinian infiltration. Thus, it was Cairo's lack of interest in Gaza that made Israeli deterrence at all possible. But this very lack of interest left the Gaza authorities on their own, even though they did not have at their disposal a force equivalent to the Jordanian Arab Legion. The Civil Guards included Palestinians with a mission to arrest Palestinian misbehavior, and this rendered Israeli deterrence only partially successful at best.

Mid-1954 witnessed the first buds of externalization of the RCC's policy orientation and search for legitimacy, a process that created substantial interest in belligerence toward Israel. Some of the pressures to externalize were internal, such as severe domestic economic problems and the inability of the Agrarian Land Reform to balance austerity measures. The need to balance the Ikhwan's (Moslem Brotherhood's) popularity pushed propaganda in the direction of Islamic orthodoxy, sent Nasser to Mecca, and prompted the RCC spokesman to talk about "Arab unity." Local press and radio became increasingly xenophobic, attacking both Christians and Jews.[88]

87. A. I. Dawisha, *Egypt in the Arab World*, p. 10.
88. R. Hrair Dekmejian, *Egypt under Nassir: A Study in Political Dynamics* (Albany, N.Y., 1971), pp. 38–39; Berger, *Covenant and the Sword*, p. 176. Despite these problems, by

In April 1954 the Northern Tier began to take shape as the Turco-Pakistan Pact was signed. Nasser's feeling of isolation in his anti-imperialist position grew, and he saw the pact as a snubb to his advocacy of noninvolvement in Western alliances by Arab states.[89] Sawt el-Arab greatly expanded its broadcasts to the Arab masses, taking on the roll of a major champion of Arab nationalist causes. Slowly, Nasser moved Egypt further into the Arab world and gradually appropriated a leadership position in it, as this July 1954 speech celebrating two years of revolution suggests: "Compatriots, Egypt has started a new era of relations with Arabs—an era based on true and frank fraternity. . . . The aim of the Revolutionary Government is for the Arabs to become one nation with all its sons collaborating for the common welfare. . . . The revolution also believes that the weight of the defence of the Arab states falls first and foremost on the Arabs and that they are worthy of undertaking it."[90] In late 1954 and early 1955 he embraced Ahmed Ben Bella's Algerian revolution against the French, lending it both moral and material support. The FLN made its first public broadcast over Sawt el-Arab.[91]

This process continued into 1955 and intensified as Nasser sought leadership not only of the Arab states but in the Third World as well. It was the pursuit of leadership in the Arab East that created the need to harass Israel. Nasser's leadership bid involved "force" and "Palestine" as central idioms. Demonstration of Arab power and the will to use it was the means to recognized Egyptian leadership in (a) promoting the Palestinian cause, (b) avenging "the disaster" of 1948, (c) fighting imperialism, and (d) providing a viable alternative to Western alliances, such as the Baghdad Pact, as a source of Arab power[92]—and Israel was ideal

---

midyear Nasser's internal position was greatly improved. The Officer Corps's support had been secured and Neguib disposed of as a serious opponent. Discussions of the internal consolidation of power include Dekmejian, *Egypt under Nassir*, chaps. 3, 4; P. J. Vatikiotis, *The Egyptian Army in Politics: Pattern for New Nations?* (Bloomington, Ind., 1961), chap. 4; Stephens, *Nasser*, chap. 5. Egypt also appeared more independent as of July, with the initialing of an accord with Great Britain for the removal of her troops from the Suez Canal. For negotiations with Great Britain at the time over the future of the Sudan and the Canal, see Nutting, *Nasser*, pp. 20–21, 35, 48–49; Lacouture, *Nasser*, pp. 120–25; Stephens, *Nasser*, pp. 110, 129–31. On the quashing of the Ikhwan in October, see Stephens, *Nasser*, pp. 135–36; Vatikiotis, *Egyptian Army in Politics*, pp. 91–94.

89. Nutting, *Nasser*, pp. 76–81; A. I. Dawisha, *Egypt in the Arab World*, p. 11; Berger, *Covenant and the Sword*, p. 176.

90. Quoted in Blechman, "Consequences of the Israeli Reprisals," p. 83.

91. Ahmed Hamroush, *Nasir Wil'Arab* [Nasser and the Arabs], (Beirut, 1976), pp. 380–83. Hamroush was one of the outer circle of the original revolutionary group in Egypt. The cited work is one of a four-volume history of the revolution and its aftermath. I am indebted to Ruth and Arnon Gross for their help in translation.

92. For Nasser's "war" on the Baghdad Pact and competition with Iraq, see Nutting, *Nasser*, chap. 5; A. I. Dawisha, *Egypt in the Arab World*, pp. 12–16, 103, 129–30.

as the proving ground for all four. Obviously central to the first two, she could serve for the third. And the successful application of Egyptian force against Israel could establish the viability of Arab power under Egyptian leadership—the fourth.

In *The Philosophy of the Revolution*, Nasser wrote of the lessons learned from the Palestine War, in which he had participated:

> I believe that what was happening in Palestine could happen, and may still happen today, in any part of this region, as long as it resigns itself to the factors and the forces which dominate now. . . . After the siege and the battles in Palestine I came home with the whole region in my mind one complete whole. . . . An event may happen in Cairo today; it is repeated in Damascus, Beirut, Amman or any other place tomorrow. . . . One region, the same factors and circumstances, even the same forces opposing them all. It was clear that imperialism was the most prominent of these forces; even Israel itself was but one of the outcomes of imperialism. If it had not fallen under British mandate, Zionism could not have found the necessary support to realize the idea of a national home in Palestine.[93]

These externally driven interests in the harassment of Israel converged with a need generated internally. The defeat in 1948 was as Egyptian as it was Arab, and there was intense desire to avenge that debacle. In 1954–55 the army was apparently not yet insisting on a general war but demanded at least some belligerence. Nasser and the RCC had risen from within the army, and with the army as their main power base, they could not well afford to ignore these demands, especially as Nasser's pan-Arab legitimacy was to rest on proven Egyptian power. Years later Nasser described this relationship with the army: "The army is my parliament. The army has [not] carried out the Revolution simply to make me a ruler and then leave me and go. I have to satisfy the army that the demands for which the Revolution was carried out are being realized."[94]

In late 1955 the Czech arms deal revolutionized the perceived balance of power, enhanced the self-confidence of the Egyptian army, and helped the desire for vengeance commute from the realm of the fanciful to that of the possible. The regime's interest in violence grew some more. It was not in violence to gain any physical object but simply to inflict pain. This confronted Israel with a formidable bargaining problem, for how could she deter an interest in violence with the threat of

93. Gamal Abdel Nasser, *The Philosophy of the Revolution* (Buffalo, N.Y., 1959), pp. 65–66. The original was published in Cairo in 1953. See also Harkabi, *Arab Attitudes to Israel,* p. 159.

94. *Al-Ahram,* 15 November 1968, quoted in A. I. Dawisha, *Egypt in the Arab World,* p. 115.

violence? How could she threaten object denial when the immediate object was violence? She did not overcome this problem.

I can dispense with an elaborate discussion of Israeli interests, for by now they should be clear enough. Briefly, from Israel's perspective, the Egyptian challenge was to both intrinsic and power interests. In other words, infiltration and blockade challenged Israel's integrity, her very sovereignty. Infiltration created economic hardships and difficulties in settling outlying areas. It complicated farming, caused high numbers of casualties, and was extremely demoralizing. The naval blockade disrupted development of commercial and other ties with Africa and Asia, so important to the locally isolated country; and Ben-Gurion's plans to develop the Negev, and economic development generally, were apparently retarded by Israel's inability to use her southern port.

It would appear that the balance of interests was in Israel's favor, for she was defending central and intrinsic interests. Yet an explanation for her inability to deter a challenger who pursued political or power values must lie elsewhere, not in this typological ordering of interests. Resorting to vitalness of interests explains nothing, for Egypt's interest in harassing or destroying Israel was nowhere as vital as Israel's in survival and sovereignty. Yet deterrence failed, so either we do not know how to measure the intensity of interests, or else relative interests is not a useful variable, or both. Probably it is simply not a sufficient variable; analysis so far hints at the balance of power as a critical variable, a point I come to shortly.

Finally, in a strict sense, Israel's coercive relationship changed from one of compelling the Gaza regime to curb infiltration to one of deterring Cairo from pursuing state violence. Contrary to what theory would predict, Israel fared better at compellence than deterrence, and again explanation of outcomes must lie elsewhere.

Political Asymmetries

THE INTERNATIONAL SYSTEM

Examination of Israeli and Egyptian positions in the international system reveals highly asymmetric freedom of violent action. Western interests on both sides of the local conflict, and strong Soviet interests only in Egypt, severely proscribed the credibility of Israeli threats of both small-scale retaliatory action and general offensive war, led to the arming of Egypt, and left her free to harass and lay maritime siege. Competition for hegemony in the regional system together with the advantage in the global arena led to the proscription of Egyptian action, not by imposing ceilings on, but rather floors under, allowable Egyptian belligerence.

Egypt's pursuit of Pan-Arab unity and leadership put her in conflict with all three Western powers. Her support of the FLN in Algeria, "war" on the Baghdad Pact, Czech arms deal, and manipulation of internal Jordanian politics should have worked in Israel's favor, but for two facts. By opening the door to Soviet arms, Nasser destroyed the West's control of relative power in the Middle East and thereby released Egypt from Western leverage; and despite Nasser's behavior, because of Egypt's size, potential for leadership, and physical situation along the Suez Canal, the West continued to woo Nasser at Israel's expense until spring of 1956.

Some notable examples of this predicament stand out. Having little to do with Israel yet indicative of America's attitude was the American decision not to join the Baghdad Pact with more than observer status so as not to alienate Egypt. The blockade was basically ignored by the Western powers who, after the Soviet veto of the New Zealand resolution in 1954, would have no more to do with it. Even after the canal was nationalized in July 1956 Israel could not get herself invited to the Suez Canal Users' Conference in London. Throughout 1955, after signing the Baghdad Pact and more so after the announcement of the Czech arms deal, Eden and Dulles persisted in recommending that Israel pursue peace and security not through Western pacts, guarantees, or even her own force but through territorial concessions.

Israeli attempts to balance Egyptian military growth in 1955 failed miserably. Even assuming an American commitment to her survival, Israel was caught in a classic perceptual divergence with her ally. The United States insisted that, even with the Czech arms deal, there was no real danger to Israeli survival. Israel did her best to change the assessment, but neither appeals nor threats that weakness would require preventive war convinced the United States.[95] As the United States could veto the delivery of such NATO weapons as fighter aircraft, Israel's covert attempts to secure French weapons led nowhere.[96]

As for violence across the frontier, the Western powers were simply not interested and could not be engaged except in the few cases where Egypt was damaged substantially or where the danger of general war seemed real. Thus the Gaza and Khan Yunis raids were followed by

95. On Israel's attempts and failures to secure Western support in 1955 and early 1956 see Stock, *Israel*, pp. 171–75; *New York Times*, 9, 18 October, 13 November 1955; *Divrei ha-Knesset*, 2 January 1956; Brecher, *Decisions in Israel's Foreign Policy*, p. 258; Bar-Zohar, *Ben-Gurion*, pt. 3, pp. 1158–60.

96. On the U.S. control over French arms supplies, see Sharett, *Yoman Ishi* 5:1518.

unanimous censuring of Israel, and when in April 1956 war appeared imminent Hammerskjold tried to work out a stable cease-fire. Even here, though, I believe that sending Hammerskjold was a way out for the Western powers, who either did not take the dangers seriously or could not afford politically to intervene, for doing so would have forced them to take sides directly. The Security Council resolution in June 1956, after Hammerskjold's visit, reflected great care by the Western powers to avoid supporting Israel's demands that the debate be expanded to a general consideration of Israeli-Egyptian problems.[97] In early 1956, General Burns suggested interposing a U.N. force between Israel and Egypt. As he describes it, the idea was not adopted because the Western powers were insufficiently concerned about the problem.[98]

Israel's reliance on the West, given the West's reactions to Israeli-initiated violence, acted as a damper on Israeli reprisals. Israeli leaders were highly sensitive to the contradictory requirements of impressing the Arabs and pursuing supportive relations with outside powers. This was especially true of Eban and Sharett, who complained bitterly that by pursuing reprisals Israel displaced proper concern for basic security—achievable only through enhanced external relations—with concern for fleeting and dubious achievements in current security.[99]

There may be a temptation here to reason backward, from the fact of the Sinai Campaign, and to ask why the threat ex ante of offensive and general war did not provide deterrence. To reason so is a serious error. The alliance of Britain, France, and Israel, formed in October 1956 to wage war against Egypt, although it was an Israeli prerequisite for war, was nonetheless an unforseeable event. Before Nasser's nationalization of the Suez Canal in July 1956, the idea of such an alliance would have been ridiculous, so that throughout most of the crisis period of this case there was not even a whiff of this threat. Even given the nationalization, it is difficult to reconstruct a hypothetical political analysis that could have predicted Britain's alliance with Israel to invade Egypt, behavior so obviously contrary to British interests in the Middle East.[100]

Ben-Gurion indeed believed that Israel's freedom to opt for general war was severely proscribed by the international system. Especially after taking control of the cabinet in November 1955, he advanced

97. Berger, *Covenant and the Sword*, p. 201.

98. Burns, *Between Arab and Israeli*, pp. 136–37. From a similar perspective Dan Scheuftan argues that the border war was simply too small to involve the superpowers and therefore did not create for Egypt an entangling dependence on the Soviet Union; see his "Harta'ah Yisraelit be-Sikhsukh Yisrael-Arav," p. 16.

99. Aronson and Horowitz, "Ha-Estrategiya shel Tagmul Mevukar," p. 83; Sharett, *Yoman Ishi* 2:405, 5:1305.

100. On the uniqueness of this alliance see Allon, *Massakh shel Khol*, p. 93.

international considerations for abstinence from war. Along with the fear of endangering Western strategic support in the long run by going to war, Ben-Gurion was sincerely afraid of British military intervention on Egypt's behalf—a far cry from anticipating an Israeli-British alliance![101]

In sum, facing an opponent who was both isolated and hampered by systemic dampers on the ability to decide on violent action, a reasonable Egyptian observer between 1954 and 1956 would have felt justifiably secure in his ability to harass Israel with impunity.

Nasser's bid for pan-Arab leadership and Israel's role in his grand strategy limited Nasser's ability to refrain from belligerence, even where he may have wished to conciliate. A good example was Egyptian behavior in the local bilateral negotiations of summer 1955. Success in the global system, specifically conclusion of the Czech arms deal, amplified these regionally imposed constraints. Nadav Safran writes of the deal:

> Whatever his own motives for the conclusion of the transaction, the Arab masses saw in it the only prospect for a successful showdown with Israel before too long. Nasser cashed in on his mastery of the streets in order to isolate Iraq and prevent the accession of Syria and Jordan to the Baghdad Pact; but he was also impelled to respond to expectations placed in him with regard to Israel by immediately adopting a tough line toward it.[102]

Thus, the same "coup" that so enhanced Nasser's Arab leadership and freedom of action also narrowed his options on launching violence, forcing his hand. These externally generated expectations and constraints coincided with internal ones, which brings us to a consideration of domestic politics.

DOMESTIC FACTORS

Domestic factors on both sides of the border militated against effective Israeli deterrence of Egyptian harassment. Israeli policies, politics, and political culture in the early 1950s undermined the credibility and clarity of Israeli threats, either to persist in reprisals or to launch general war. Egyptian politics created strong interests in challenging Israel and at the same time diminished Cairo's sensitivity to possible and actual Israeli reactions.

Until the Czech arms deal in late 1955, Israeli spending priorities were heavily skewed toward development and away from the military. Ben-

---

101. Aronson, *Conflict and Bargaining*, pp. 15–16. See Ben-Gurion's explanation to Dayan of his resistance to general war, in Dayan, *Avnei Derekh*, pp. 174–75.
102. Safran, *From War to War*, p. 51.

Gurion's grand design envisaged the path to national growth and ultimate power through immigration, absorption, settlement, and investment. In 1952, Chief of Staff Yigael Yadin resigned over these priorities, which, in his view, led to insufficient investment in the military. Dayan replaced him and joined the search for ways to cut military spending. He fired a large number of civilians and career officers and launched internal discussions of proposals to shorten mandatory service from two and a half years to two. The Southern Regional Command was briefly abolished as an economy measure.[103] In the early years Dayan's main emphasis was on developing the quality of the IDF—command and morale—not hardware or size. For deterrence these are difficult values to mobilize, as the next section shows.

With such clear priorities Israel could not have hoped to project a militant image or even a mild propensity to launch general offensive war. Obviously she was not preparing for one. Two circumstances could have mitigated this impression on the Egyptians. First, the limitations on defense spending were in part attributable to external constraints already discussed, and indeed, through November 1955 the forces of Egypt and Israel were kept at roughly equal levels by virtue of the Tripartite Declaration. Second, Israel's economic growth at the time was about 11 percent per year,[104] which translated consistently low spending priorities for defense into constantly increasing real defense outlays.

In the early 1950s Israel discovered her sensitivity to casualties and costs, an attitude important in retarding retaliation and ultimately abandoning it as policy. It also severely depressed the propensity for general war. After Israel's last retaliatory raid in Jordan, just weeks before Sinai, Peres said, "The real problem is not whether it [the raids] influences Jordan. The real problem is how long we can bear it, because the price we paid today is very heavy. It is not heavy from a military perspective, but who does that console. Tonight we had 18 dead and 50 wounded . . . . we cannot afford this for long."[105] Similar sentiments were expressed by Dayan and other officers.[106]

---

103. For these developments and policies, see Daniel Shimshoni, *Israeli Democracy: The Middle of the Journey* (New York, 1982), p. 197; Aronson, *Conflict and Bargaining*, p. 11; Dayan, *Avnei Derekh*, pp. 109, 131; A. Ayalon, "Bitkhonah ha-Leumi shel Yisrael be-35 Shnoteyhah" [Israel's national security throughout her 35 years], *Skirah Hodshit*, nos. 2–3 (February–March 1983); Teveth, *Moshe Dayan*, chap. 15.

104. Shimshoni, *Israeli Democracy*, pp. 233, 236.

105. Peres, *Hashlav haba*, pp. 27–28. Peres was at the time director-general of the Ministry of Defense.

106. Dayan, *Avnei Derekh*, p. 250. For a general discussion of Israel's sensitivity to casualties, see Ben-Horin and Posen, *Israel's Strategic Doctrine*, pp. 21–23.

In considering general war Ben-Gurion was extremely sensitive to the prospect of civilian casualties in Israel's cities. He would not approve the Sinai Campaign until absolutely sure of effective air cover for Israel's civilian population, a requirement that rendered Israel's decision for war dependent on an alliance with a European power. A domestic trait thus amplified the intrusion of the international system, already inimical to Israeli deterrence. In a conversation with Dayan in December 1955 Ben-Gurion explained his opposition to preventive war: "One consideration—is the tremendous destruction that every war causes. There is no doubt that a war, even one in which we would be entirely victorious— the implication is tremendous destruction to the settlements, the economy, and a retreat almost of five–seven years."[107]

The democratic nature of Israeli decision making was harmful to Israeli deterrence through high- and low-level threats. Decisions on retaliatory raids were made centrally and at a high level, usually in the cabinet. I have already discussed the depressing effect this had on the propensity for continuous violent activity: every decision on a small operation was substantial, difficult, interdependent with previous ones, and sensitive to the influence of raids on Israel's broader foreign relations. Added to the disciplined nature of the IDF, the result was the very small number of reprisal operations in Egypt between 1953 and 1956.

In late 1955 and well into 1956 the Knesset was the platform for a continuous debate on the merits of preventive war.[108] The debate does not seem to have produced a single dominating signal, but it must have made two strong impressions. First, there had been a change in the political balance when Herut became the second largest single party (after Mapai) in the elections of July 1955. The tremendous growth in Herut's popularity greatly increased the party's confidence, militancy, and vocality in demanding a preventive war.[109] The second dominant impression must have been the public posture adopted by Ben-Gurion in this debate. True, referring to infiltration and the blockade, he did

107. Quoted in Dayan, *Avnei Derekh*, p. 174. In this regard U.S. Ambassador Lawson's briefing to the JCS in May 1956 is quite interesting. Lawson claimed that "activist" Ben-Gurion had become quite conservative, that Israel was unlikely to attack Egypt, and mainly because of fear of attack by Arab air forces on Israeli cities. This appears in an internal JCS memo, subject: "Middle East Roundup," dated 4 May 1956 (see n. 72).

108. For a discussion of the debate, see Stock, *Israel*, chap. 7. For early Herut demands for war and Sharett's response, see *Divrei ha-Knesset*, 30 August, 1 September 1954. For the debate in 1955–56, see examples: ibid., 19 October, 2 November 1955, 2, 9 January 1956.

109. The Egyptians indeed noticed this development, as indicated by broadcasts over Sawt el-Arab (6 August 1955), cited in "Korot ha-Yamim," *Hamizrah he-Hadash* 7, no. 1 (1956):36.

warn Egypt on 2 November that "this unilateral war must stop, for it cannot remain unilateral for long." But that very day he said, over the same podium, "We cannot obtain security through military victory— not even the most complete. We do not want, we are not permitted, and we cannot annihilate tens of millions of Arabs in the Middle East, and no war-like rhetoric can change this. Our defense lies in constant readiness and increasing our strength in every field and front."[110] In January he told the Knesset that "the maintenance of peace is preferable even to victory in war."[111] How the Egyptians read this debate and what about it impressed them—Herut's gains and militancy or Ben-Gurion's defense of inaction—we do not know. What is clear is that the signal was not clear.

Nasser's dependence on the army for internal legitimacy gave it considerable leverage in the definition of Egyptian interests, an influence not enjoyed by the IDF. The Egyptian army's desire to harass translated directly into policy, whereas, for example, Dayan's theory of degeneration to war through skirmishes could not (see n. 61). From the perspective of the military organizations, then, the Egyptian challenger enjoyed greater freedom of action than the Israeli defender.

The Israeli war of reprisal was waged against the Egyptian army, partly as an instrument of upward convertibility to strategic deterrence. We have no hard evidence but can surmise that the internal politics of a large and growing military organization would have rendered it immune to coercion by low-level harassment. A small number of low-level failures would probably have led, at most, to changes in personnel, and not to general reevaluations of relative strategic power.[112]

Critical to Israeli deterrence was the Egyptian regime's attitude toward Gaza. Small in population, geographically isolated, and not integrated into Egypt, events there were of little intrinsic concern to Cairo. In 1952 a visitor described Gaza as follows:

> It is, in fact, occupied territory. The Egyptians are exceedingly strict about permitting Palestinians to enter Egypt and they are even more strict about them securing employment there. . . . When in Cairo I asked Egyptian officials why they did not treat Gaza as a part of Egypt. They replied that that would be at variance with armistice agreements. It is possible that the Gaza Strip is considered by Egypt as a white elephant from political,

110. Quoted and translated in Stock, *Israel*, p. 161.
111. Ibid.
112. In another context Uri Ra'anan argues that even the infamous Gaza raid could not possibly have been militarily significant to the Egyptian army; see *The U.S.S.R. Arms the Third World* (Cambridge, Mass., 1969), pp. 46–47.

military and economic points of view. The people of Gaza have no passports, as they are a stateless population.[113]

This attitude did not change over the years. In June 1955, Egyptian officials complained that Gaza was merely a money drain. In September 1955, *Al-Ahram* reported that an Egyptian court had established that—for legal purposes—Gaza was not Egyptian territory.[114] The circumstantial evidence is also striking. Nasser visited Gaza only twice in the four years before the Sinai Campaign. The first visit was right after the February 1955 Gaza raid, the second after the Fedayeen attacks in April 1956.[115]

The Egyptian attitude helps account for both early Israeli deterrence and later failure. In 1953 and into 1954 the Egyptian lack of interest in Gaza and Israel left the Gaza authorities to face Israel on their own, making Israeli coercion possible, within limits. Later, Egypt developed an interest in harassing Israel, but because no similar Egyptian concern for Gaza developed, Israel found herself with no meaningful countervalue threat. This is not to say that Egypt could have allowed herself to ignore Israeli attacks against Palestinians had these materialized, but their effect could not have been the same as similar attacks in Jordan. Disruption in Gaza had nowhere the life-threatening implications for the state that similar operations did in Jordan, and in any event dead Gazans were not dead Egyptians.

For the same reasons Cairo did not treat the Israeli threat to capture the Gaza Strip with strategic urgency. Egyptian leaders appear to have been sure that Israel could capture the Strip at will but that ultimately they would recapture it.[116] Nothing strategically catastrophic seemed to be involved in such an exchange.

Power Asymmetries

The two physical determinants of Israel's difficulty in deterring Egypt were size and geographic arrangement. Egypt's putative power was so much greater than Israel's that the existing balance of actualized power must have seemed unstable and easy to overturn. In the first years after

113. Totah, *Dynamite in the Middle East*, p. 40.

114. *Al-Ahram*, 6 September 1955, cited in "Korot ha-Yamim," *Hamizrah he-Hadash* 7, no. 1 (1956):36. Note that this happened almost simultaneously with the tremendous escalation of Fedayeen activity from Gaza in late August.

115. "Korot ha-Yamim," *Hamizrah he-Hadash* 7, no. 4 (1956):289.

116. *New York Times*, 13 June 1955. For Egyptian assessments of Israeli capabilities and intentions, see Ya'ari, *Mitsrayim veha-Fedayeen, 1953–1956*, pp. 15, 26.

the Egyptian Revolution, actualized power was in physical or quantitative balance. After the Czech arms deal the actualized balance became much more precarious, pitting Israeli quality against Egyptian quantitative superiority—a problematic balance from the perspective of deterrence. Geographically, Egypt was in the enviable position of being close to Israel, yet far away. Her forces and the Fedayeen were deployed near Israeli targets; yet given the Egyptian attitude toward Gaza and Gazans, she provided no hostages in return. Similarly, the naval blockade was implemented far away from Israel, part of it actually *within* Egypt.

The putative power differences explain the David-and-Goliath imagery often invoked in the conflict. In 1954, Egypt enjoyed a GNP about three times the size of Israel's and a population fifteen times as large: 22 million versus less than 1.5 million. By mobilizing a somewhat smaller proportion of GNP than did Israel, and one-twentieth the fraction of her population, Egypt could still outspend Israel two-to-one on defense and raise a standing army roughly equal in size to Israel's. The Israelis were sensitive to the delicacy of an actualized balance that rested on such putative differences. In February 1956 at a conference in Tel-Aviv on Egyptian affairs the following analysis was presented: "The quality of Egypt's population is so low in terms of health and education, that Egypt can only mobilize one percent of her population, some 200,000. . . . But it is important to remember that one percent of Egypt's population is equal to the entire mobilizable potential of Israel, and should Egypt achieve just two percent . . . things could become very unpleasant."[117]

Before the Czech arms deal the protagonists were kept fairly equally unequipped for mobile desert warfare. Each had some two hundred tanks and fifty jet aircraft. It is difficult to imagine either protagonist believing it had an offensive advantage and, most important, that Israel was likely to engage in an offensive campaign.[118] In June 1955 the Egyptians conceded their local disadvantage in Gaza but were confident in the strategic balance and in their ability to reverse any Israeli achievements. The influx of Soviet arms beginning in late 1955 immediately altered the putative balance with immense quantities of military equipment that Israel could not hope to match. It was only a matter of time before these armaments would be absorbed and the actualized balance would be revolutionized as well. Assessments of the exact quantities involved vary considerably among sources, but there is little disagree-

117. Y. O., "Mishtar ha-Hafikhah ve-Otsmatah shel Mitsrayim" [The revolutionary regime and Egypt's potential], *Hamizrah he-Hadash* 7, no. 3 (1956):177. For statistics on GNP and defense expenditures, see Safran, *From War to War*, pp. 147–52, 156–65.

118. Brecher, *Decisions in Israel's Foreign Policy*, p. 230.

ment as to the order of magnitude or the imbalancing effect. According to Dayan, the deal included 230 tanks, 200 armored personnel carriers (APCs), 100 self-propelled guns, 200 jet fighters, and assorted naval craft.[119] According to Robert Stephens, the American official estimate included 80–100 Mig fighters, 30–40 light bombers, and 100 tanks. The British numbers were similar, with higher estimates of tanks.[120] Dayan wrote of the deal that it "wiped out in a flash the delicate balance of forces that existed between the Arab states and Israel."[121]

Much has been made of French balancing on Israel's behalf, of which we must be wary. In reality, relative to the magnitude and quality of Soviet shipments to Egypt, little of consequence reached Israel before July 1956. While the French had been willing to sign a number of moderate agreements in 1954 and 1955, the United States intervened to veto actual deliveries. Only in April, with accession to power of the French Socialists and Dulles's growing disaffection toward Nasser, were meaningful accords pursued and executed, especially those on jet aircraft and tanks. Much of this equipment reached Israel only weeks before the Sinai Campaign. In fact, in the campaign Israel relied on French air cover of her cities because by late October she could only fly 16 Mystere jets herself.[122] In sum, throughout the period under discussion (1953–56), actualized power was either in balance or in the process of shifting in Egypt's favor.

One note on air power: at no point after the War of Independence did Israel attempt to acquire the capability for, or develop a doctrine of, strategic bombing; she concentrated instead on the development of a tactical air force.[123] Regardless of whether it would have been efficacious, Israel therefore could not balance the perceived Egyptian threat of countervalue bombing. Most obviously absent was an ability to threaten nonmilitary Egyptian values beyond Sinai in the event of hostilities.

Throughout late 1955 and into 1956 Egypt absorbed her new weapons and raised her force levels in eastern Sinai. By spring of 1956 she had deployed 60,000 troops in the peninsula, 42,500 along the border.[124] An internal U.S. Joint Chiefs of Staff (JCS) report from late fall 1955 de-

119. Dayan, *Yoman Ma'arekhet Sinai*, p. 10.
120. Stephens, *Nasser*, p. 161.
121. Dayan, *Yoman Ma'arekhet Sinai*, p. 10.
122. Safran, *From War to War*, pp. 223–24; Aronson, *Conflict and Bargaining*, p. 17.
123. Handel, *Israel's Political-Military Doctrine*, pp. 27–29.
124. See Appendix C to the following JCS memo, subject: "Plans for Protective Military Measures in the Middle East," for Commander in Chief, US Naval Forces, Eastern Atlantic and Mediterranean (SM-338-56), dated 27 April 1956. For deployments just before hostilities in October 1956, see Dupuy, *Elusive Victory*, pp. 146–47, 212.

scribed the Egyptian army as increasingly self-confident since completion of the arms deal.[125]

Whatever Israeli equality or superiority existed at the time could only
have been attributable to intangibles. But if these existed, not only were
they invisible to the Egyptians but to most Israeli decision makers as
well—Dayan excepted.[126] Ben-Gurion was quite skeptical about Israel's
power relative to Egypt. Michael Brecher's study of decision makers'
perceptions in mid-1956 shows that Ben-Gurion, Meir, and Peres were
convinced of Israel's growing inferiority, even with the flow of French
arms.[127]

Should not the Egyptians have feared an Israeli blitzkrieg? Just as it
would have been wrong to reason backward from the Sinai Campaign
to the political analysis, it would be wrong to do so for power assessment. It is important to remember that Israel did not possess, at the
time, the blitzkrieg army or the first-strike strategy it would develop
later. True, the general principle of an offensive approach had been
stated and accepted by Ben-Gurion, Dayan, and other leaders; and
Dayan did much to instill an offensive mentality through the creation of
Unit 101 and other measures.[128] But, Israeli general Israel Tal cautions:

> In the Sinai Campaign was embedded the principle of waging war deep
> within the enemy's territory. We struck the first blow because of the
> special circumstances and the specific plan, and not because the theory of
> first strike had achieved the status of first principle in our national security
> strategy. The opposite is true: only after the Campaign . . . the principle
> of first strike in all cases of a forming threat was established.[129]

And Michael Handel writes of the doctrine:

> As for the general development of the IDF's doctrine during Dayan's
> period as chief of staff, it continued to remain basically a classic infantry
> army until the Sinai Campaign, both in its psychological attitude and its
> material. Dayan, although having a good understanding of the principles

---

125. Report dated November 1955 (no "subject" or addressee), located in the Modern
Military Section, U.S. National Archives, Washington, D.C., in file CCS 381 EMMEA (11–
19–47) sec. 24.

126. Ya'ari discusses the joint Egyptian-Syrian intelligence assessment of May 1956, in
which they concluded that Israel was relatively weak; see *Mitsrayim veha-Fedayeen, 1953–
1956*, p. 26.

127. Brecher, *Decisions in Israel's Foreign Policy*, pp. 246–47.

128. See Ben-Gurion to the Knesset in 1950, quoted in Ben-Gurion, *Yechud ve-Ye'ud*,
p. 142.

129. Israel Tal, "Torat ha-Bitakhon, Reka u-Dinamikah" [The principles of security,
background and dynamics], *Maarachot* 253 (December 1976):4.

of mobility and deep penetration, had little understanding of armored warfare.[130]

As for the Israel Air Force, despite development of a tactical fighter force, Israeli leaders, including the chief of staff, expressed little confidence in its preemptive capability, so important for successful blitzkrieg, and which we now take for granted.

Another component of Israeli doctrine not developed before the campaign was the notion of destroying enemy forces. The operational orders for the Sinai Campaign did not define the mission's purpose as "to destroy the enemy's forces," the idiom of most subsequent Israeli planning, but rather "to disrupt the Egyptian forces in Sinai, and cause their collapse."[131]

On the ground, at least, Israel did fight an almost classic blitzkrieg in 1956; yet only because one person—Dayan—changed his approach literally in the few weeks prior to the campaign—and did so in the face of much opposition within the general staff. It was also for the most part a blitzkrieg fought on foot and in mobilized milk trucks. In the Sinai Campaign the IDF "discovered" armored warfare more than it applied it. In sum, a reasonable Egyptian in 1956 may be excused for not having correctly predicted Israeli strategic and doctrinal behavior when the Israelis themselves did not know how they would act.

In October 1956, Ben-Gurion explained to the Knesset the problems inherent in trying to deter with a qualitative and intangible superiority when it had to compete with extreme quantitative inferiority. First he quoted Dayan: "The IDF is strong not because it has weapons superior to its enemies'. It is powerful because it does not condition its fighting on having superior arms. . . . The IDF is strong because its sailors, pilots and soldiers are young men and women whose readiness to serve their country's security knows no bounds." But, Ben-Gurion continued, the problem was not to *win* a war; rather,

we want to *prevent* war, and to secure our rights, prestige and security, and there is only one means to achieve this: if our friends . . . supply us with enough defensive arms which will not fall in quality from that of our enemy's. . . . Only if we receive enough weapons of superior quality— this will deter our enemy. . . . Only when the enemy knows that we are well supplied by his standards—he will not dare attack us, and peace in

130. Handel, *Israel's Political-Military Doctrine*, pp. 25–26.
131. Dayan, *Yoman Ma'arekhet Sinai*, p. 182; Zvi Lanir, "Political Aims and Military Objectives: Some Observations on the Israeli Experience," in Zvi Lanir, ed., *Israeli Security Planning in the 1980s: Its Politics and Economics*, JCSS Book (New York, 1984), p. 21.

the region will reign. The Arab leaders do not know as we do to value the quality and spirit of the fighting person.[132]

The geopolitical arrangement contributed to Israel's lack of coercive leverage. With Egyptian intrinsic insensitivity to events in Gaza, the next closest nonmilitary value was in Egypt proper, over 200 kilometers across the desert. Egypt was well insulated. Even had Israel been sure her forces could make it to Egypt, the mere image of the IDF dealing with a nation of 22 million is ridiculous.

The blockade was actuated at two points, both distant from Israel. Crossing the Sinai and actually capturing the Suez Canal must have seemed a dubious prospect and indeed was not planned seriously by the Israelis. Perhaps less fanciful was the threat to capture the Straits of Tiran, because of their fairly neutral location at the tip of the Sinai Peninsula. The idea of capturing the straits occurred to Israeli decision makers a number of times. The evidence indicates that the IDF had serious difficulties in dealing with such a distant objective. The Israel Navy had virtually no forces at its disposal, especially in the Red Sea. Nevertheless, in February 1954 an attempt to reach the Straits was made—and failed for technical reasons. When, in August 1955, Dayan and Ben-Gurion discussed the possibility of a limited action to test the blockade and if necessary capture the straits, they concluded that it would take ten months to organize.[133] As for overland access to the straits, there were no roads to speak of over the 300-kilometer route from Eilat, and the near impossibility of passage was demonstrated in the Sinai Campaign itself. The Egyptians were presumably well acquainted with the terrain and had good reason not to expect an Israeli overland attack.[134]

The preceding discussion raises an important problem of quality-based superiority. The Israeli victory in 1956 can essentially be attributed to surprise, to doing the unexpected at strategic, tactical, and doctrinal levels. Had the Egyptians really understood the sources and details of Israeli superiority, had they known what and how Israel was planning, would they have been deterred? Or would they have therefore known how to prepare and hence been undeterred? If such victory is possible only when unexpected, and if making it expected renders it also unlikely, then we must conclude that quality-based deterrence is highly unlikely to hold. These are the contradictory and unresolvable knowledge requirements of victory and deterrence explored in Chapter

132. *Divrei ha-Knesset*, 15 October 1956.
133. Dayan, *Avnei Derekh*, pp. 112, 150.
134. In the event, the overland route was indeed only barely passable; see descriptions in Dupuy, *Elusive Victory*, pp. 194–200; Dayan, *Yoman Ma'arekhet Sinai*, pp. 168–78.

1, where I also suggested a solution: general, detail-free reputation, to which I turn shortly.

Escalation and Brinkmanship

One might have expected Israeli reprisals to create deterrence through the following logic: they would "hurt" sufficiently to engage Cairo and give Egypt a stake in the status quo; they would demonstrate general Israeli military superiority; and they would introduce a shared risk of uncontrollable escalation to general war. In this manner an initially nonstrategic game would be made strategic by creating an Egyptian stake in it. Brinkmanship—the threat of inadvertent escalation to war with a demonstrably superior foe (the IDF)—would induce Egypt to desist and Western powers to intervene.

Until mid-1954 the threat of escalation was not really necessary. As long as Israel contended with the Gaza authorities, merely the threat of continued reprisals engaged their interests and put them at unbearable risk, leading them to oppose infiltration. In mid-1954, with the independent growth of Cairo's interest in the Arab-Israeli conflict, Israeli operations may have hastened Egyptian engagement in the bilateral conflict as Israeli reprisals hurt Egypt's Arab prestige and that of her army. Unfortunately for Israeli deterrence, the nature of Egyptian interests, their policy of "neither peace nor war," and the positive value they derived from violence made it impossible to deter through such escalation and engagement.

There is ample evidence that Israeli leaders conceived of reprisals as a tool of brinkmanship, to demonstrate that the results of general war would be unpleasant for Egypt and to create a risk of inadvertent escalation to such a war. We have seen that Dayan believed that low-level confrontations could cause escalations and that Ben-Gurion and Dayan believed that these confrontations demonstrated to the Egyptians the nature of the outcome of such escalation. Why did this not work?

In discussing domestic factors I noted that slapping around a few infantry companies was unlikely to convince an opposing army of equal size and superior armaments of its overall strategic inferiority. The discussion of power asymmetries suggested that the Egyptians had good reasons to have faith in their relative strength. The joint Egyptian-Syrian intelligence evaluation (of May 1956) in fact stated explicitly that the purpose of Israel's reprisals was to try and project power that simply did not exist![135] In a sense, converting small demonstrations to a general

135. Ya'ari, *Mitsrayim veha-Fedayeen, 1953–1956*, p. 26.

image of power raises problems similar to those of projecting power through quality instead of quantity.

I have found no way to uncover what the Egyptians made of the implicit and explicit Israeli threat of "involuntary" degeneration from skirmishes to war. One can imagine a reasonable Egyptian observer concluding that this was highly unlikely. We know, for example, that for Sharett and Ben-Gurion, reprisals were not only not necessarily a path to war but a way to avoid it. In the public debate the Israelis surely behaved as though they considered general war a large social-political decision, to be made at the highest level and as the outcome of a national consensus. Observing Israeli reprisals against Egypt reveals a small number of well-planned and precisely executed operations, centrally ordered and directed. With the exceptions of the ambush of reenforcements in the Gaza raid and the April 1956 shelling of Gaza (the town), there is little evidence of loss of control, of the army pursuing its own policy, or of local commanders pursuing "personal" wars. In sum, an observer would have found little evidence of irrational Israeli decision making or uncontrollable implementation; Israel was not, to the detriment of brinkmanship, a crazy state.

The Egyptians could expect to suffer little damage even in the unlikely event of inadvertent Israeli escalation. With their faith in ultimate victory in case of war and with the West's proven tendency over the years to discourage Israeli aggression and to reverse Israeli military gains, the Egyptians could expect any degeneration to be short lived and reversible.[136]

The Israelis did possess one instrument of brinkmanship: mobilization. Had Israel called up her reserves she no doubt would have created an independent risk of war because of her inability to remain mobilized for long. Once Israel mobilizes, she must either resolve the crisis immediately or use her forces. But Israel did not mobilize, remaining on the safe side of the war/no-war decision. In 1955 a small number of reserves were twice called up, after which Dayan wrote in a letter to Ben-Gurion that Israel could not afford to do so: "It seems to me that it will only be justified to mobilize the reserves only [sic] after we decide on initiated operations."[137] Mobilization, then, was a big economic and political decision, which made it impossible to stumble into the one act from which it might have been possible to stumble into war.

---

136. For Israel's capitulation to Great Britain's forceful intervention during the First Sinai Campaign (of 1948–49), see Bar-Zohar, *Ben-Gurion*, pt. 2, pp. 858–63; Dupuy, *Elusive Victory*, pp. 112–13.

137. Dayan, *Avnei Derekh*, p. 164.

Deterrence, Spiraling, and De-escalation

Much has been made of the argument that Israeli reprisals motivated general escalation by Egypt. Essentially, the argument goes, Israeli tactical escalation caused both strategic and tactical Egyptian escalation—in other words, a spiral. Most writing has focused on the Gaza raid of February 1955 as the main tactical Israeli operation that led to a general change in Egyptian policy, in motivating both the search for arms (leading to the Czech arms deal) and the policy of direct harassment. Explanations revolve around the humiliating effect of the raids on Nasser's prestige and ability to project power in his bid for Arab leadership and the effect on the army, which reacted to humiliation with increased demands to harass the Israelis. Recall that after the Gaza raid, the Egyptian army increased its presence in Gaza and Sinai, organized the Fedayeen, and was further involved in direct confrontations with the IDF and in harassment of Israeli villages.

Of the Gaza raid Evron wrote:

> As it happened, the Gaza attack had far-reaching effects on the way in which the Egyptian-Israeli conflict developed. Shortly after the attack had been carried out, the Egyptian leadership formed the famous Fedayeen squads and launched them against Israel. . . . The tenet that violence breeds violence became a reality in the Egyptian-Israeli conflict. . . . One direct result of the Gaza raid was the complete breakdown of communications between the two sides.[138]

As already noted, Sharett had been convinced long before the Gaza raid that blows delivered to the Egyptian army could only result in spiraling. Colonel A. Ayalon, a senior IDF historian, wrote of the entire period (through 1956): "The paratroopers were activated according to the Biblical principle—'a tooth for a tooth,' which says: he who hurts you, you hurt him, not only to avenge, but also to disrupt, warn, and prevent his actions and deter him. But this principle has an attendant result of degeneration."[139]

I do not wish to argue with the conclusion that Israeli reprisals had an escalatory effect. But analysis of Egyptian harassment suggests that it was not, at base, motivated by Israeli belligerence or fear thereof.

138. Evron, *Middle East*, p. 38. See also Nutting, *Nasser*, p. 97; Lacouture, *Nasser*, p. 277. For a thorough summary of the literature in this vein, see Brecher, *Decisions in Israel's Foreign Policy*, pp. 256–57, text and notes.

139. Ayalon, "Bitkhonah ha-Leumi shel Yisrael," p. 42. See also Itamar Rabinovich, "Seven Wars and One Peace Treaty," in Alvin Z. Rubinstein, ed., *The Arab-Israeli Conflict: Perspectives* (New York, 1984).

Rather, Egypt had positive strategic interests in escalation unrelated to Israeli actions, and in this sense Israel and Egypt were not in a spiral. Also, short of her own capitulation, Israel did not possess specific values desired by Egypt, so that despiraling through strategic appeasement was not a viable option.

The systemically induced interest of the Revolutionary Command Council in harassing Israel intensified between 1954 and 1956 as Egypt fought formation of the Baghdad Pact and then the accession to it of others. A number of Egyptian actions reflect this need and appear unrelated to Israeli activities. The most obvious is the persistent tightening of the blockade. I can find no Israeli actions to explain its imposition, its tightening in January 1954 to include the straits, its relaxation and reimposition in February and October 1954, and its escalation to include air travel in September 1955.

The press and radio campaign against Christians, Jews, imperialism, and Israel started in mid-1954, well before the Gaza raid, as did serious and apparently state-directed infiltration at the frontier. Indeed, the first recorded instance of direct (if small-scale) Egyptian army involvement in harassment occurred in January 1955, some five weeks before the Gaza raid.[140]

Some of the specific post-Gaza incidents across the ADL in 1955 also place in question the notion of Israeli-induced spiraling. The collapse of negotiations in August 1955 and the subsequent wild attacks on Israel by both Fedayeen and army can only reflect Nasser's inability to conciliate and a drive to escalate motivated by his other relationships. The same must be said for the Egyptian decision to challenge the status quo at the Auja DMZ in October 1955, which presumably resulted from confidence enhanced—and pressures engendered—by the Czech deal.

The Czech arms deal was most likely not an escalatory reaction to Israeli deterrent activities. Before the deal the balance of power was carefully maintained within the guidelines of the Tripartite Declaration. Wish for arms she may have, but until the Czech deal Israel failed to acquire them, so Egyptian arming was not a spiraling reaction to Israeli military growth. Evidence indicates that the request for Soviet weapons was motivated chiefly by Nasser's competition with Iraq and the Baghdad Pact for Pan-Arab leadership through "war" on Western imperialism.[141]

So far in this discussion I have been treating the strategic and tactical levels of interaction as one, or I have conceived of the tactical as an

140. Stock, *Israel*, p. 71.
141. Ra'anan, *U.S.S.R. Arms the Third World*, p. 54, chap. 3.

expression of the strategic and concentrated on the latter. But if tactical actions are reflections of the strategic relationship, then what happens at a lower level may indeed have a second-order effect on the higher level relationship. Viewing the Egyptian-Israeli confrontation from such a perspective suggests the possibility of a tactical-strategic spiral.

We have seen how Egypt's domestic and external politics generated an interest in anti-Israeli violence per se, but this is not the complete picture. Bidding for a position of Arab leadership probably converged with needs of the army to require not merely violence but successful violence. Egypt and its army needed to look good, and even small Israeli successes hurt Egyptian interests, further centralizing the bilateral conflict and enhancing its importance. As Comdr. Elmo Hutchison says, those who overthrew Farouk largely for his regime's military weakness could hardly allow themselves to appear unequal to ongoing Israeli challenges.[142] Egypt had to take action. The result: a tactical-strategic spiral. But the extent and importance of this kind of spiraling in the case at hand should not be overstated. In a meticulous study of the Czech arms deal—probably the single most significant escalatory step—Uri Ra'anan shows that it was not a reaction to the Gaza raid of February 1955. It appears that negotiations for Soviet arms transfers began before the Israeli raid. Keith Wheelock argues that, at most, the Gaza raid was used as an excuse to explain the deal.[143]

Israel did make modest attempts to conciliate at the strategic level. After Ben-Gurion welcomed the July Revolution, Israel persisted through September 1954 in offering concessions, like transit rights over the Negev between Jordan and Egypt, refugee compensation, and Arab use of Israeli ports. Israel's policy on the blockade was explicitly conciliatory. Except for the Bat Galim and Essek ha-Bish episodes in late 1954, Israel lived meekly with the blockade. Appeasement proved nonconstructive, however, because Egypt had strategic interests in harassment not directly related to these bilateral issues.

The discussion of tactical-strategic spiraling suggests that Israel could have pursued constructive appeasement by assuming a purely defensive posture in dealing with harassment. Execution of such a policy entails, however, constructing a formidable physical barrier—a fence, for example—dispersing mines, engaging in patrols and ambushes, and increasing guard duty at the border; and remember that Israeli leaders were extremely reluctant to commit the IDF to guard duty for

142. Hutchison, *Violent Truce*, p. 122.
143. Ra'anan, *U.S.S.R. Arms the Third World*, pp. 46–47; Wheelock, *Nasser's New Egypt*, p. 233.

fear of retarding the army's development. Whether it would really have harmed the IDF I am not sure, but one cannot help noting that at the time, Israel had less than two standing infantry brigades and faced violent frontiers many hundreds of kilometers in length. Much larger forces would have been required. It is also not clear that Israel, in a deep economic recession in the early 1950s, could have made the capital investments.

Because of Egypt's positive interests in violence, one could be skeptical about the strategic efficacy of tactical conciliation. Although it might have allowed Israel to avoid creating a greater Egyptian interest in escalation and violence, tactical conciliation would not have addressed basic Egyptian interests. It is likely therefore that such a policy would have affected the rate, but not the fact, of escalation, just as ignoring the blockade could not induce its termination. Even so, there are strong arguments to support this approach. One is the imperative to experiment, given the tenuous and speculative business of identifying and assessing interests. Where the risk is not too overbearing it may be wise to try, and this may have been such a case. Also, in a world of dynamic asymmetries and changing balances, the pace of events may be most important to a defender. The ability to influence the "when" of challenge and the pace of acceleration and escalation can be critical if a defender can put time earned or resources saved to good use.

Back at the strategic level, Israel's only potentially efficacious conciliatory policy option would have been to make grand concessions, which Egypt could have paraded as strategic victories for the various causes she led. These concessions could have been large territorial ones or repatriation of hundreds of thousands of refugees. Yehoshafat Harkabi explains how Israel's geography and the maximalist nature of Palestinian demands rendered these possibilities moot:

> Israel because of its smallness enjoys very limited latitude in making concessions. Israel may suspect that any territorial concession is of importance to the Arabs if it is calculated to weaken Israel as a step towards a final onslaught. . . . Israel, by the nature of her position, will prefer living dangerously, rather than offering a concession incurring the danger of nonexistence. Any concession which may weaken Israel is too big for her; for the Arabs it is too small if it leaves the existence of Israel intact.[144]

Reputation and Knowledge

Israeli failure to deter Egyptian harassment demonstrates why reputation is so necessary yet so difficult to create and apply. Reputation was

144. Quoted in Jabber, *Israel and Nuclear Weapons*, p. 103.

necessary to generalize shared knowledge of Israel's superior ability and will because sharing detailed knowledge could only have been detrimental to deterrence. But the reputation Israel brought into the crisis period proved irrelevant and ineffective.

Had Israeli and Egyptian understanding of the structure of their relationship been perfected, deterrence would not have been salvaged—quite the opposite. Suppose Israeli decision makers had understood perfectly Egypt's attitude to Gaza, its need for "neither war nor peace," and its assessment of its own superiority? The only imaginable conclusion would have been to stop attempting deterrence by reprisal and to choose among living with harassment, experimenting with defense, or initiating general war sooner than 1956. Enhanced knowledge would have led to abandoning deterrence, not to achieving it by innovative means. And suppose Egypt understood the political constraints on Israeli violence, the rationality of Israeli decision making and implementation, Israeli military doctrine, Ben-Gurion's lack of confidence in the IDF and the chief of staff's in the Air Force. Such knowledge could only have increased Egyptian self-confidence and sense of impunity.

Was no useful knowledge created by virtue of the extended nature of the crisis? Useful, perhaps, but detrimental to deterrence. Extended observation of Israeli and other actors' behavior could only have enhanced Egyptian self-confidence. Israel appeared acquiescent to the blockade, and her reaction to physical provocation was intermittent reprisal operations, with which Egypt could live. Western countries that had some control over Israeli behavior proved repeatedly that they could be counted on to keep Israel on the defensive, regardless of Egyptian behavior. As for the Israeli theory of repeated small demonstrations of strategic superiority, it could not work because of the limits to upward convertibility already discussed.

Information prior sharing of which would have strengthened deterrence was not really knowable in advance. An example is the tripartite Israeli-French-British alliance, which came as a surprise to everyone, Israelis included, and was only made even remotely possible after July 1956. Another example was Israel's ability to blitz across the Sinai, the success of which surprised the Israelis themselves and depended on surprising the Egyptians, that is, on secrecy of doctrine, tactics, organization, and mobilization. In sum, what Israel needed for deterrence was a credible general threat—a reputation.

The War of 1948 ended in a resounding defeat for the Egyptian army. The largest and most powerful Arab contingent in the war, it suffered the most unambiguous humiliation; Israel might afterward have expected her reputation in Egypt to be well established and robust. Not so. Examination of developments after 1949 shows that so much changed in the Israeli-Egyptian relationship that there was, by 1956, little similarity to the situation of 1949. The game, alas, was not a repeated game, and Israel's reputation was not applicable.

First, the Israeli victory.[145] Initial Egyptian successes in 1948 brought their forces to a distance of 32 kilometers from Tel-Aviv. But in July the IDF began an offensive that ended in the complete routing of the Egyptian force of some twenty thousand men. Toward the end of the war Israeli forces under Yigal Allon's command carried out two large operations that ended in Israel's first Sinai campaign.[146] In these operations the IDF maneuvered highly mobile division-sized forces, favored deep penetration movements over attrition, and achieved local air superiority by preemptively destroying Egyptian aircraft on the ground. Allon sent his forces barreling rapidly into central Sinai in a move aimed at bringing about the collapse of Egypt's forward forces in Gaza. Only U.S. and U.N. pressure, combined with the threat—made real by demonstration[147]—of British military intervention worried Ben-Gurion enough to order Allon to stop his attack and retreat. This outside intervention and the Egyptian government's agreement to a cease-fire saved the Egyptian army from total ruin and prevented Israeli capture of large portions of the Sinai.[148]

The Egyptians did not deny this disaster in Palestine; yet their explanations of it denied Israeli superiority, resting instead on transitory and remediable causes. They viewed the 1952 Revolution as partially the outcome of the Egyptian and Arab social and political deficiencies that had caused the Palestine defeat and saw the new regime as acting vigorously to correct them. By 1954 and surely by 1955, they perceived a *new* Egypt, no longer the Egypt of 1948.

Although the Egyptians tended to blame themselves for the defeat in Palestine, there was little inclination to lay blame on the soldiers or field formations. In 1955, Nasser complained that the Egyptian army had not been fully committed to the Palestine War: "We were not defeated in Palestine in 1948, for the Egyptian army did not fight in 1948."[149] Fault

145. The following description is based primarily on Dupuy, *Elusive Victory*, pp. 54–59, 71–72, 80–83, 91–99, 105–11.
146. The earlier operation was the Yo'av Offensive of 15–22 October, in which the northern Negev and Beer Sheva were liberated; the Faluja Pocket was cut off, and its four thousand soldiers, among them Lt. Col. Nasser, remained surrounded until the end of the war. The second operation was the Horev Operation of 22–29 December.
147. On 5 January 1949 the Royal Air Force sent five aircraft against Israeli forces in the Sinai; Israeli planes shot down all five.
148. Yigal Allon, *The Making of Israel's Army* (New York, 1971), pp. 47–48; Bar-Zohar, *Ben-Gurion*, pt. 2, pp. 858–61. On the sad state of the Egyptian army at the end of the war, see Safran, *From War to War*, pp. 32–33.
149. Quoted in Harkabi, *Arab Attitudes to Israel*, p. 374.

rested at the level of the supreme political-military leadership. Much blame was ascribed to the corrupt leadership of King Farouk's administration, which had provided poor equipment and imposed politically motivated decisions on the army, undermining its ability to fight effectively. The Egyptian administration was not vigorous and not prepared. In 1953, Nasser stated, "The leadership in their speeches said 'so-called Israel' and did nothing but speechify about so-called Israel."[150]

Guilt was also externalized. Much at fault was Western Imperialism, depicted as critical to the establishment and arming of Israel. Nasser declared, "We know that the Palestine downfall was not a downfall at all, but a plot of Imperialism against the Arab people with the aim of dividing it and imbuing it with a spirit of defeatism."[151] The failure of Arab unity in the war allowed Egypt to transfer much of the blame to Abdullah of Jordan, who in truth stood passively by while the IDF routed the Egyptian army. Indeed, the fact that sometimes Israel actively fought only one army at a time should have undermined her image as simultaneous victor over five Arab armies. What probably made the various explanations of defeat and optimistic expectations for the future seem reasonable were the putative power differences in 1948 that had not in fact been actualized. Safran writes, "Given the apparent glaring disparities in gross size, numbers and resources between Israel and the Arab states, or even between Israel and Egypt alone, it was impossible for the Arab elites and governments not to entertain the notion that, with better planning and preparation, it should be possible in the future to reverse the decision of arms of 1948 and take revenge, wash out the humiliation of defeat, and restore justice all at once."[152]

Israeli strategist General Tal agrees, warning that the quantitative imbalance in the War of Independence was not what we normally make of it, for "in the area of balance of forces, the entire Arab power potential was not realized."[153] The differences in power potential had not changed in a fundamental manner since 1948.

Radical transformation of the Egyptian army took place after 1952. If in the War of Independence it was capable of fielding 18,000–20,000 of its 55,000 troops, in 1956 the active garrison in Sinai alone was about 60,000 soldiers. After the Revolution the old "pasha-type" officers were sacked and younger ones promoted. The system of career and pay inducements was changed to make the army attractive to high-quality

---

150. Quoted in ibid., p. 373; see also Nasser, *Philosophy of Revolution*, pp. 26, 31; Vatikiotis, *Egyptian Army in Politics*, pp. 32–33.

151. Quoted in Harkabi, *Arab Attitudes to Israel*, p. 377; see also Nasser, *Philosophy of Revolution*, pp. 64–65.

152. Safran, *From War to War*, p. 41.

153. Tal, "Torat ha-Bitakhon, Reka u-Dinamikah," p. 4.

officers and men.[154] Indeed, the revolution was not just political but social as well and, by implication, would create a new society that, once liberated from its regressive shackles, would also be more powerful. And once powerful it could complete the circle and avenge the past proof of its impotence.[155] In September 1955 the Czech arms deal catapulted the Egyptian army into a different league. While paying due homage to the army Nasser expressed a new sense of confidence: "Today we are in 1955. We are different from the past, and so I say to Israel and those who threaten us in her name. . . . Today I say to her: The Egyptian Army under the command of Abd al-Hakim Amir is no different from the Egyptian Army before, but the methods which led to our defeat in the past have been completely changed and will not be restored."[156]

In another critical sense the situation after 1952 was different from that of 1948. During the War of Independence the IDF had demonstrated its prowess at thwarting a poorly organized attack and then counterattacking against hastily formed defenses. This particular reputation may actually have stuck, but the question remains whether this ability was transferable to the situation in 1955--56, where some sixty thousand troops were stationed in well-planned and static defensive positions. One suspects not.

Finally, all the visible constraints on Israeli action might have been overcome had she had the reputation, which some say she now has, of a crazy state willing to escalate low-level conflagrations to general offensive warfare against all odds and despite all visible constraints. Crazy-state behavior had never yet been demonstrated by Israel on any front. If Israel had a strong reputation in 1955, it might have been for excellence and vigor in *reprisals*, which Egypt did not fear. It would take the Sinai Campaign to revolutionize Israel's reputation.

Success or Failure

There is no conceivable way to salvage success by resorting to relativism in the case of Egyptian harassment. As in the earlier consideration of infiltration from Jordan, both Dan Horowitz and Barry Blechman discover a short-term decline in Egyptian violence immediately after most Israeli reprisals. Blechman shows that positive results (from Israel's perspective) were normally limited to twenty days.[157] If we look at

154. Safran, *From War to War*, p. 208.
155. Y. O., "Mishtar ha-Hafikhah ve-Otsmatah shel Mitsrayim," p. 177.
156. Quoted in Harkabi, *Arab Attitudes to Israel*, p. 379.
157. Horowitz, *Hatfisa ha-Yisraelit shel Bitachon Leumi*, pp. 20–23; Blechman, "Consequences of the Israeli Reprisals," pp. 162–65.

Table 5. Infiltration induced by Egypt, and Israeli-Egyptian military exchanges, 1953–1956

	Infiltration		Military exchanges
	via Egypt	Fedayeen via Jordan	
July–December 1953	(2)*	—	—
January–June 1954	(17)*	—	14
July–December 1954	100	—	30
January–June 1955	75	—	44
July–December 1955	30	16	87
January–June 1956	85	33	104
July–October 1956	33	71	49

Sources: Barry M. Blechman, "The Consequences of the Israeli Reprisals: An Assessment" (Ph.D. diss., Georgetown University, 1971), tables 3, 5, 6; idem, *Military Event Data Set*, Computer Tape 0483 (Inter-university Consortium for Political and Social Research, 1972).

Note: I have included Fedayeen infiltration from Jordan since much (if not all) of the serious infiltration from Jordan after June 1955 was exported violence, paid for and organized by Egyptian authorities and agents.

*Clearly not state directed.

the whole period, there is no evidence of a decreasing challenge. The blockade was not affected in either direction by Israeli policy, nor was the trend of violence across the ADL, if we consider it in six-month increments (table 5).

By the fall of 1956 Israeli leaders recognized that active deterrence-by-reprisal had failed on all fronts. Reprisals against Egypt had been all but discontinued since the previous fall. After a series of large operations in September–October 1956 in Jordan, Peres declared, "I am convinced that the Israeli government will have to decide shortly on how to continue. I do not believe that continuing the reprisal operations will be a repeat of Hussan and Qalqilya."[158] On 14 October, Dayan's diary reports of a general staff meeting: "On the central subject of the meeting, the 'principle' of reprisal, the general opinion is that the present method requires revision."[159] Dayan recommended either further escalation, to include daytime combined-arms operations, or the capture of territory for bargaining. He concluded, again in his diary, that "not in the General Staff, not in the [Knesset's] Defense and Foreign Affairs Committee, and not in conversations with the prime minister was anything definite decided, but it is clear to all of us that we are at the end of the chapter of night-time reprisal operations."[160]

158. Peres, *Hashlav haba*, p. 28.
159. Dayan, *Avnei Derekh*, p. 250.
160. Ibid., p. 251.

The Sinai Campaign can be seen as a declaration of the failure of deterrence, a recognition that the threat of continued reprisal was not deterring and that the threat of escalation to general war was either not credible or not worrisome to the challenger. But from this very expression of failure came a decade of classic success for Israeli deterrence. What the astounding victory accomplished was the demonstration of both will and capability; it established a reputation that would last for many years.

True, Israel was forced to relinquish her territorial gains in the war, and Nasser emerged a hero from his confrontation with imperialism and Zionism. But Nasser changed his Israel policy dramatically, in ways that reflected Israeli deterrence success. The overall Egyptian force levels in Sinai were reduced by at least one-half, and the eastern Sinai was basically demilitarized.[161] The Fedayeen units—destroyed in the campaign—were not reconstituted, and harassment across the border and through Jordan virtually ceased. The blockade of the straits was lifted, not to be reimposed till 1967. It is significant that even though Israel refused to allow the stationing of U.N. troops on her side of the frontier, Nasser permitted the deployment of the United Nations Emergency Force in the Gaza Strip and at the straits,[162] as Jean Lacouture explains:

> However unfortunate the operation for the reputation of the Jewish state, it [the Campaign] revealed itself to be profitable from the strategic point of view: the Egyptians opened the Strait of Tiran, which commanded access to Elath, and accepted, although the Israelis had not, the installation on their soil of the blue helmets of the United Nations. This attitude is very revelatory of the state of military inferiority to which Nasser again found himself reduced. He preferred the humiliating shield of the United Nations to a confrontation with Moshe Dayan's army.[163]

Nasser stated quite explicitly that one lesson of the Sinai Campaign was that escalation could not assuredly be controlled and that if a small war should escalate, Israel might win. The campaign had breathed life into Israeli brinkmanship. Speaking to the legislative council of Gaza in 1962 Nasser explained that to initiate quasi-military operations would be unwise: "How can I be sure that Ben-Gurion will not perform

---

161. Yair Evron, *The Demilitarization of Sinai*, Jerusalem Papers on Peace Problems, No. 11 (Jerusalem, 1975), pp. 6–10.

162. "Ba'ayot ha-Bitakhon shel Yisrael ba-Assor akharei Kadesh" [The security problems of Israel in the decade after the Sinai Campaign], *Skirah Hodshit* (September–October 1966): 231–33; Evron, *Middle East*, p. 47; Safran, *Israel*, p. 368.

163. Lacouture, *Nasser*, pp. 288–89.

sharper [larger?] operations against us, and not necessarily quasi-military operations." And he warned of the possible outcomes: "If I make a certain decision, I must be sure that I can impose my views on my forces and my forces on Ben-Gurion himself and those who stand behind him, and I would not come to gamble on the fate of my country and enter a second holocaust like that of 1948."[164]

The Sinai Campaign showed that Egypt could not use Israel with impunity to generate values in domestic or international arenas or harass Israel casually for any purpose. In other words, the bilateral Israel-Egypt relationship became much more central and strategic to Egypt than it had been before.[165] The most telling evidence of this change was Egypt's negative reaction in the early 1960s to Syrian demands for escalation of the conflict.

The first Arab summit in Cairo, in January 1964, was a desperate attempt by Nasser to regain his declining position as leader of Arab unity. His main rival was Amin Hafez of Syria, and the main substantive issue was the formulation of an Arab response to Israeli diversion of Jordan River waters to the Negev. Despite his defensive position, Nasser did his best throughout the conference to moderate demands for belligerent action. He successfully led the forum to decide on nonviolent action, like diversion of the Jordan headwaters, and formation of "unified commands."[166] In 1965, Nasser spoke to the Second Convention of the Palestine Liberation Organization (PLO) immediately after Israeli destruction of Syrian diversion equipment. His message was that if Syria chose to pester Israel prematurely, then Egypt felt no obligation to help her.[167]

Active deterrence is both possible and necessary. This is the central lesson from the pre-Sinai failure of deterrence and its subsequent success. Reputations are necessary, possible to establish, yet mortal and in need of rejuvenation. The numerous barriers to credibility of skill and will along with a priori disbelief in the pain of war make reputations so necessary. The experience with Egypt suggests that useful reputations can be established, but only through full-scale warfare. The ability and will to execute small operations of company size do not convert upward

164. Quoted by the Israel Government Broadcast Monitoring Service, *Broadcast Abstracts*, 27 June 1962.

165. This argument is made by Scheuftan, "Harta'ah Yisraelit be-Sikhsukh Yisrael-Arav," p. 19.

166. Sela, *Achdut*, pp. 26–37.

167. *Skirah Hodshit*, May 1965. For similar expressions by *Al-Ahram's* Mohammed Heykal, see Cairo Radio, 25 November 1966, quoted in Israel Government Broadcast Monitoring Service, *Broadcast Abstracts*, 24, 26 November, 2 December 1966.

to a national willingness to wage general war or establish one's overall strategic superiority. General war may also serve as a reminder or lesson that war is hell—a painful affair. Together with their effects on reputation major wars may change the very nature of a bilateral relationship, centralizing and making it more strategic and more similar to a game of Chicken, in which the status quo is relatively stable.

Whereas in nuclear contexts Armageddon cannot be forgotten or denied, memories of the statesmen of nonnuclear states may fade and reputations may dissipate with time. Reputations may be limited to the game structure in which they are established; yet the dynamics, additivity, and relativism of conventional forces are such that one should not expect a relationship to remain static in structure. It changes unavoidably in response to actions of both direct and more distant actors.

What the Israelis demonstrated in 1948 was indeed impressive but simply irrelevant to the completely altered Egyptian state of 1955. The lessons taught in the small-scale actions between 1954 and 1956 were not convertible. The full-scale exhibition of will, ability, and pain in 1956—this time to the "new" Egypt with her international independence of action and large modern army—would remain relevant for many years, but alas it too would be forgotten by 1967.

[4]

Egyptian Attrition, 1967–1970

As the IDF was formulating its final plans for the now-famous blitz-krieg of June 1967, newly appointed minister of defense Moshe Dayan sounded the following warning to the general staff: "Should the IDF reach the Suez Canal the war will never end. The Egyptians will not be able to afford the IDF's presence at the Suez Canal, and neither will the Soviets allow it. Possibly they [the Soviets] will even intervene, perhaps with indirect military means."[1] And to the cabinet Dayan said, "He who values his life will keep a distance from the canal. Should we reach the canal Nasser will refuse to cease fire, and the war will continue for years."[2] Well, the IDF did reach the canal, the war did continue for (three) years, and the Russians did intervene—directly. And in the end, Israel lost the war.

The 1967 war left Israel with unprecedented and unquestionable strategic superiority. She had virtually destroyed three Arab armies and their air forces, occupied vast tracts of land, and sat but miles from Cairo, Damascus, and Amman. In the south the war had basically reversed the pre-June strategic relationship. Two hundred miles of desert buffer were now in Israel's possession; Egypt Air Force (EAF) flight time to Israel had quadrupled to fifteen minutes, whereas for the Israel Air Force (IAF) flight time to Egypt was cut to about four minutes. Israeli ground forces occupied the entire Sinai Peninsula (map 5) and were deployed on the east bank of the Suez Canal, directly threatening the economy and population of the canal's west bank with its four large cities and industrial plant. But, for all of this, it turned out that Dayan had been prescient.

1. Quoted in Shabtai Teveth, *Moshe Dayan*, p. 575.
2. Ibid., pp. 575–76.

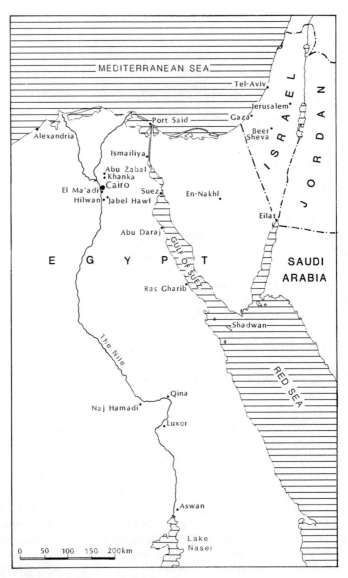

5. Israel and Egypt, 1967–1973

Two and one-half months after the Six Day War, Egyptian armed challenge began, a challenge moderate and intermittent at first but steadier and more violent over time. Egyptian belligerence took the form of small arms fire, small-scale cross-canal operations for mining and sabotage, a few company-sized attacks, air raids against Israeli positions, and perhaps most characteristic, massive and lengthy artillery attacks. By the spring of 1969 Egyptian belligerence and Israeli response intended to end it had reached, in the words of U.N. Sec. Gen. U Thant, a "virtual state of active war,"[3] and so it continued without respite until August 1970.[4]

In the spring of 1970 the armed challenge was revolutionized by direct Soviet intervention, first with surface-to-air missile (SAM) operators and later pilots on operational missions. On 8 August 1970 the shooting war ended with an accord to cease fire, reached when Israel's local superiority had been nullified and both protagonists were attrited indeed. Under cover of the cease-fire the Egyptian-Soviet challenge continued in cold form for about six weeks, as the Egyptians advanced enough SAM batteries toward the canal (in violation of the accord) actually to reverse the local power balance.

This chapter tries to explain why Dayan had been so right; why Israel's June 1967 victory, the strategic reality in its wake, and all she did through September 1970 did not suffice to deter the Egyptian challenge.[5]

Israel and Egypt agreed on one aspect of the postwar situation: the need for a political solution. But this brought them no closer to resolving their differences, for the political goals and expectations of Egypt and Israel were irreconcilable, which set the stage for conflict. Furthermore,

3. Quoted in Daniel Dishon, ed., *Middle East Record*, vol. 5 (1969–70) (Jerusalem, 1977), p. 505. Henceforth this volume is cited as *MER* (1969–70).
4. In this war with Egypt, Israel suffered over 1300 casualties, of them 367 deaths. The figures for Egypt are much disputed but tend to run into the thousands of deaths. See Jehuda Wallach, Moshe Lissak, and Shimon Shamir, eds., *Atlas Carta le-Toldot Medinat Yisrael: Assor Sheni* [Carta's atlas of Israel: The second decade] (Jerusalem, 1980), p. 103; *MER* (1969–70), pp. 166, 172.
5. The War of Attrition is normally defined more narrowly than the three-year period I have chosen to deal with; traditionally it is March 1969–8 August 1970. See for example the treatment in the following works: Yaacov Bar-Siman-Tov, *The Israeli-Egyptian War of Attrition, 1969–1970: A Case Study of Local Limited War* (New York, 1980); Zvi Lanir, "Political Aims and Military Objectives"; Ahmed S. Khalidi, "The War of Attrition," *Journal of Palestine Studies* 3 (Autumn 1973). Two semiofficial histories by the IDF cover the entire three-year period, but only until the cease-fire of 8 August: Yitshak Arad, ed., *Elef ha-Yamim, 12 Yuni 1967–8 August, 1970* [1000 days, 12 June 1967–8 August 1970] (Tel-Aviv, 1972); Mordechai Naor, *Hamilhama leachar ha-Milhama* [The war after the war] (Tel-Aviv, [1970?]). Lawrence Whetten treats the entire six-year period between 1967 and 1973, in *The Canal War: Four-Power Conflict in the Middle East* (Cambridge, Mass., 1974).

each of the protagonists had faith in military power as the basis for a political solution, thus setting the stage for *armed* conflict. Israel believed that the unqualified superiority she had demonstrated in the Six Day War would support her bid for a political revolution: peace with Egypt, a turning forward of history's pages. But Egypt's political goal was to eject the Israelis from Egyptian territory and return to the status quo ante: to turn history's pages back. This was to be achieved by military manipulation of political interests and processes. Force, then, took on special meaning as Egypt turned to challenge and Israel to deter.

A History

June–December 1967

On 9 June 1967, Nasser declared that his goal was to "remove the traces of aggression," and he immediately set out to pursue it.[6] The strategy with which to achieve this goal developed slowly during the first months after the June debacle, as Nasser experimented with various approaches and tested his environment. At first the Egyptians hoped for a political ejection of Israel from Sinai, expecting outside powers, Western and Eastern, to intervene as they had in 1957 to force Israeli withdrawal. Nasser gave his blessing to a mission of King Hussein to President Johnson to demand American assistance in returning lost territories.[7]

The Soviets and Americans were in no hurry to intervene on Egypt's behalf. Johnson refused to repeat Eisenhower's arm twisting of Israel, and the Russians apparently told the Egyptians to "accept the logic of their defeat and change their position on their conflict with Israel."[8] If purely political interests could not induce superpower intervention, Egypt hoped that closure of the canal would create in Europe and the United States economic pressure to intercede. By late summer it was clear that a closed Suez Canal or even a threatened Arab oil embargo would not engender appropriate Western behavior.[9]

6. Quoted in Dishon, *Middle East Record*, vol. 3 (1967) (Jerusalem, 1971), p. 256. Henceforth this volume is cited as *MER* (1967). See also Bar-Siman-Tov, *Israeli-Egyptian War*, p. 43; Whetten, *Canal War*, p. 45.

7. *MER* (1967), p. 259.

8. Evron, *Middle East*, pp. 80–81. On early Soviet-American collusion to find a compromise solution, see Alvin Z. Rubinstein, *Red Star on the Nile: The Soviet-Egyptian Influence Relationship since the June War* (Princeton, N.J., 1977), pp. 24–29.

9. On attempts to apply economic pressure, see *MER* (1967), pp. 261–62, 296.

In the weeks immediately after the cease-fire, Egypt was militarily helpless before the victorious Israelis and saw herself as a defender as well as a potential challenger. Israel indeed intended to expand somewhat her territorial claims and in late June tried to capture the northwest corner of the peninsula around Port Fuad (map 6), which had remained in Egyptian hands. In July Israel tried to define the de facto cease-fire line down the center of the canal by sailing small vessels along the east bank. Egyptian military action and escalation thwarted Israeli designs and forced Israel to withdraw both claims permanently.[10] Egypt tried to transfer her strategic deterrence problem to the Soviet Union. Nasser offered to hand over command of the EAF to the Soviets and to elicit a mutual defense pact from them.[11] The Russians refused but did accede to his demands for massive rearmament, a project they pursued with such vigor that within six months between 60 and 80 percent of the arms lost in June were replaced. Egyptian fears of an Israeli "walkover" dissipated.[12]

In July and August, while failing to extract extraregional support for his challenge of Israel directly, Nasser began to maneuver for support through the Arab system. After much Egyptian pressure the Arab states convened for a summit meeting at Khartoum (29 August–1 September).[13] Egypt's behavior at the summit reflected her pursuit of a political solution, perhaps in an attempt to impress the Americans and alter the American position of apathy.[14] Nasser succeeded in overruling Syrian, Palestinian, and Algerian objections to the resolution calling for "political efforts at the international and diplomatic level to eliminate the effects of the aggression."[15]

Now that Egypt had a real (intrinsic) problem with Israeli occupation, Nasser lost interest in his own prewar theoretical and ideological hubris

10. For descriptions and discussions of these incidents, see *MER* (1967), p. 297; Heykal, in *Al-Ahram*, 8 August 1969; Arad, *Elef ha-Yamim*, p. 28; Eli Landau, *Suez: Fire on the Water*, trans. from Hebrew by R. Ben-Yosef (Tel-Aviv, 1970), pp. 17–24; Naor, *Hamilhama leachar ha-Milhama*, pp. 12–14.

11. Jon D. Glassman, *Arms for the Arabs: The Soviet Union and War in the Middle East* (Baltimore, 1975), pp. 66–67; Rubinstein, *Red Star on the Nile*, p. 18.

12. By the end of 1967 the Egyptians had deployed the equivalent of three divisions at the canal. At their disposal were 550 artillery pieces. In contrast, the Israelis quickly demobilized the 1967 army and remained with one brigade on the east bank, with a small number of artillery pieces in support. See Edgar O'Ballance, *The Electronic War in the Middle East 1968–1970* (London, 1974), pp. 31–32.

13. Discussion of the Khartoum Summit is based on these sources: *MER* (1967), pp. 262–66; Sela, *Achdut*, pp. 67–80; Lacouture, *Nasser*, pp. 324–25; Malcolm H. Kerr, *The Arab Cold War: Gamal Abd al-Nasser and His Rivals, 1958–1970*, 3d ed. (New York, 1971), pp. 137–40.

14. On the political solution as a tactical move, see *MER* (1967), pp. 269–70.

15. Quoted in ibid., p. 264.

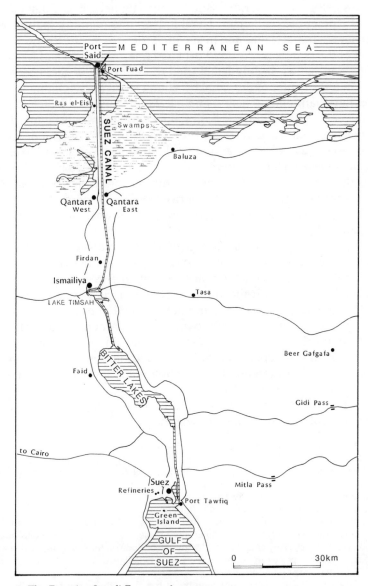

6. The Egyptian-Israeli Front, 1967–1973

and rhetoric regarding Israel's destruction and got the conference to concentrate on his practical need to eject Israel. Unfortunately, the most memorable resolution of the summit was not the call for "political efforts" but rather the concomitant declaration of "Three Noes": no direct negotiations, no formal peace, no recognition.

In September, Egypt made her first direct and blatant armed challenge of Israel at the canal. In a number of separate incidents (on 4, 5, 6, 12, 21, and 27 September) Egyptian forces instigated large conflagrations that included massive artillery barrages against Israeli forces. The IDF responded with ground fire. Egyptian forces and artillery batteries were deployed in residential areas, and as a result Israeli return fire caused damage and civilian deaths and created refugees as residents fled the combat zone. In all, during September Israel suffered some forty casualties, twenty-five on 27 September alone.[16]

After these exchanges, on 30 September 1967, Nasser announced his decision to evacuate the canal cities, a decision he was not able to execute immediately but one that would become an important element of his strategy for dealing with Israel. From a bargaining perspective this was a decision to nullify Israel's access to Egyptian hostages.[17]

Except for minor activity, the front was quiet until the INS Eilat incident. In the early evening hours of 21 October, Egyptian missile boats, using Styx-type surface missiles, sank the Israeli destroyer and flagship INS Eilat in the vicinity of Port Said. Israeli casualties were high: of 198 crew members 47 died and 91 were wounded.[18]

On 24 October the IDF responded with intensive shelling of the Suez refineries and oil installations. The damage was severe, with the burning of hundreds of thousands of tons of oil and asphalt and the destruction of a number of factories. The severity can also be understood from the official Egyptian government statements to the effect that the shelling was "indeed a serious blow" to the economy and that "it was not the price we should expect to pay for trying to defend ourselves."[19] On 27 October, Nasser announced that his forces would have to "cool" the front for a while: "We have plans for retaliation . . . but when will we step up these plans? . . . Escalation today would not be in our favor."[20]

16. Ibid., pp. 299–300; Naor, *Hamilhama leachar ha-Milhama*, pp. 24–25.

17. *MER* (1967), pp. 582–83; Heykal, in *Al-Ahram*, 8 August 1969, cited by Israel Government Press Monitoring Service, *Press Abstracts*, 8 August 1969.

18. Descriptions of the incident may be found in Landau, *Suez*, pp. 70–93; Arad, *Elef ha-Yamim*, pp. 53–54; Schiff and Haber, *Lexikon le-Bitahon Yisrael*, p. 39; *MER* (1967), pp. 301–2.

19. *MER* (1967), p. 303; Naor, *Hamilhama leachar ha-Milhama*, p. 26; Schiff and Haber, *Lexikon le-Bitahon Yisrael*, p. 100.

20. Quoted in *MER* (1967), p. 303.

And indeed, for the most part the Suez front relaxed for a full year until the fall of 1968.

How do we interpret Egyptian belligerence at the canal in September and October, especially in light of the Khartoum resolution calling for political and diplomatic efforts? At least in part, military activism was an attempt to appease the demands of the army, which naturally needed to prove its worth and raise morale. Also the nation needed a restoration of honor and prestige, be it limited by the relatively modest capabilities of a recently purged and physically demolished army.[21] But there was more to it than that.

After the Khartoum Summit we find increasing attention to the need for force as a lever for achieving the desired political solution. The threat of force is portrayed more and more as establishing a strong political bargaining position, especially one from which to pressure external actors to intervene and resolve the conflict. Kol Yisrael [Israel Radio] first noted this connection in Egyptian policy after the September incidents: "The maintenance of unrest is obviously part of an official policy designed to impress the world in general and the UN in particular . . . that the Suez Canal constitutes a major international area of unrest and thereby bring to bear the pressure of international opinion on Israel with a view to extracting concessions."[22] The London *Times* seems to have realized the destabilizing nature of Nasser's actions, just as he would have had Western leaders understand it: "Ships of one navy do not sink ships of another unless they are at war or spoiling to start a war."[23]

From the early months there is little direct Egyptian rhetorical evidence that this was the policy but some of a circumstantial nature. For example, immediately after the October incidents Nasser sabotaged King Hussein's "peace offensive" in the United States although he had endorsed it earlier.[24] Mohammed Heykal wrote that a political solution was no longer possible. One speculates that it was no longer possible because Israel was getting the better of Egypt's forces at the canal and neither Israel nor the outside powers seemed terribly concerned by the violence. Stopping short Hussein's trip to Washington was one way to impute urgency to the situation.

In November and December the connection between military and political moves became more explicit in Egyptian statements, which

---

21. Ibid., pp. 302, 557–58; Whetten, *Canal War*, pp. 60–61; O'Ballance, *Electronic War*, pp. 32–33.
22. *MER* (1967), p. 301.
23. *Times* (London), 23 October 1967, quoted in ibid., p. 302.
24. *MER* (1967), p. 268.

appear to have been aimed at foreign audiences. In early November the Egyptian government spokesman directly threatened violence unless the United Nations found a political solution to Israeli occupation. In December, Heykal wrote, "If the enemy does not withdraw . . . we will be compelled to force them. . . . If no political solution is found, there is no alternative to the resumption of fighting. . . . Is there anything wrong or excessive in what we say?"[25] After adoption of U.N. Resolution 242 in late November, Nasser announced that "what is taken by force cannot be restored except by force," an assertion quickly explained by his spokesman to mean *unless* a political solution were found![26]

What we see here is the crude expression of the following principles of political-military strategy: (a) outside powers might be induced to intervene by credibly threatening instability in the region, and (b) a political settlement should not be pursued from a position of inferiority. Thus, the violent incidents may have been intended to establish the ability to cause instability. When Israel's ability to silence the Egyptians proved this threat not credible, *serious* political negotiations were terminated, although rhetorical political efforts, such as acceptance of 242, were maintained along with rhetorical belligerence.

The Six Day War revolutionized Israel's grand strategy overnight (or over a week). In the decade before 1967 the Israeli approach to war was, in the words of Zvi Lanir, one of "denial." The central tenet of this approach was that war had no immediate political aims beyond survival of the state, and its only purpose was to preserve the status quo.[27] The outcome of the June war had two major effects on Israeli goals and strategic thinking. First, the survival problem appeared solved, and second, therefore, positive political and strategic goals could be pursued to reflect the new strategic balance. Frontier revisions and true peace seemed within reach.

Early Israeli optimism was evident in both word and deed. Reflecting the new faith in geostrategic superiority and her ability to survive, Israel rapidly demobilized its military reserves. Deployment at the Suez Canal was treated rather casually, with soldiers digging into foxholes (and not bunkers), with a rather small order of forces in a loose organizational structure. The Egyptians, went the faith, could and would do very little of a belligerent nature.[28] Rapid conversion from denial to belief in

25. Quoted in ibid., p. 269.

26. Ibid.

27. Lanir, "Political Aims and Military Objectives," pp. 22–25.

28. On the relaxed attitude and lack of serious fortifications in the postwar period, see Landau, *Suez*, pp. 100–4; Naor, *Hamilhama leachar ha-Milhama*, pp. 15–16; Avraham (Bren) Adan, *On the Banks of the Suez* (Novaro, Calif., 1980), pp. 42–43.

positive benefits of war was given expression by Prime Minister Levi Eshkol at the Knesset on 12 June: "On the wings of victory perhaps will arrive a new era of changing values, relations and borders. Victory in the war can bring with it the victory of eternal peace."[29] Foreign Minister Abba Eban told the Knesset that there were no intermediate states between war and peace, and to the United Nations he spoke of Israel's demand for direct negotiations: "Our insistence on direct negotiations is not a matter of procedure. . . . A refusal to negotiate is inherently identical with a refusal to live in peace."[30]

By mid-July the telephone had not rung, and Israeli leaders began to develop a longer view of the problem. Preservation of the status quo as pressure on Egypt began to emerge as a central tenet of Israeli strategy, similar to the earlier idea of deterrence-by-frustration. Eban had said in 1965, "Our policy of containment and deterrence . . . has two objectives. In the specific context of security it aims to protect our land and lives. In its political aspect, it aims to induce new currents of thought in the Arab mind. We want to create doubt—and eventually resignation and despair—about the dream of eliminating Israel from the world's map."[31] Now, with more positive goals, continued frustration was expected to lead to peace. On 31 July the Israeli government decided formally that no withdrawal from the cease-fire lines would occur except as a result of direct negotiations.[32]

After the Khartoum Summit in early September, Israeli leaders revised their expectations downward but did not change their approach. The prospects for immediate peace receded, but the long run still seemed promising. And with the new frontiers and strategic balance, long-term frustration appeared possible. In an official press release the cabinet stated that in light of the Khartoum "noes," Israel would "continue to maintain fully the situation established by the cease-fire agreements, and to safeguard her position, taking into account the vital needs of Israel's security and development."[33] In a sense, the situation seemed optimal for Israel. Frustration would either lead to peace or not, but either way Israel felt secure, with both time and the new frontiers working in her favor.[34]

29. *Divrei ha-Knesset*, 12 June 1967.

30. *MER* (1967), pp. 274–75.

31. From an interview with the *Jewish Observer and Middle East Review*, 2 July 1965.

32. *Haaretz*, 31 July 1967. Note that in negotiations after the July incidents over canal navigation rights, Defense Minister Dayan insisted that *neither* side navigate, so as to freeze the status quo; see *MER* (1967), p. 299.

33. Quoted in ibid., p. 275.

34. See Yigal Allon in *Haaretz*, 5 September 1967; Dayan, quoted in *MER* (1967), p. 276; Lanir, "Political Aims and Military Objectives," p. 28.

Egyptian belligerence in September and, more so, the October attack on the INS Eilat sat Israeli leaders on the painful horns of a dilemma. Retaliation was deemed necessary for deterrence but would play into the hands of Nasser's destabilization policy. In September the IDF minimized its response, firing only at the offending Egyptian units; but the shelling of the Suez refineries after the Eilat incident was a shift to countervalue reprisal, intended to demonstrate pain and threaten *more* should the Egyptians continue to violate the status quo.[35]

The Israelis understood their predicament. In September a Kol Yisrael radio commentary expressed the view that though Egypt desired unrest in order to manipulate outside powers, "peace and quiet along the Canal are in Israel's interests," precisely to keep extraregional actors out.[36] After the shelling of Suez in October, Dayan hurried to stress that it had been a discrete reprisal for a particular violation and that the IDF would strive to maintain the cease-fire henceforth.[37]

In December, Dayan expounded publicly the emerging Israeli theories of deterrence by countervalue threat and frustration:

> Sinking the Eilat cost them the refineries. . . . the Egyptians will have to realize that we were capable of hitting the refineries even before [the Eilat incident], that the oil tanks and oil pipes are in the range of our artillery and tanks. We knew before hand that there was oil and that it could be ignited, but we had no interest in doing so. But if the Egyptians pressure us and heat up the lines, we shall act similarly and shell the other bank of the Suez. . . . Our policy is to strive not for hot lines but for cold lines, and we have no interest in incidents. . . . We must sit at the Suez Canal until we achieve our goals of peace. It is difficult but possible. We must be prepared for a long sitting and to operate so that we do not surrender to pressure.[38]

1968

During the first eight months of 1968 the canal front was relatively quiet as Nasser pursued diplomatic and verbally coercive attempts to force an unconditional Israeli withdrawal. The basic strategic approach remained as before, but throughout 1968 it was further developed, refined, and given more eloquent and public expression ultimately as

35. On the return to reprisals see Whetten, *Canal War*, p. 60.
36. *MER* (1967), p. 301.
37. Ibid., p. 303.
38. Quoted in Moshe Dayan, *Mapa Hadasha: Yakhasim Akherim* [A new map: New relations] (Tel-Aviv, 1969), pp. 89–90. This source is a collection of public statements made by Dayan between 1967 and 1969.

Nasser's theory of stages. In September and October, Egypt escalated the violence, a direct implementation of this theory.

By early spring Nasser was most likely finally convinced that no purely political solution to his problem was likely. In January, Egypt apparently tried to reopen the canal unilaterally, but Israeli fire on Egyptian surveyors cut this effort short. The lack of *any* Western reaction should have buried any lingering hopes for economically induced pressure on Israel.[39] In addition, Egypt's acceptance of U.N. Resolution 242 was paying no dividends, and Gunnar Jarring's U.N. mission to advance an accord was leading nowhere.[40]

More and more public and private statements by Egyptian leaders stressed the need to involve the superpowers directly so that they might impose a solution. In March Nasser reportedly wrote to DeGaulle that "a solution to the crisis in the Middle East must, in the Egyptian view, have as [a] starting point an agreement of the four Great Powers."[41] Throughout the spring Spokesman Zayyat and Foreign Minister Mahmoud Riyad expressed their belief that intervention by the powers was imperative to force the "correct" implementation of 242.[42] But how was such intervention to be effected?

The idea was to engage in a kind of offensive brinkmanship, a threat that things might get out of control and involve the superpowers in a conflict they so feared. And so, throughout the spring and summer one sees continuous threats of the possible consequences of not resolving the conflict and numerous repetitions of the axiom that "what was taken by force cannot be restored except by force." War would result if the political process failed, and it seemed to be doing just that. Heykal wrote in August 1968: "I have become convinced of the difficulty and even the impossibility of finding a political solution. . . . All this leaves only one field in which the Middle East crisis can find a solution—the battlefield. . . . This course is imposed on us because no other way is open to us after reviewing all the factors and circumstances."[43] The real target of these threats of instability was the United States, which Nasser and Heykal came to see as unique in its ability to influence Israel. Heykal described the United States as "the only power that can arouse Israel from its stupor."[44]

39. Evron, *Middle East*, pp. 92–94; Dishon, *Middle East Record*, vol. 4 (1968) (Jerusalem, 1973), pp. 263–70. Henceforth this volume is cited as *MER* (1968); Rubinstein, *Red Star on the Nile*, p. 53.

40. Rubinstein, *Red Star on the Nile*, p. 55; Whetten, *Canal War*, pp. 55–57.

41. Quoted in *MER* (1968), p. 210.

42. Ibid.

43. Quoted in ibid., p. 208.

44. Quoted in ibid. See also Shimon Shamir, "Nasser and Sadat, 1967–1973: Two

Force, real and proven, was necessary to threaten instability credibly. After discovering in late 1967 the futility of trying to bargain without the backing of successfully used force, the Egyptians increased their attention to the necessity of military power. Said Nasser, "If we accept and follow the course of political action, the outcome depends on our preparedness for battle,"[45] and Riyad, "Political action to achieve justice cannot succeed without force to back it. However much we may talk about the justice of our cause, we will not be able to achieve what we want or to obtain our rights without force to back them."[46]

In August, Heykal pulled many of these ideas together in a rare exposition of the military-political strategy of offensive brinkmanship:

> If escalation of the crisis occurs—and this is more likely than many people think—it will turn into a problem between the great powers. . . . What I am trying to say is that it is not enough if we ourselves feel that the field of battle is the only alternative left us. It is important that many others too should be of the same opinion and that they should be fully convinced that this is the choice forced on us. . . . Thus we shall see that the USA and the USSR cannot ignore what happens in the Middle East. If they do not succeed in moves to bring about real peace in the region, they will not be able to stand aside from the fighting that will inevitably ensue, fighting that will settle the fate of the region. Therefore the very fact of reaching the brink of war demands precisely political activity on our part, massive patience and staying power—until we reach our goal.[47]

Amassing the necessary power and creating the required instability depended on the ability to mobilize both the Arab system and the Soviet Union. Aside from the financial support of the oil states, Egypt demanded military assistance in the form of a second active front against Israel. Throughout 1968, Nasser made repeated attempts to goad Syria, Iraq, and Jordan into opening the so-called Eastern Front against Israel—with no success. Despite its official launching in October, the Eastern Front (or Command) never really materialized to assist Egypt in upsetting the local balance.[48]

Approaches to a National Crisis," in Itamar Rabinovich and Haim Shaked, eds., *From June to October: The Middle East between 1967 and 1973* (New Brunswick, N.J., 1978), pp. 193–94; Bar-Siman-Tov, *Israeli-Egyptian War*, p. 51.

45. Quoted in *MER* (1968), p. 207.

46. Ibid.

47. *Al-Ahram*, 23 August 1968. This translation is from Bar-Siman-Tov, *Israeli-Egyptian War*, pp. 50–51. See also Lt. Col. Yona, "Mediniut ha-Maavak shel Abd Al-Nasser" [Nasser's policy of (for) struggle], *Maarachot* 223 (June 1972):31.

48. *MER* (1968), pp. 160–64. This is not to say that Israel's other borders were peaceful throughout the period. Between 1967 and 1970 Israel waged almost continuous warfare

The Soviet Union provided vast quantities of weapons, advice, advisers, and instructors. There were reports of between one and four thousand Soviet personnel in the United Arab Republic, including advisers down to field unit and squadron levels. Some three hundred Egyptian pilots received advanced training in the Soviet Union during the year. In the course of the year, agreements were signed for hundreds of T-54/55 tanks, self-propelled artillery, 150 Mig-21 interceptors, torpedo and missile boats, and more, which were then delivered.[49]

The Soviet role in the Egyptian strategy was pivotal, for they were to provide the power necessary for credible offensive brinkmanship. But the threat of inadvertent escalation was the threat to involve the superpowers directly and against each other, and so the Soviets were caught in a conflict of interests, which they resolved by pressing Nasser to moderate his plans for offensive action at the canal. To make sure, they refused to supply certain offensive weapons systems in quantities sufficient to execute large operations against Israel.[50] Nasser did maintain the freedom and ability to engage in limited attrition, which he attempted in the fall, as a direct application of his theory.[51]

It was in March and April that Nasser publicly expounded this theory of stages of action against Israel. He envisaged four consecutive escalatory steps of Egyptian military action:

1. Standing firm (in which Egypt had been engaged since June 1967)
2. Deterrence, or active defense
3. Erasing the traces of aggression
4. Final victory

Stage 3 referred to the 1967 aggression, stage 4 to the liquidation of Israel.[52]

---

against Fedayeen infiltration and shelling across the Jordanian, Lebanese, and Syrian frontiers. There were also sporadic clashes with the Jordanian and Syrian armies. This activity was troublesome and painful but of little strategic significance or assistance to the Egyptians. For overviews of these other wars, see Wallach, Lissak, and Shamir, *Atlas Carta: Assor Sheni*, pp. 115–23, 128–34; Arad, *Elef ha-Yamim*, passim.

49. *MER* (1968), pp. 35–37.

50. Whetten, *Canal War*, pp. 67–69; *MER* (1968), pp. 32–33; George W. Breslauer, "Soviet Policy in the Middle East, 1967–1972; Unalterable Antagonism or Collaborative Competition?" in Alexander George, ed., *Managing U.S.-Soviet Rivalry: Problems of Crisis Prevention* (Boulder, Colo., 1983), pp. 71–72, 83–91.

51. Oded Eran, "Soviet Policy between the 1967 and 1973 Wars," in Itmar Rabinovich and Haim Shaked, eds., *From June to October: The Middle East between 1967 and 1973* (New Brunswick, N.J., 1978), p. 33.

52. Yona, "Mediniut ha-Maavak shel Abd Al-Nasser," passim; *MER* (1968), pp. 271–72.

Such a presentation of future history must have been meant to impart a sense of a sure path to ultimate success. Given both inter-Arab and domestic Egyptian pressure for action despite the relatively pacific reality since October, the theory of stages may have been an attempt to enjoy in the present the fruits of future activity. The theory as presented also allowed a separation of ideology and practicality. Stage 4 was essential for Pan-Arab legitimacy, yet in practical terms Nasser's agenda included only the first three (Egyptian) stages. The fourth was postponed to the very distant future, and the fundamental fight against Zionism was placed in the mythical and long-run idiom of the war against the Crusades.

Nasser provided no time table with his program, insisting that progress from stage to stage would be both slow and conditional upon the mobilization of force and resources. This, I believe, reflected Nasser's practicality, his intention not to get involved in unsustainable adventures such as the Six Day War. But it also can be seen as integral to his general strategy.

The conditionality in the theory and of the program should have pressured the Eastern Front to form. Also, the promise of slowly yet unalterably escalating belligerence is perfect rhetorical support for offensive brinkmanship. Nasser can be seen as serving notice on the United States and Israel that either the conflict must be resolved or else it would become larger and larger ("What you see now is only the beginning") until strategic destabilization would occur.

It was possible to observe the dynamics of expectations and action being created. In June and July the United Arab Republic instigated a number of small artillery incidents; upon returning from the Soviet Union in July, Nasser announced that stage 2 was indeed about to begin.[53] On 8 September the Egyptians surprised Israeli forces at the canal with a three-and-a-half-hour artillery barrage covering nearly the entire length of the canal. The Israelis suffered ten dead and eighteen wounded. On 9 September the beginning of stage 2 was officially announced.[54]

On 26 October the Egyptian army launched what could only be described as a "coordinated and well planned" artillery attack along the entire front. Under cover of the artillery fire two infantry platoons crossed the canal to ambush and mine. Israeli forces returned fire, targeting Egyptian artillery, the Suez refineries, and oil storage tanks. Damage was severe. Israel Defense Forces casualties were again high:

53. Ibid., p. 43.
54. *MER* (1968), pp. 358–59.

fifteen dead and thirty-four injured.[55] Demonstrating seriousness of purpose and an irrevocable dedication to escalation, Nasser continued to evacuate the canal cities throughout September and October. For example, according to official sources, by mid-September the town of Suez had only 60,000 of its original 260,000 citizens, and Ismailiya 5000 of 173,000.[56]

Egyptian pessimism about the prospects of a quick, neat political resolution was mirrored by growing Israeli despair at the realization that the continuing situation would not lead to peace. As 1968 progressed, Israeli leaders expressed gloomier and gloomier prognoses. In August, Meir stated that as long as Nasser ruled Egypt there was no hope for peaceful developments and that "under the present circumstances we have nobody to talk with in the Arab states."[57] These views were echoed by other leaders such as Eshkol, Yigal Allon, and Dayan.[58] Even Eban, who objected to the "nihilistic concept of the inevitability of war," saw in Egypt "hardening of the ideological intransigence, extreme adherence to the principles formulated in Khartoum, and total refusal even to dream of peace with Israel."[59]

These new understandings of the problem did not move Israeli leaders to consider fundamentally new approaches. Before the Egyptian escalation of October, quiet had reigned for nearly a year, and even if challenges were offered by Egypt, such as the shelling in September, at least the new line at the canal provided strategic security. Perhaps, too, peace would come eventually. For Israel, sitting as she was at the canal seemed a maximin strategy. Only after the serious Egyptian escalation on 26 October did the Israelis turn to reassess Egyptian intentions behind local belligerency and to seek new means of deterrence for both the long and short runs.[60] These came in the form of the first in-depth commando raid, at Naj Hamadi, and the construction of the Bar Lev Line.

During the night of 31 October, IDF airborne commandos penetrated to the heart of Upper Egypt and sabotaged three strategic targets: (a) the Naj Hamadi Bridge and dam on the Nile, (b) the Naj Hamadi transformer station, and (c) the Qina Bridge, some 50 kilometers east of Naj

---

55. Ibid., pp. 359–61; O'Ballance, *Electronic War*, pp. 40–41.

56. *MER* (1968), p. 359; Naor, *Hamilhama leachar ha-Milhama*, p. 44; Whetten, *Canal War*, p. 61.

57. *Jerusalem Post*, 7 August 1968, cited in *MER* (1968), p. 255.

58. See Dayan's pessimistic speech in August, quoted in *Mapa Hadasha*, p. 29.

59. *Lamerhav*, 22 September 1968, cited in *MER* (1968), p. 255.

60. See Dayan's reaction to the incident of 26 October in *Avnei Derekh*, pp. 513–14.

Hamadi. The unit accomplished its mission and returned to Israeli territory unharmed.[61]

What were the principles behind the raid? Why in such depth in the very heart of Egypt? The choice of deep targets was an attempt to let the Egyptians know that despite the tremendous preponderance of force at the canal, the Egyptian army was impotent against deep incursions into Egypt, where the IDF could roam at will. The choice of civilian or economic targets was a demonstration that not only could the Egyptian army not defend itself but its actions put Egypt proper at risk. These blows at the economy deep inside Egypt, and hence also to the prestige of the regime, would continue, went the threat, as long as Egyptian belligerence at the canal did not let up.[62]

For the first time since reprisals in Jordan in 1953, the Israelis readopted the classic countervalue reprisal by incursion for active deterrence. Both Allon and Dayan expressed belief in the efficacy of Israel's countervalue threats in 1968, especially in the effect of possible damage to the canal cities.[63] Gen. Avraham Adan argues that the Naj Hamadi raid was a result of Nasser's evacuation of the canal cities: having lost one countervalue threat, the Israelis began to seek others.[64]

The shift from shelling the canal cities to in-depth raids was a major change in deterrence principle: from causation of real and substantial pain to reliance on the threatening effect of demonstration, be it of Israeli superiority, of Egyptian impotence, or of the possibility that Israel might escalate horizontally and not confine her activities to the canal zone where Egypt had the quantitative advantage. As Dayan explained at the Knesset two days before the raid, "If they [the Egyptians] believe that the large forces that they have amassed on the west bank of the Canal—and they have deployed there large forces—immunize them from military blows and military blows by us, then I believe that they are wrong. . . . I fear that they will be proven wrong in their calculus, that the forces at their disposal insure them against military blows, which might come if the cease-fire is violated."[65] The Israeli press commented that the purpose had indeed been to teach the Egyptians that evacuating the cities did not force Israel to accommodate

61. Find descriptions in Naor, *Hamilhama lechar ha-Milhama*, p. 45; Landau, *Suez*, pp. 121–26; *MER* (1968), pp. 361–63.

62. Dayan, *Mapa Hadasha*, pp. 88–89; *MER* (1968), p. 362.

63. Zeev Schiff, *Knafayim me'al Suez* [Phantom over the Nile: The story of the Israeli Air Corps] (Haifa, 1970), p. 190; Allon, *Massakh shel Khol*, p. 389.

64. Adan, *On the Banks of the Suez*, p. 43.

65. Dayan, *Mapa Hadasha*, pp. 88–89.

Egypt's desire to fight a static, artillery-intensive war and "emphasized [Israeli] warnings . . . that, fighting need not be confined to the Suez Canal front."[66]

The Naj Hamadi raid stunned the Egyptians. They announced the immediate establishment of the Popular Defense Organizations, a kind of civil guard to defend installations and potential objectives throughout Egypt. They also reportedly changed civil aviation air routes to help prevent infiltration through them of enemy aircraft.[67] Most important, they desisted from belligerent activity at the canal for four months, until March 1969. Nasser had been pushed back to stage 1.

If the Naj Hamadi raid was an attempt to put an immediate stop to Egyptian belligerence, the Bar Lev Line was to make possible the frustration of Egyptian hopes of upsetting the status quo by violence. It was to enable the IDF to "not surrender to pressure," as Dayan had said earlier. Like the raid at Naj Hamadi, its construction and the organizational changes attending it resulted from changing Israeli assessments of Egyptian attitudes and intentions regarding the status quo. Israel expected that sooner or later the Egyptians would resume their challenge to the status quo by fire, or even by canal crossings of some scale. The Bar Lev Line would be the answer to these challenges.

The new Israeli attitude was immediately reflected in a decision to raise the force level in western Sinai from less than two loosely organized brigades to three brigades (two of them armored). The enhanced force was organized as a standing division, Israel's first.[68]

Given the government's mandate of inflexible defense of the territorial status quo, the IDF had to choose between two contending approaches to implementation.[69] Generals Ariel Sharon and Israel Tal envisioned a mobile defense of the east bank, a system of mechanized patrols and operations that would ensure Israeli control. Chief of Staff Haim Bar Lev and Gen. Adan believed in the necessity of continuous and contiguous immovable physical presence at the canal.

66. *MER* (1968), p. 362. One principle behind the raid that had little to do with deterrence was the IDF's need to live by its traditional ethos of initiative and offense. This drive comes up again shortly, intruding on Israeli attempts to devise appropriate defensive strategies.

67. Saad el-Shazli, *The Crossing of the Suez* (San Francisco, 1980), p. 12; Anwar el-Sadat, *In Search of Identity: An Autobiography* (New York, 1978), p. 196; *MER* (1968), p. 362.

68. Adan, *On the Banks of the Suez*, pp. 43–44; Hanoch Bartov, *Daddo: Arbajm ve-Shmoneh Shanah ve'od Essrim Yom* [Daddo: 48 years and 20 more days] (Tel-Aviv, 1979), pp. 176–77. The latter is the award-winning biography of the late chief of staff, David Elazar.

69. The discussion of the concepts behind the Bar Lev Line is based on Zeev Schiff, *A History of the Israeli Army (1870–1974)* (San Francisco, 1974), pp. 243–44; Bartov, *Daddo*, pp. 174–76; Adan, *On the Banks of the Suez*, pp. 44–49; Dayan, *Avnei Derekh*, p. 515.

The Bar Lev Line was a compromise solution, advanced by Adan and supported by Tal. Thirty strongholds (maozim), impenetrable to artillery and ground attack, would sit "on" the canal, providing an immovable foothold. The maozim would be spaced about 10 kilometers apart, and each would hold some twenty soldiers. Artillery and mobile forces would deploy in the rear, the artillery close enough to provide fire support, and the armor to race to the canal as required. For low-level current defense purposes, the maozim would provide a continuous presence at the canal, establishing Israel's obstinate adherence to the status quo. In the event of more substantial Egyptian attempts to cross the canal, the maozim would provide a fixed presence regardless of temporary Egyptian advances and could also provide intelligence and forward observation for the bulk of the forces deployed behind, who would counterattack as tactically required.[70]

In November a special team was put together under Gen. Adan to effect the required organizational changes and construct the Bar Lev Line. Their work was made possible in large part by the Egyptian reaction to the Naj Hamadi raid. Four months of relative quiet allowed them nearly to complete the new construction before the Egyptians renewed their attacks in early March.

November 1968–February 1969

During the four-month interlude the Israelis concentrated on construction and organization, making it explicit policy to ignore sporadic Egyptian sniping and other low-level activities.[71] Prime Minister Eshkol died on 26 February and Meir replaced him on 7 March. The change of leadership had no visible effect on the National Unity Government or its policies toward Egypt.

In the wider political arena, events seemed at first to vindicate Nasser's belief in the possibility of forcefully causing strategic instability and superpower intervention. Nasser must have derived much satisfaction from one of Nixon's first statements as he assumed office in January: "I consider it [the Middle East] a powder keg, very explosive . . . because the next explosion in the Mideast, I think, could involve very

---

70. As in the considerations driving the retaliatory raid policy, so here a driving motivation for adopting the approach was the desire to fight mobile warfare even when defending. With only six hundred "static" soldiers, the rest of the defending force would act as though it were in offensive mobile warfare. Naor, *Hamilhama leachar ha-Milhama*, pp. 68–69; Schiff, *History of the Israeli Army*, p. 245. See a comment to this effect in Ben-Horin and Posen, *Israel's Strategic Doctrine*, p. 31.

71. MER (1968), pp. 277–78; MER (1969–70), pp. 123, 172.

well a confrontation between the nuclear powers, which we want to avoid."[72]

By February 1968 it was clear that the Jarring Mission was not going to succeed.[73] The United States responded by appearing more and more open to participating in two- and four-power talks, which, despite protestation, carried the implication of an externally imposed solution—clearly anathema to Israel.[74] But Egypt had discovered once again, in December, that strategic destabilization also scared her patron. The Soviets apparently put pressure on Egypt to accept and support their forthcoming "December 30" peace plan, with its several clauses antithetical to Egypt's positions, most important among them the possibility that future borders be determined in local negotiations.[75]

Thus, potential destabilization had created the prospect of superpower collusion at Egypt's as well as Israel's expense. The Egyptian conclusion was a reaffirmation that favorable politics could only result from a favorable military and power balance. In January 1969, Heykal wrote that "no progress can be made by military or political action unless the military front is the starting point for such progress."[76] He also called for "an Arab action that would change the existing military reality and in turn the political reality."[77] On 24 February in anticipation of the coming "Arab action," Nasser declared a national state of emergency.[78]

8 March–18 July 1969

On 8 March, Nasser launced what later became known as the War of Attrition, which lasted continuously, and indeed escalated, until August 1970. What were the Egyptians trying to achieve in this protracted static war, and how? It is critical to the understanding of Egyptian strategy to realize that Nasser did not embark on what this war became.

72. Quoted in William B. Quandt, *Decade of Decisions: American Policy toward the Arab-Israeli Conflict, 1967–1976* (Berkeley and Los Angeles, 1977), pp. 81–82.

73. Touval, *Peace Brokers*, pp. 152–53.

74. For Israeli protestations of unhappiness with four-power talks and imposed solutions, see *MER* (1969–70), pp. 10–11; Dayan, *Mapa Hadasha*, pp. 75–76. For Egyptian support of the talks see *MER* (1969–70), p. 101.

75. For details of the Soviet plan and Soviet-Egyptian discord, see Rubinstein, *Red Star on the Nile*, pp. 73–79; Whetten, *Canal War*, pp. 68–69; Breslauer, "Soviet Policy," pp. 72–73. For Egyptian fear of superpower collusion, see Bar-Siman-Tov, *Israeli-Egyptian War*, p. 52. For reports of Soviet pressure for Egyptian restraint, see *MER* (1969–70), p. 10.

76. *Al-Ahram*, 21 January 1969, quoted in Rubinstein, *Red Star on the Nile*, p. 77.

77. *Al-Ahram*, 3 January 1969, quoted in *MER* (1969–70), p. 101.

78. *MER* (1969–70), p. 1230.

Rather, in March, Nasser and his army began a well-defined, limited offensive campaign intended to last but a few months. By the end of this period the Egyptians expected to have upset the strategic balance and the territorial status quo, so that Israel would be less willing to continue the fighting and her occupation, and the United States would be willing to help eject Israel from the Sinai. Only in late July, when it was clear that this plan was not working, did Nasser announce a war of attrition—"harb il-istinzaph." Let us first examine the logic and application of the Egyptian program, then turn to the Israeli response.

As well as I can make out from less than perfect sources, the Egyptian plan worked out by March 1969 was an attempt to restart stage 2 (active defense) as a brief prelude to stage 3, erasing the traces, or liberation. These two stages were incorporated into a single four-step plan as follows:[79]

1. *Attrition,* a six- to eight-week period of massive shelling aimed at destroying large parts of the Bar Lev Line and inflicting heavy casualties
2. *Limited crossings* of commando units (for short durations) to complete destruction of the line
3. *Extensive east bank operations* by large units for extended periods of time
4. *Large-scale crossing* with the intention of capturing and keeping at least portions of the east bank

Zeev Schiff suggests that the entire program was to be completed by the end of the summer. Clearly, "attrition" was merely one tactical step in the overall strategy.[80]

The program was intended to remedy the apparent weaknesses of Egypt's destabilizing policy. The intended offensive was deemed severe enough to attract major superpower concern. Definitively changing the territorial status quo and at least the local balance of power would bias in Egypt's favor any resolution through superpower intervention. Egyptian success in destroying the line and eroding Israel's willingness to fight would convince her and the United States of the futility of trying to maintain the status quo. A successful Egyptian

79. Bar-Siman-Tov, *Israeli-Egyptian War,* pp. 58–59; Khalidi, "War of Attrition," pp. 62–63; Schiff, *Knafayim me'al Suez,* pp. 22–25.

80. On the importance of at least a few footholds or limited achievements on the east bank, see Mohammed Heykal, *The Road to Ramadan* (New York, 1975), p. 60; idem, *Al-Ahram,* 11 April 1969, quoted in *MER* (1969–70), p. 18; Schiff, *Knafayim me'al Suez,* pp. 21–25.

offensive was also deemed necessary to make the Soviets take Egypt seriously and support her positions in forthcoming negotiations. It would also serve as a catalyst in activating the Eastern Front, which, once in action, would help ensure Egyptian success.[81]

There is also in this Egyptian strategy a sense in which they were trying to overcome a salient point, or "focal point," to use Schelling's term.[82] If the IDF could not prevent an Egyptian crossing of the canal, then Israel and her supporters would have to reassess her ability to hang on by force to "pieces" of the Sinai. The implication was that if part of it fell, all of it would follow. In April, Heykal told his readers how a limited victory would work: "It would destroy the myth of the invincibility of the Israeli army; destroy or shake the belief of Israeli society in its army's ability to protect it . . . undermine the basis of Israeli strategy . . . and it would cause the United States to change its policy towards the Middle East crisis."[83] Some readers will recognize in this statement the very principles behind the Yom Kippur War four years later, in 1973.

Nasser and the Egyptian general staff believed that they could impose a limited war, that Israel could not or would not escalate. Egyptian analysis portrayed Israel as having an interest in de-escalation and as definitely unlikely to wage offensive warfare. In a limited yet relatively protracted war, Egyptian commanders expected to achieve local superiority and prevail, but in any event, the Egyptians expected that Israel's sensitivity to casualties and the balance of interests would cause her to lose her resolve long before Egypt did.[84]

Egyptian actions between 8 March and 18 April appear to reflect implementation of step 1, attrition. On 8 March, Nasser declared a national blackout and began two days of massive shelling of Israeli positions along the entire length of the canal. Israel suffered four fa-

81. *Al-Ahram*, 7 March 1969, in Israel Government Press Monitoring Service, *Press Abstracts*, 7 March 1969.

82. For a discussion of the importance of focal points in bargaining, see Schelling, *Strategy of Conflict*, chap. 3.

83. *Al-Ahram*, 11 April 1969, in *MER* (1969–70), p. 18. On these points see also ibid., 21 March 1969, in ibid., p. 18; ibid., 28 March 1969, cited by Israel Government Press Monitoring Service, *Press Abstracts*, 28 March 1969; Nasser, in *Al-Ahram*, 21 January 1969, cited by Khalidi, "War of Attrition," p. 77; Bar-Siman-Tov, *Israeli-Egyptian War*, p. 56. On the desire to influence the Soviets, see Glassman, *Arms for the Arabs*, p. 69.

84. See the analysis portion of this chapter for detailed discussions of the logic of these assessments. See also Bar-Siman-Tov, *Israeli-Egyptian War*, pp. 52, 57; *Al-Ahram*, 7 March 1969; Khalidi, "War of Attrition," pp. 78–79; Safran, *Israel*, p. 262; O'Ballance, *Electronic War*, p. 54; Schiff, *Knafayim me'al Suez*, pp. 20, 23; Janice Gross Stein, "Calculation, Miscalculation, and Conventional Deterrence, I: The View from Cairo," in Jervis, Lebow, and Stein, eds., *Psychology and Deterrence*.

Table 6. IDF casualties on the Egyptian front, March–July 1969

	Total	Killed	Wounded
March	36	7	29
April	50	17	33
May	43	13	30
June	41	7	34
July	106	30	76

Source: Daniel Dishon, ed., *Middle East Record*, vol. 5 (1969–1970) (Jerusalem: Israel Universities Press, 1977), p. 172.

talities and twenty-three injuries. An Israeli spotter plane was downed by a SA-2 missile, the only Israeli plane to be so hit until June 1970. Israeli return fire was directed at both military and civilian targets, hitting batteries, factories, the Suez refineries, and private residences. On 9 March, Egyptian chief of staff Riyad, author of the Egyptian program, was killed by an Israeli shell.

Throughout March and April the Egyptians maintained the pressure of artillery barrages almost daily. Israeli casualties were alarmingly high: thirty-six in March and fifty-five in April (table 6). Neither counterbattery and other counterforce actions nor countervalue responses seemed to have any effect on Egyptian activity. To strengthen his position, Nasser ordered that Port Said, the only canal city still left intact, also be evacuated.[85]

On the night of 19 April, Egypt advanced to step 2: limited crossings. A fifteen-man unit crossed the canal in the Ismailiya sector under cover of intensive artillery fire. They attacked a maoz but after penetrating one of the bunkers were repulsed.[86] Before April was out a number of additional confrontations occurred on the east bank, though none quite as bold as the first.

Hinting at a new stage, the Egyptian newspaper *Jumhuriyya* described the first raid as "a new development," and Radio Cairo announced that "the initiative passed to Egyptian forces."[87] On 24 April the Egyptian government spokesman announced that the 1967 cease-fire was invalid. On 1 May, Nasser announced that 60 percent of the Bar Lev Line had been destroyed, an achievement that, had it been true, would have

85. *MER* (1969–70), p. 1238; Arieh Avnery, *Pshitot ha-Tagmul: Milhemet ha-Hatasha* [The Israeli commando: A short history of the Israeli commandos—1950–1969, vol. 4, The War of Attrition] (Tel-Aviv, [1970?]), pp. 67–68.
86. Landau, *Suez*, pp. 164–66.
87. *MER* (1969–70), p. 126.

allowed Egypt to progress according to plan and on schedule.[88] In reality, not one maoz had been seriously damaged.

On the night of 29 April, Israel launched a retaliatory raid in the Naj Hamadi area similar in style and choice of targets to the first Naj Hamadi raid eighteen months earlier. Egyptian raids then fell off for the month of May but resumed with three in rapid succession on 21, 23, and 24 June, the last of these by a fifty-commando unit on a maoz in the Firdan area. It was repelled. The Israelis tried again to deter Egyptian raids through more retaliatory operations, but two Israeli actions in May, two in June, and one on 1 July had no effect.[89]

On 7 July a force of about seventy Egyptian commandos attacked a maoz at the Bitter Lakes. Failing, the Egyptian unit retreated, leaving nine bodies behind. On the next night a commando unit crossed at Port Tawfiq under cover of heavy artillery fire. This time the Egyptians scored: they disabled or destroyed two Israeli tanks, killed six Israeli soldiers, and carried one wounded prisoner back with them. The IDF spokesman called it "the most successful [operation] . . . carried out by Egyptian forces since the Six Day War."[90]

If Egyptian commando activity was intermittent, their artillery fire and other ground-based harassment escalated almost continuously through mid-July. The IDF also continued to sustain a high casualty rate: 45 in May, 42 in June, and 108 in July. To understate: Israeli deterrence was not working.

Activity by the two air forces was minimal during these months. The Egyptians tried to penetrate Sinai a number of times and were usually intercepted. A few Mig-21s were shot down after causing little damage. On 17 June two Israeli Mirages buzzed Cairo, marking a changed Israeli conception I discuss presently, and on 24 June and again on 26 June dogfights occurred over the Gulf of Suez when Migs challenged Israeli patrols. Three Migs were felled. On 2 and 7 July there were more encounters over the gulf. Six Migs plunged. In all of these events not a single IAF fighter plane was hurt.[91]

Back in March and April the Israelis did not understand the transformed Egyptian challenge. They saw it as before: an attempt at offensive brinkmanship executed mainly by fire and small-unit and small-scale raids, not intended to lead to more substantial conflict. Israeli

---

88. Ibid., p. 128.
89. For a description of events in this period, see ibid., pp. 126–130.
90. Quoted in ibid., p. 130; Avnery, *Pshitot ha-Tagmul*, p. 92.
91. Schiff, *Knafayim me'al Suez*, pp. 35–37; *MER* (1969–70), pp. 124, 128–29.

leaders attributed Egyptian escalation at least partly to attempts at influencing the two- and four-power talks just getting under way.[92]

The Israeli approach to the problem thus remained unchanged. To counter Egypt's attempts to influence the international system, Israeli leaders portrayed Egyptian policy as a futile attempt to create concern where there was really no danger of escalation. Eban told a press conference in the United States that the Egyptians were trying "to give the Big Powers a sense of alarm so as to force a half-baked solution."[93] Dayan declared that the Egyptians were trying to create a "false impression" that the Middle East was a powder keg.[94] Prime Minister Meir expressed similar views to the Knesset, and Allon said that "the comparative aggravation of the security situation along the cease-fire lines is a direct result of the Four-Power meetings and the Arabs' desire to influence the discussions."[95]

Israeli military policy continued to be low keyed, defensively oriented, and basically reactive. The intention was not to cause or permit escalation.[96] Looking for a nonescalatory way to force Egypt to desist Israel attempted to repeat the countervalue approach of the previous fall by shelling civilian targets and later—only after the first Egyptian commando raids—by repeating the Naj Hamadi in-depth operation. Statements by Israeli leaders after the second Naj Hamadi raid show a continuing faith in the efficacy of both countervalue actions and demonstrations of Egyptian inferiority.[97] And given the de-escalatory imperative, frustration of Egypt remained a central tenet of the Israeli approach. In late April Dayan stated in public that "Israel must remain at the June 1967 cease-fire lines if only to prove that she is powerful enough to do so for a long time."[98]

In June and July two concerns made Israeli leaders reconsider both Egyptian intentions and appropriate Israeli actions. First there was the pressure of casualties. As Egypt had suspected, Israel was having serious difficulties with a protracted, seemingly endless war with high

---

92. Dayan, *Mapa Hadasha*, p. 86; *Haaretz*, 13, 27 March 1969. See Haim Herzog's comments on the radio, in *MER* (1969–70), p. 126. See also, Bar-Siman-Tov, *Israeli-Egyptian War*, pp. 65–66.

93. Quoted in *MER* (1969–70), p. 18.

94. Quoted in *Mapa Hadasha*, p. 77.

95. Quoted in *MER* (1969–70), p. 26.

96. Dayan in a talk to students, *Haaretz*, 30 April, 1969.

97. See Allon's radio address, *Haaretz*, 12 March 1969; *Maariv*, 30 April 1969; editorial in *Haaretz*, 10 March 1969; *MER* (1969–70), p. 127; Bar-Siman-Tov, *Israeli-Egyptian War*, pp. 73–74.

98. *Haaretz*, 30 April 1969; see also ibid., 9 April 1969.

numbers of casualties. Also, within the IDF there was growing pressure at all levels to use available power to put an end to this dragged-out affair.[99] Second there was the national security community's reassessment of Egypt's intentions. In June, the Israelis became convinced that Egypt's activity was leading, as indeed it was, to a wider conflict. By late June, IDF Intelligence concluded that the Egyptians intended to work themselves up to a canal crossing in force. The deterrence problem had been revolutionized.[100]

As in the past the IDF sought to deter strategic challenge through small-scale demonstration of its superiority and the Egyptian army's impotence in defending either itself or the Egyptian nation. This is another explanation for the series of spectacular, immaculately executed Israeli raids in June against economic and military targets both in the gulf area and in the Egyptian heartland. Now that the Egyptians were considering more serious action, it also became important for Israel to demonstrate superiority in the area tactically critical for a canal crossing: air power. To do so in as nonescalatory a manner as possible, Israel chose to lure the EAF into air battles over the Gulf of Suez. This explains the dogfights of late June and early July. Buzzing Cairo was probably another part of this strategy.

As for the potential large-scale offensive challenge, the Israelis may not have had such cause for alarm by mid-July. There is at least some, if imperfect, evidence to suggest that by mid-July, Nasser was still very far from advancing to step 3 and was in fact stuck somewhere between steps 1 and 2. On 18 July, one day *before* the change in Israeli policy, Heykal explained that immediate war had been postponed, warning, "In reality, the advocates of the peaceful path have learned and so have the advocates of immediate war . . . that the challenge before us is bigger than the excited theories."[101]

We do not know why Nasser did not go ahead with his four steps as scheduled, but it does seem that in three important ways his plan was not panning out. First, propaganda aside, the Bar Lev Line was holding up just fine and the Israelis were maintaining air superiority, returning a spirited fight, and did not seem about to fold. Second, the war was not bringing activation of the Eastern Front; in July Nasser was still fighting alone.[102] Third, Nasser's patron continued to apply moderating pres-

99. On the new importance of reimposing the cease-fire, see Bar Lev's introduction to Arad, *Elef ha-Yamim*, p. 2; Naor, *Hamilhama leachar ha-Milhama*, p. 47.

100. Schiff, *Knafayim me'al Suez*, p. 27; MER (1969–70), p. 19; Landau, *Suez*, p. 176.

101. *Al-Ahram*, 18 July 1969, in Israel Government Press Monitoring Service, *Press Abstracts*, 18 July 1969.

102. MER (1969–70), pp. 562–65.

sure throughout the spring.[103] In May, Soviet-American collusion was producing compromise resolutions not entirely to Egypt's (or Israel's) liking. The Soviets also tried to force moderation through their armaments policy. They apparently persisted in not meeting Egypt's demands for specific weapons and quantities of ammunition required for a sustained offensive.[104]

But from the Israeli perspective all of this was opaque. After the Egyptian raid at Port Tawfiq on 8 July the failure of Israel's deterrence policy appeared self-evident. The time series of all important indicators—fire incidents, casualties, commando raids—showed a steady rise in total disregard of Israeli deterrence efforts. With all elements of her deterrence policy apparently failing, Israel initiated on 19 July a new and different approach.

19 July 1969–January 1970

On 19 July Israel began a major tactical escalation in which the IAF played the dominant role. This Israeli escalation, which also included ambitious ground operations, reflected a critical transformation of approach. From a basic reliance on defensive and reactive behavior, the IDF moved to offensive and initiated action. In part, this change reflected the gradual substitution of deterrence by victory for deterrence by frustration. Deterrence by victory was to follow from a forceful remaking of the actual bilateral balance of power, made possible by offensive air operations.

The full transformation of the Israeli approach did not occur overnight but developed rather gradually in July and August. By September it was in final form. In mid-July the main Israeli opponent to activation of the air force, Dayan, changed his mind and agreed to support a one-time use against targets in the canal zone. The reason for the change, it seems, was perception of an impending Egyptian attack, so that activation of the IAF could be understood to be a preemptive strike.[105] Minimal escalation was still a central guiding principle. In the face of an impending Egyptian attack, limited but substantial use of air power seemed less escalatory than other options, such as a preemptive ground attack.[106]

103. Mohammed Heykal, *The Sphinx and the Commissar: The Rise and Fall of Soviet Influence in the Middle East* (New York, 1978), p. 193.

104. Breslauer, "Soviet Policy," pp. 77–78; Glassman, *Arms for the Arabs*, p. 72. For discussions and accounts of Soviet-Egyptian tensions at the time, see Rubinstein, *Red Star on the Nile*, pp. 81–89; *MER* (1969–70), pp. 19–20.

105. Schiff, *Knafayim me'al Suez*, p. 47. See also Bar-Siman-Tov, *Israeli-Egyptian War*, p. 86.

106. Dayan, in *Haaretz*, 5 August 1969; Bar-Siman-Tov, *Israeli-Egyptian War*, p. 86.

During the night before the massive air attacks of 20 July an elite Israeli unit performed one of the most daring commando-style operations in IDF history. The target was the impregnable fortress on Green Island near the southern entrance to the canal. The spectacular raid left a destroyed fortress and forty dead Egyptians. The operation was a blatant demonstration of Israel's ability to exact punishment and her general superiority on the ground as well as in the air, which she was about to show.[107]

On the afternoon of 20 July the IAF executed a sustained air attack on Egyptian positions, mostly in the northern sector of the canal.[108] The IAF attacked and destroyed the one SAM-2 battery in the nothern sector, artillery batteries and mortars, commando bases, bunkers, and the Sweet Water Canal.[109] Two hours into the attack the EAF attempted to intervene and lost five jet fighters. The IAF lost two planes, the last it would lose in July.

Two days later the IAF resumed its attacks on Egyptian positions in the northern sector, and this time the EAF did not come close. On 24 July the IAF attacked across the entire front and basically destroyed the SAM-2 network along the canal. In response, later in the day, the EAF attempted a massive attack by some forty aircraft on Israeli positions. They caused little damage while losing seven planes. Israeli air raids continued through 28 July, meeting no Egyptian resistance. In all, between 20 and 28 July the IAF executed about one thousand sorties and caused some 250 Egyptian deaths.[110] After 28 July the Israelis desisted.

The fact that the Israeli offensive stopped after a week supports the notion that at first the Israeli leadership did not conceive of continuous application of the air force but rather saw it as a one-time preemptive action to remove the immediate threat of an Egyptian offensive. For deterrence it was important to desist in order to convert the attack into a conditional threat. This Dayan, Bar Lev, and Meir tried to do after the

107. For descriptions of the operation, see Schiff and Haber, *Lexikon le-Bitahon Yisrael*, p. 122; Wallach, Lissak, and Shamir, *Atlas Carta: Assor Sheni*, p. 108; Avnery, *Pshitot ha-Tagmul*, pp. 95–101. In the operation an important air defense radar was also destroyed in preparation for the coming air attacks. See the explanation by a senior IDF officer in *Maariv*, 21 July 1969.

108. Description of IAF activities in July is based on *MER* (1969–70), pp. 131–33; Schiff, *Knafayim me'al Suez*, pp. 47–52.

109. The Sweet Water Canal is an open conduit used to transport water from the Nile to the Ismailiya area and from there north and south along the Suez Canal to the cities.

110. This was a substantial effort on the part of the IAF. To perform one thousand sorties in one week with a fleet of three hundred aircraft would require that about half the force be in action every day.

attack, by depicting it as a one-time demonstration of what would happen in the event of further Egyptian belligerence.[111] As I have stated earlier, the demonstration was not merely of superiority but of an ability to inflict substantial damage and pain.

During the week-long attack and in its aftermath Israeli leaders tried to convince the public, and presumably the superpowers, that Israel was engaged in *tactical* escalation only with the ultimate purpose of de-escalating the conflict. Already on 21 July senior IDF officers pointed out that the change was only in means, not ends, and that Israel was attempting to "prevent escalation, not to encourage it." This point was repeated by Chief of Staff Bar Lev on 25 July and by Meir to the Knesset on 27 July.[112] In early September, Bar Lev made the case most eloquently:

> If what we are speaking about is not the means of warfare but the state of the hostilities in a situation of confrontation between ourselves and the Egyptians, then the introduction of an additional means of warfare does not necessarily aggravate the situation. For example, I am prepared to say that putting planes into action currently on the Canal is "escalation for the sake of deescalation", an increase of activity for the purpose of securing a reduction of activity.[113]

Between 28 July and 12 August the IAF did not operate at all at the front, and the Israelis discovered that the Egyptians were intent on continuing the newly christened War of Attrition as before. During the week of attacks in July the Israelis had been surprised by the effectiveness of aircraft against ground targets, and in mid-August they began to incorporate the IAF in a classic deterrence policy of conditional response. The Israelis told and showed the Egyptians that any artillery activity would bring the IAF into action, mostly against the offending units.[114] But by 19 August it was evident that this approach would not intimidate the Egyptians into inaction, and their belligerent activity at the canal continued unabated.

In August, Israeli attention began to turn from deterring an impending crossing (which no longer appeared so immediate) to the War of Attrition itself. But not completely. Dayan conceived of the challenge facing Israel as "the battle for the battle of the Canal."[115] Implied here

---

111. Dayan, in *Haaretz*, 1 August 1969; *MER* (1969–70), p. 133; Bar-Siman-Tov, *Israeli-Egyptian War*, pp. 88–89.

112. *MER* (1969–70), pp. 132–33.

113. *Bamahaneh*, 8 September 1969, trans. by Bar-Siman-Tov, *Israeli-Egyptian War*, p. 87. *Bamahaneh* is the popular weekly magazine of the IDF.

114. Schiff, *Knafayim me'al Suez*, p. 53; *MER* (1969–70), pp. 133–34.

115. *Haaretz*, 5 August 1969.

was the notion that Egypt's propensity for large-scale offensive action would be determined by their success and ability to escalate in attrition warfare. In this way, conceptually, deterring low-scale violence became a strategic mission. Furthermore, in a subtle way, if what was going on was a battle in a war, then it would have to be won; indeed, after conditional response failed in August, Israel decided to focus on reimposing the cease-fire by winning the war.[116]

Obviously the Israelis did not think in terms of a 1967 victory, but they began to pursue demonstrations of strategic superiority and actual changes in the local balance of power through military pressure. Winning this kind of war required seizing the initiative and pursuing meaningful offensive action, all within the framework of limited war. The IAF seemed to be the perfect instrument for such a policy.

In operational terms, Israeli decision makers hoped to accomplish the following: (a) force the Egyptians to disperse their forces away from the canal; (b) achieve total air superiority over the canal, thus completely neutralizing the EAF; (c) apply constant and real pressure on their forces at the canal so as to reduce their current activity; and (d) create (but not use) free aerial access to the Egyptian hinterland, thus establishing a credible threat of penetration bombing. To minimize escalatory danger IAF activity was to be limited to a 20-kilometer strip on the west bank and was to attack only military targets. On 15 August, Dayan announced that the IDF would no longer react but would now seize the initiative. In September, Israel started implementing this policy, commonly known in Israel (suggestively) as "attrition of the attrition."[117]

The Israeli offensive began with the much-celebrated armored raid of 9 September, code-named Operation Raviv. In a fairly complex combined-arms operation, an Israeli force of six tanks and three APCs was ferried across the Gulf of Suez. Landing at 3:40 A.M. just north of Abu Daraj, the task force traveled south along the gulf, covering 50 kilometers in ten hours. With both air and artillery support from the east bank, the force destroyed vehicles and radar stations and overran camps and posts. The IAF took the opportunity to destroy a SAM-2 battery in the vicinity of the operation. When it was over the force was ferried back across the gulf, leaving in its wake over 150 dead Egyptians and substantial damage. The fatalities included one Egyptian general and a senior Soviet adviser. The Israelis suffered one injury.[118]

116. See Dayan's references to the need to win in *Haaretz*, 19 August 1969; Avnery, *Pshitot ha-Tagmul*, pp. 214–15.

117. *Haaretz*, 15 August 1969; Schiff, *Knafayim me'al Suez*, p. 54; Bar-Siman-Tov, *Israeli-Egyptian War*, p. 90.

118. For descriptions see Arad, *Elef ha-Yamim*, p. 185; Wallach, Lissak, and Shamir, *Atlas Carta: Assor Sheni*, p. 109; MER (1969–70), pp. 134–35.

For the Egyptians the operation was a major embarrassment, and in the aftermath Nasser fired his chief of staff, Ismail 'Ali, commander of the navy and theater commander of the Red Sea area.[119] As damaging as the operation itself was the fact that the Egyptian command did not figure out what was happening before it was over.

From 12 September through December the IAF executed almost daily raids on Egyptian military targets along the canal and the Gulf of Suez. The attacks grew in boldness and in the target area they covered, spreading from short daylight raids in the north to long and sustained actions in all sectors, at times even at night. The two main types of targets were field artillery and the antiaircraft system, be it SAMs, antiaircraft artillery, or radar. The IAF persistently destroyed and then redestroyed SAM-2 batteries and radar installations at the canal, along the gulf, and even along the Egyptian Mediterranean coast.[120]

On 10 November the IDF reported that the Egyptians had no SAM system left at the canal; in mid-December the Egyptians tried to replace seven destroyed batteries. In an all-day operation on 25 December the IAF destroyed the replacements.[121] We get a sense of what the Israelis were trying to accomplish from the assessment found in the semiofficial IDF history of the war:

> The largest air attack since the Six Day War, on the 25th of December, renders a decisive blow to the AA system along the Canal. During eight hours the IDF attacks military targets to a depth of 20 kilometers along the entire canal and opens a wide gate into Egypt. One should note that the attack of 25 December sums up a long and consistent aerial campaign, which destroyed the Egyptian AA system along the Canal. . . . This attack teaches that Egypt can no longer defend herself. The Egyptian army *at the front and in the rear* is vulnerable to the IAF.[122]

Throughout the fall the IDF continued its limited offensive on the ground as well. In the static confrontation at the canal this was expressed in purposeful instigation of incidents by the IDF and in constant attempts to harass the Egyptians with tanks and artillery. The IDF also continued to perform commando raids,[123] and in a truly spectacular coup it stole an advanced air-defense radar in a heliborne operation on 26 December. Aside from providing knowledge essential for Israeli

---

119. *MER* (1969–70), p. 136; Wallach, Lissak, and Shamir, *Atlas Carta: Assor Sheni,* p. 109.

120. O'Ballance, *Electronic War*, p. 86; *MER* (1969–70), p. 137.

121. *MER* (1969–70), p. 141; Schiff, *Knafayim me'al Suez*, p. 66.

122. Arad, *Elef ha-Yamim*, p. 205 (my emphasis).

123. For descriptions of these, see Wallach, Lissak, and Shamir, *Atlas Carta: Assor Sheni,* p. 108; *MER* (1969–70), pp. 139, 141.

air operations, theft of the radar was intended to be another statement and demonstration of Egypt's complete "powerlessness," and "confusion."[124]

The immediate Egyptian response to Israeli escalation in July was to abandon Nasser's four-step program formally, or at least greatly expand its time frame from months to years. A number of prominent Egyptians published apologias for the new situation and policy. For example, strategist Taha el-Magdoub argued that

1. Egypt's strategy of escalation should not be seen as requiring monotonically increasing violence,
2. Escalation is not limited to the military realm. One should look for it in other areas, such as politics or economics,
3. Offensive brinkmanship can be a two-way street. One must control it very carefully lest one lose the initiative, and
4. Egypt should expect the Israelis to seize the initiative.

Therefore, wrote Magdoub, the road ahead was long and arduous and called for great patience. Magdoub warned the Egyptians against "being in a pendulum—between heights of hope and depths of despair."[125]

On 28 July, Nasser declared—and coined the phrase—a War of Attrition (harb il-istinzaph), explaining that a long struggle to exhaust the enemy was planned. Thus, as Bar-Siman-Tov describes it, attrition commuted "from tactics to strategy,"[126] and it appears that Bar Lev was correct when he concluded in September that "one achievement [of IAF activity] is in postponing the war."[127]

Egypt intended to continue protracted low-level belligerence, which she did throughout the fall despite the blows of the IAF. Where necessary the Egyptians modified their activity but never stopped it. At the canal they were forced to moderate their use of field artillery, but they clearly compensated with an increase of mortar and small arms fire, as table 7 shows.

Egyptian commando activity on the east bank also continued unabated, with eight raids between October and January.[128] These included

124. MER (1969–70), p. 142; O'Ballance, *Electronic War*, p. 100; Avnery, *Pshitot ha-Tagmul*, pp. 224–26.

125. *Al-Ahram*, 27 July 1969, in Israel Government Press Monitoring Service, *Press Abstracts*, 4 August 1969. See also Heykal's article in *Al-Ahram*, 8 August 1969, in ibid., 8 August 1969.

126. Bar-Siman-Tov, *Egyptian-Israeli War*, pp. 104–6.

127. *Haaretz*, 8 September 1969.

128. Description of the events in this and the following paragraph may be found in *MER* (1969–70), pp. 137–42; Naor, *Hamilhama leachar ha-Milhama*, pp. 87–89; Schiff, *Knafayim me'al Suez*, pp. 63–64.

Table 7. Incidents initiated by the United Arab Republic, May–October, 1969

	May	June	July*	August	September	October
Light arms	158	71	85	225	186	345
Mortar	1	4	47	209	187	165
Artillery	63	311	207	72	56	117
Total	222	386	339	506	429	627

Source: Daniel Dishon, ed., *Middle East Record*, vol. 5 (1969–70) (Jerusalem: Israel Universities Press, 1977), p. 167.
*IAF activated.

two attempted attacks on maozim and a number of ambushes of Israeli vehicles and troops. On 5 October, Egyptian commandos performed a daytime ambush on the east bank, a first in initiative and courage. In these raids and ambushes the IDF suffered six dead, fifteen wounded, and two prisoners. Another mode of activity Egypt pursued was naval; on 8 November two Egyptian destroyers shelled Israeli targets along the Mediterranean coast about 20 kilometers from the canal.

For a time the EAF tried to maintain a presence both in defending Egyptian air space and in countering IAF blows to their ground forces with its own but with little success and a loss of a large number of planes. On 11 September the EAF lost eleven aircraft, one of them to a Hawk missile. In late September and October the EAF innovated with nighttime raids and for a short time experimented with quick hit-and-run attacks on the Bar Lev Line, but these were ineffectual. Between August and November the EAF lost twenty planes to Israel's three and in December stopped flying altogether.

Surveying these events and developments Dayan had to admit in late fall that Israel was not achieving its second deterrence goal, imposition of a cease-fire: "The intense operations of the Air Force and its total mastery of the skies of the Canal eased somewhat the pressure on the units on the line. But Egyptian military activity did not diminish, and the cadence of war—increased."[129] Insofar as casualties were central to the Israeli definition of success, then the offensive was clearly not paying off. Table 8 shows no substantial decline in the course of the campaign.

In the fall and winter Nasser made two bids to mobilize his potential external sources of support: the Soviet Union and other Arab states. He was not very successful in either, though perhaps more so in the former. Toward the end of the fall, as Egypt went on the strategic defensive, the Soviets apparently began to fear another defeat. This fear motivated them to decide in principle to intervene to save the regime

129. Dayan, *Avnei Derekh*, p. 516.

Table 8. IDF casualties, May–December 1969

	Total	Killed	Wounded
May	43	13	30
June	41	7	34
July*	106	30	76
August	65	11	54
September	47	19	28
October	56	10	46
November	39	12	27
December	30	12	18

Source: Daniel Dishon, ed., *Middle East Record*,
vol. 5 (1969–70) (Jerusalem: Israel Universities
Press, 1977), p. 172.
*IAF activated.

should that become necessary. But even in late December, Moscow did not consider the Israeli threat severe enough to warrant a supply of SAM-3s or other more sophisticated weapons. In December, Vice-president Sadat traveled to Moscow in search of arms. He received numerous declarations of support, and little else.[130]

Nasser did better on the diplomatic front. Egyptian and then Israeli escalation in late summer and early fall had apparently scared the Soviets into supporting a reopening of two-power talks in the hope of reaching a diplomatic solution. Renewed U.S.-Soviet collusion led to the Rogers I peace initiative, which Egypt found offensive. Nasser apparently succeeded in forcing the Soviets to drop their support for it.[131]

In late July, Nasser launched a six-month effort to mobilize the Arab system. In his 23 July "War of Attrition" speech Nasser said that everything had changed, including "the disposition of our forces . . . the enemy's methods . . . [and] the international situation. . . . All this calls for joint consultations at the highest level so that the Arab decision will be final. . . . The battle no longer needs only material support. . . . More than ever before, the battle requires joint thinking, joint planning and joint action."[132]

Nasser made repeated attempts throughout the fall to actuate an Arab summit by convening various Arab forums and trying to motivate the

---

130. On the early decision "in principle," see Rubinstein, *Red Star on the Nile*, pp. 100, 103–5; Schiff, *Knafayim me'al Suez*, p. 209; Glassman, *Arms for the Arabs*, pp. 73–74. On the difficulty of obtaining concrete assistance, see Whetten, *Canal War*, p. 78; Bar-Siman-Tov, *Israeli-Egyptian War*, p. 137.

131. Breslauer, "Soviet Policy," pp. 86–87; Bar-Siman-Tov, *Israeli-Egyptian War*, p. 115.

132. Quoted in *MER* (1969–70), pp. 528–29.

representatives.[133] He had to contend with Saudi opposition, which he only overcame in November, finally paving the way for the Rabat Summit in December. At Rabat, Nasser hoped to win acceptance of his war minister's program for joint Arab action. The Fawzi Plan proposed specific responsibilities and contributions of each Arab state in the upcoming *very long* conflict with Israel.[134]

Saudi-Arabia, Algeria, and Kuwait were not prepared to commit vast sums of money to a long-term project of uncertain prospects. By 23 December it was clear that Nasser would not get the resources he desired. After a bitter attack on the summit's participants and especially Saudi-Arabia, Nasser said dejectedly, "I am a tired man, because I have the impression that I am a lonely man."[135] He then got up and left the summit.

January–August 1970

Her active deterrence failing, on 7 January, Israel took one further step in escalation for de-escalation and executed the threat she had created earlier: bombing of targets deep inside Egypt. On 8 August the long-awaited cease-fire went into effect. But oddly, instead of relief and satisfaction, acceptance of the cease-fire caused the disintegration of the National Unity Government. For when it finally came, the cease-fire reflected not Israeli deterrence but deterrence of Israel, not Israeli power but Israeli weakness, not Israeli choice but acceptance of imposition, and not Israeli victory—rather, defeat.

Before surveying the unfolding of events, we should explore briefly the Israeli theory of strategic bombing. Israeli military and political leaders agreed that the deterrence goals remained as before: to reimpose a cease-fire and to discourage any ideas of an Egyptian crossing of the canal. Dayan wrote in his autobiography that "in order to press the Egyptians and compel them to implement the cease-fire, I asked the Ministerial Committee for Security Affairs on 6 January 1970 to autho-

133. Throughout the fall Nasser convened a number of forums (e.g., the Arab League and the Arab Joint Defense Council); he even tried unsuccessfully to activate the Eastern Front directly by convening the first Confrontation State Conference; see Sela, *Achdut*, pp. 83–86; *MER* (1969–70), pp. 529–33. On Nasser's frustration with the Eastern Front, see Heykal, *Road to Ramadan*, p. 81.

134. The Fawzi Plan had been presented and accepted by the Arab Joint Defense Council in November. See *MER* (1969–70), pp. 533–36; Sela, *Achdut*, pp. 85–86.

135. *Le Monde*, 24 December 1969, in *MER* (1969–70), p. 541. On Nasser's failure at Rabat and Egypt's subsequent "loneliness," see *MER* (1969–70), pp. 538–44; Sela, *Achdut*, pp. 88–96; A. I. Dawisha, *Egypt in the Arab World*, pp. 56–57; el-Sadat, *In Search of Identity*, p. 199.

rize air attacks on military bases deep within Egypt."[136] Bar Lev explained in an interview that Israel's goals were "A, postponement of the war. B, attainment of a situation as near as possible to a cease fire along the frontier."[137]

In some respects, strategic bombing relied on the same mechanism and concepts that had motivated the initial activation of the IAF in July 1969. Perhaps the most important motivation was the need to demonstrate unequivocal superiority. If establishing local air superiority and destroying the antiaircraft system had not sent a clear enough signal, then a further *demonstrative escalation* was necessary. It would require bombing throughout the Egyptian heartland to bring to every Egyptian citizen and soldier undeniable proof of Israel's total superiority.[138]

It is important to understand that Israeli strategic bombing was not strategic countervalue bombing in the tradition of World War II. Neither the military nature of the targets nor the number of bombing sorties and missions would support an argument that the Israelis were trying to beat the Egyptian people physically into submission. In this sense the choice of instrument and its application reflect, as before, an attempt to minimize escalation. And again, from a deterrence perspective, it left open a threat of potential further escalation.

Although intended to have a demonstrative effect, proven superiority was supposed to deliver victory. Instead of victory through a change in the physical balance of power (as expected in the fall), it was now victory achieved politically, by undermining the Nasser regime, for which Israel hoped. Demonstrative strategic bombing was intended to cause an internal loss of faith in the regime, confuse it, and compel it either to change course or fall.

No Israeli leaders directly admitted to having this purpose in mind, but the number of times and the manner in which this goal was disclaimed is incriminating. A sample statement by Meir will suffice: "The attacks by our Air Force deep inside Egypt are not intended to reach the Egyptian capital or bring down Nasser's regime. It is not we who are

---

136. Dayan, *Avnei Derekh*, p. 517.

137. *Maariv*, 6 May 1970. See also Mordechai Gazit, *Tahalikh ha-Shalom (1969–1973)* [The peace process (1969–1973)] (Tel-Aviv, 1984), pp. 36–37; Avi Shlaim and Raymond Tanter, "Decision Process, Choice, and Consequences: Israel's Deep-Penetration Bombing in Egypt, 1970," *World Politics* 30 (July 1978):491–92.

138. Dan Margalit, *Sheder meha-Bayit ha-Lavan: Aliyatah u-Nefilatah shel Memshelet ha-Likud ha-Leumi* [Message from the White House: The rise and fall of the National Unity Government] (Tel-Aviv, 1971), p. 40; Naor, *Hamilhama leachar ha-Milhama*, p. 101; Khalidi, "War of Attrition," p. 66; Yigal Allon, "The Soviet Involvement in the Arab-Israel Conflict," in Michael Confino and Shimon Shamir, eds., *The U.S.S.R. and the Middle East* (Jerusalem, 1973), p. 152.

responsible for his being Egypt's ruler and we have not taken it on ourselves to overthrow him. That is the task of the Egyptian people. I can't say we shall weep if he does fall."[139]

Israeli leaders were not willing to show any political flexibility concurrently with the strong military blows delivered by the IAF. The government seemed to be seeking a total and unconditional victory. Thus Meir moved quickly and viciously to quash Eban's proposal that Israel launch a peace offensive in search of possible solutions, and she put to rest Interior Minister Haim Moshe Shapira's suggestion of a unilateral bombing halt for a number of days.[140]

When Israeli leaders sat down in December and early January to assess the feasibility of the proposed policy they concluded that there were neither military nor political obstacles to its pursuit. By December 1969 the IAF had opened the skies into Egypt. There was nothing, so it seemed, that the Egyptians could do about it: neither Migs nor SAMs posed much threat to Israeli aircraft. In addition, the recent acquisition of F-4 Phantoms gave the IAF, for the first time, the capacity to deliver efficiently large quantities of ordnance to distant targets.[141]

The Israelis also concluded that neither superpower would change its current policy in response to Israeli bombing. The United States, they believed, would continue to supply arms and give tacit approval of Israeli actions. The Soviets, they expected, would continue delivering verbal condemnations of the Zionists and transferring arms to Egypt as before but would be unlikely to intervene directly.[142]

Israel's strategic bombing campaign lasted from 8 January to 13 April. During this period the IAF hit thirty-four targets inside Egypt on twenty occasions. Through 26 February objectives included military camps and headquarters, EAF storage depots, and ammunition dumps. Targets were usually chosen in the vicinity of major cities in both Upper and Lower Egypt, and a number of attacks were purposefully within visible

---

139. *Haaretz*, 2 March 1970. The translation is by Bar-Siman-Tov, *Israeli-Egyptian War*, p. 124. On pp. 123–25 Bar-Siman-Tov presents twelve such statements by Israeli leaders. On this purpose, see also Shlomo Aronson, *Conflict and Bargaining*, p. 117; Khalidi, "War of Attrition," p. 66; Paulus (columnist), in *Haaretz*, 23 January 1970.

140. Margalit, *Sheder meha-Bayit ha-Lavan*, pp. 61–64; Whetten, *Canal War*, p. 89.

141. Schiff, *Knafayim me'al Suez*, p. 190; O'Ballance, *Electronic War*, p. 102; Evron, *Middle East*, pp. 104–5; Shlaim and Tanter, "Decision Process, Choice, and Consequences," p. 491. For the revolutionary capabilities of the F-4, see Schiff and Haber, *Lexikon le-Bitahon Yisrael*, pp. 429–30; O'Ballance, *Electronic War*, p. 81.

142. For the Israeli expectation of superpower behavior, see Margalit, *Sheder maha-Bayit ha-Lavan*, pp. 37–43; Gazit, *Tahalikh ha-Shalom*, pp. 37–38; Schiff, *Knafayim me'al Suez*, pp. 191–92; Aronson, *Conflict and Bargaining*, p. 117; Yitzhak Rabin, *The Rabin Memoirs* (Boston, 1979), p. 165; Allon, *Massakh shel Khol*, pp. 417–18.

and audible range of Cairo's residents. For example, on 13 January the IAF raided the EAF storage camp at Khanka (20 kilometers from Cairo center), and on 18 January it attacked Jabel Hawf (5 kilometers from Hilwan) as well as targets adjacent to Cairo International Airport. On 28 January the Ma'adi Camps were attacked, just 10 kilometers south of the capital. These raids were indeed small in number and basically demonstrative but performed with extreme accuracy and highly damaging to the targets.[143] Not a single Israeli plane was lost in three months of activity.

On 22 January the IDF performed another of its spectacular and large ground operations. A large airborne force landed on the island of Shadwan in the Gulf of Suez, captured it, and destroyed the installations. The Egyptians suffered seventy dead and yielded sixty-two prisoners.[144] The raid was similar in timing and size to the Green Island raid that had accompanied the introduction of the IAF in July, and the message would seem to have been the same: we may primarily be using air power, but we also have a considerable terrestrial threat. Just as in the previous case, there was little follow-up to the raid on the ground; most subsequent offensive IDF operations were from the air.

On 12 February an Israeli airplane on a bombing mission against the EAF storage depots at Khanka (near Cairo) mistakenly hit an adjacent factory at Abu-Zabal causing seventy civilian deaths.[145] Meir told the Knesset on 17 February that the strike had been an error but that Israel would not change its policy under the international pressure growing in the wake of the mishap. On the same day and again on 26 February the IAF attacked in the Cairo-Hilwan area—for the last time.[146]

Beginning in March, Israel confined its strategic bombing to targets in the northeast Delta region, away from dense population centers, and concentrated on radar and SAM-2 sites instead of camps. Two explanations are given for this change in policy, both probably correct. First, despite Meir's bravado after Abu Zabal and a show of determination, Israel reacted as she had after Qibya in 1953. Especially in light of international reaction Israel moved to ensure that such a horrific error would not recur.[147]

The second explanation is probably of weightier import. In March the

143. Schiff, *Knafayim me'al Suez*, pp. 193–98.

144. For descriptions see *MER* (1969–70), p. 143; Wallach, Lissak, and Shamir, *Atlas Carta: Assor Sheni*, pp. 110–11.

145. Schiff, *Knafayim me'al Suez*, pp. 198–201; Schiff and Haber, *Lexikon le-Bitahon Yisrael*, p. 13.

146. *Divrei ha-Knesset*, 17 February 1970; Shlaim and Tanter, "Decision Process, Choice, and Consequences," p. 498.

147. Schiff, *Knafayim me'al Suez*, p. 204.

Soviets introduced Russian-manned SAM-3 batteries to defend the air space of major cities and the Aswan Dam. In the first small step of what would become a long retreat, Israel stepped out of the Bear's way. This appeasement, it was hoped, would prevent further Soviet intervention.[148]

But by 13 April there was irrefutable evidence that the Soviets had introduced their own aircraft and crews as part of their air defense of the Egyptian heartland. On that day Israel flew her last strategic bombing raid. On 18 April any lingering doubts about Soviet intervention were erased. An Israeli reconaissance patrol near Cairo was intercepted by fighters whose pilots conversed freely, openly, and fluently in Russian.[149]

All the while, IAF activity at the canal continued as in the past, acting as flying artillery against ground targets on an almost daily basis. In addition, the IAF continued to maintain its local control of the air space. Throughout March the IAF repeatedly thwarted Egyptian attempts to reconstruct a SAM-2 system west of the canal zone.[150]

How did Egypt, the Soviet Union, and the United States react to the Israeli campaign? Was the desired effect achieved? Inside Egypt the policy was highly counterproductive for Israel. She had brought the war home to every Egyptian, which made it possible for the regime to portray Israel's war on Egypt as total, aimed at the Egyptian nation itself. The raids thus had an integrating effect on Egyptian society and helped make Nasser a symbol of national resistance.[151]

At the Suez Canal as well, the Egyptian reaction was not as intended. After a brief two-week decline in activity in January, the Egyptians resumed the previous high level of belligerence. In fact, both the overall level of activity and the number of Israeli casualties rose steadily in the January–April period, trends visible in tables 9 and 10. One important and ominous change in Egyptian activity was the massive reactivation of their artillery. Throughout this period the role of artillery fire rose dramatically, despite antibattery activity of the IAF.[152]

Israeli strategic bombing enabled Nasser to actuate the Soviet inter-

148. *MER* (1969–70), p. 147; Schiff and Haber, *Lexikon le-Bitahon Yisrael*, p. 176; Bar-Siman-Tov, *Israeli-Egyptian War*, p. 152.

149. O'Ballance, *Electronic War*, pp. 114–15; *MER* (1969–70), p. 151; Whetten, *Canal War*, p. 95.

150. *MER* (1969–70), pp. 146, 150.

151. To help the process along, the regime announced formation of Citizens' Committees for the Battle, renewed the national blackout, and ordered automobile headlights painted blue. See Khalidi, "War of Attrition," p. 67; Schiff, *Knafayim me'al Suez*, p. 197.

152. Naor, *Hamilhama leachar ha-Milhama*, pp. 101–4; *MER* (1969–70), pp. 146–47, 151; Bar-Siman-Tov, *Israeli-Egyptian War*, pp. 141–42.

Table 9. IDF casualties on the Egyptian front, January–July 1970

	Total	Killed	Wounded
January	39	7	32
February	51	18	33
March	47	9	38
April	89	27	62
May	97	34	63
June	74	19	55
July	50	7	43

Source: Daniel Dishon, ed., *Middle East Record,* vol. 5 (1969–70) (Jerusalem: Israel Universities Press, 1977), p. 172.

vention I have described. In January Nasser traveled to Moscow, apparently to demand Soviet assistance in halting the Israeli campaign and also in providing more advanced weapons. The Soviets agreed to intervene directly to save the regime from falling but refused to fulfill his requests for advanced offensive weapons such as Mig-23 and Sukhoi-9 aircraft.[153]

This last fact underscores a point worth mentioning briefly: Russian intervention was reluctant, slow, and careful. The Soviets executed their promise two full months after making it. During that time they virtually begged the United States to call off the Israelis while they pressed Egypt to moderate her own activity at the canal. Intervention, when it finally did come through, was accompanied by great publicity. The missiles were unloaded in broad daylight and driven through the streets of Cairo, and communications among the Soviet pilots in the air were carried out in Russian.[154] The Soviets, apparently, intended to make their intervention a public and political act that might help prevent direct Soviet-Israeli confrontation.

Publicly silent at first, the United States began between January and April to distance itself slowly from identification with Israel's policy. The Abu Zabal mishap elicited expressions of concern by Undersecretary of State Elliot Richardson that such tensions might endanger a recent Israeli request for additional Phantoms and Skyhawks.[155] In private contacts, U.S. officials persistently questioned the wisdom of bombing. Finally, on 23 March Secretary of State William Rogers an-

153. On Nasser's visit, see Heykal, *Road to Ramadan,* pp. 83–90; Glassman, *Arms for the Arabs,* p. 85; Rubinstein, *Red Star on the Nile,* pp. 107–10.
154. *MER* (1969–70), pp. 48–50; Heykal, *Road to Ramadan,* p. 90; el-Sadat, *In Search of Identity,* pp. 197–98; Rubinstein, *Red Star on the Nile,* pp. 110–11.
155. *MER* (1969–70), p. 145.

Table 10. Incidents initiated by the United Arab Republic, 1970

	Light arms and bazooka fire	Mortar shelling	Artillery	Mining	Sabotage activities	Raids on Israeli positions	Clashes with patrols	Aerial incidents	Naval incidents	Total
January	118	102	98	2	1		1	6		328
February	188	105	177	2			2	27		501
March	147	162	197	5			2	7		520
April	128	290	219	7	1	2	1	7		655
May	90	504	259	3			5	12		874
June	43	605	193	9				7	1	857
July	89	548	304	5			1	5		952

Source: Daniel Dishon, ed., *Middle East Record*, vol. 5 (1969–70) (Jerusalem: Israel Universities Press, 1977), p. 167.

nounced that Nixon had decided to "hold in abeyance for now" any decision on arms to Israel.[156] In mid-April Assistant Secretary of State Joseph Sisco warned Bar Lev, Dayan, and Intelligence Chief Ahron Yariv that the United States opposed the bombing or any other Israeli escalatory activity and demanded Israeli flexibility.[157]

In April, Dayan said, "The Russians have become our central problem,"[158] thus reflecting the tremendous complexity of Israel's new deterrence problem as it had begun to emerge. Israel now had to deter the Soviet Union directly and also a more confident Soviet-backed and protected Egypt. From what challenges? The Israelis rightly feared further escalation of Soviet involvement and were concerned lest the Russians act to nullify Israel's air superiority at the canal. As for Egypt, the problem remained to reverse somehow the trend of ever escalating violence at the front.

Israeli leaders basically accepted the new reality, that Israel could not neutralize Soviet intervention on her own, and turned to the United States. This new dependence on the Americans was best reflected in a reversal of rhetoric. Whereas in the past, Israeli leaders tried to keep the superpowers out of the conflict by assuring them that it neither would nor could get out of control, beginning in April they made repeated and more and more alarmist statements indicating that Soviet-Israeli confrontation could lead to global confrontation—unless, of course, the United States acted to reverse Soviet intervention.[159]

The American reaction to all this was to open an even greater distance between itself and Israel. Although verbal support for Israel and harsh words for the Soviets were uttered on various occasions by Nixon and other officials, the administration persisted in its refusal to supply aircraft. It did agree (secretly!) to replenish those airplanes lost in the fighting. But even a letter by seventy-three senators in May did not move Nixon either to confront the Soviets or to supply the requested aircraft.[160] Yitzhak Rabin, who had been the great believer in American

156. Meir had requested a new aircraft deal in September 1969 and did not receive a reply until the decision of 23 March 1970. See my discussion of this issue in the section on political asymmetries and see also Lewis Sorley, *Arms Transfers under Nixon: A Policy Analysis* (Lexington, Ken., 1983), pp. 84–86; *MER* (1969–70), p. 47; Rabin, *Rabin Memoirs*, chap. 9.

157. *Haaretz*, 16 April 1970; Shlaim and Tanter, "Decision Process, Choice, and Consequences," p. 502.

158. Quoted in Shlaim and Tanter, "Decision Process, Choice, and Consequences," p. 505. On the growing concern over the Soviet Union, see Brecher, *Decisions in Israel's Foreign Policy*, pp. 467–68.

159. See Eban's alleged statements to Nixon, in *New York Times*, 21, 26 May 1970, and Bar Lev in *Maariv*, 5 June 1970. See also Bar-Siman-Tov, *Israeli-Egyptian War*, p. 168.

160. Whetten, *Canal War*, p. 93; *MER* (1969–70), pp. 54–55; Steven L. Spiegel, *The Other*

support for Israeli escalation, concluded in June that precisely because of the danger of U.S.-Soviet confrontation, "there is no prospect of the United States issuing a warning that a blow against Israel is equivalent to a blow against the US."[161]

Approaching the Soviets directly, the Israelis attempted appeasement and, when this failed, direct bilateral deterrence of Russian intervention. Between late March and mid-April, Dayan tried to reach a modus vivendi with the Soviets through appeasement of sorts. In a number of speeches the defense minister tried to establish spheres of activity, "agreeing" to Soviet control of the Egyptian interior in return for Israeli control of the canal zone. Israel's cessation of strategic bombing in mid-April may well have been a fulfillment of Dayan's side of the bargain.[162] But the Soviets had no interest in the arrangement Israel offered. In mid-April, Soviet intervention came to include flying. In May and June the Soviets began assisting in Egyptian attempts to reestablish control of the airspace over the canal by advancing SAM systems eastward.

The Egyptians, with Russian help, tried a number of technical and tactical approaches to establishing a "SAM Box" some 30 kilometers west of the canal and parallel to it. In May they tried to blitz-build SAM sites in a matter of days under the protection of antiaircraft artillery. The IAF foiled the attempt. In early June the Egyptians attempted to advance SAMs at night and set them up as ambushes at first light. The IAF destroyed them handily. The important point is that they kept trying new methods and that in each attempt the Soviets took a more prominent role.[163]

These direct Israeli attacks on the joint Egyptian-Soviet ventures seem to have been in direct support of the Israeli rhetorical or declaratory policy of directly deterring the Soviets from further encroachments. Dayan declared, "If we do not fight . . . the Russians will set up SAM-3s on the Canal,"[164] and when Bar Lev was asked how an Israeli pilot would behave if challenged by a Soviet aviator, he replied, "If the Russian pilot impedes him in fulfilling his mission, the Israeli pilot will continue in his mission despite the disturbances."[165] And to an American television audience he said: "We do not wish to fight the Russians.

Arab-Israeli Conflict: Making America's Middle East Policy, from Truman to Reagan (Chicago, 1985), pp. 190–93.

161. *Maariv*, 5 June 1970.

162. For example, see *Maariv*, 10 April 1970; see also the discussion in Bar-Siman-Tov, *Israeli-Egyptian War*, p. 153.

163. Schiff, *Knafayim me'al Suez*, pp. 219–20; MER (1969–70), pp. 152–53, 155.

164. Quoted in MER (1969–70), pp. 152–53.

165. *Maariv*, 5 June 1970.

But if they advance too close to the Canal or if they impede our missions when we decide to attack targets within Egypt, we shall fight them."[166]

All of this was to no avail. During the nights of 28–29 and 29–30 June the Soviets and Egyptians set up a new missile system in a "box" some 65 kilometers long and 30 kilometers west of the canal. At this distance it provided coverage of nearly the entire west bank.[167] The innovations were in technology, deployment, and tactics. Deployment was in dense clusters of overlapping SAM-2 and SAM-3 batteries and antiaircraft artillery as well. At first the system consisted of fifteen batteries. On 30 June, Israeli aircraft met the first of the massive missile barrages fired in so-called ripples.[168] In trying to tackle the new deployment the IAF immediately lost two jet aircraft, the first to missiles since 1967. They destroyed two batteries. On 5 July another Israeli plane was lost, and toward the end of the month two more.

The rate of exchange of planes for SAM batteries quickly became untenable for the Israelis. Directly confronting the Soviets revolutionized the quantitative balance problem for Israel. Russian willingness to expend masses of missiles and to replace both destroyed missiles and entire batteries put Israel in a competition she could not sustain. As July wore on, the IAF limited its activities to a very narrow strip along the west bank of the canal. The Russians advanced a number of squadrons to forward air bases.

On 30 July, Israel executed its threat to fight the Soviets directly. An IAF formation shot down either four or five Soviet-piloted Migs over the Gulf.[169] For all the sensation this caused, the Soviets had already won the battle for the Canal, and a cease-fire had been agreed upon. The famous air battle had no significance.

In April, feeling increasingly secure with the Soviet assistance, Egyptian forces at the canal had begun a static offensive that Israel was at a loss to arrest.[170] This included intensive artillery shelling, sporadic air raids on Israeli positions at the canal and along the Mediterranean coast, and a number of commando raids on maozim, sabotage, and

---

166. Ibid., 8 July 1970.

167. O'Ballance, *Electronic War*, pp. 124–25.

168. For descriptions of the IDF's unsuccessful battle with the missiles, see Schiff, *Knafayim me'al Suez*, pp. 224–26; Wallach, Lissak, and Shamir, *Atlas Carta: Assor Sheni*, p. 113; Naor, *Hamilhama leachar ha-Milhama*, pp. 119–20; Landau, *Suez*, pp. 260–62; MER (1969–70), pp. 157–58; Glassman, *Arms for the Arabs*, p. 79.

169. MER (1969–70), p. 160; Schiff, *Knafayim me'al Suez*, p. 227.

170. A sign of renewed confidence was the cancellation of the blackout and the return of light to Egyptian cities in May. The Egyptian army resumed a regular training schedule; see O'Ballance, *Electronic War*, p. 117. See also Schiff, *Knafayim me'al Suez*, pp. 218–19; *Haaretz*, 19 June 1970, in MER (1969–70), p. 151; ibid., p. 154.

mining. In mid-May, Egyptian commando forces penetrated Eilat harbor for sabotage and did some minor damage. Such aggressive Egyptian behavior continued through July, the number of incidents of all kinds increasing on a monthly basis (table 10).

Israeli attempts to silence the Egyptians contained no major innovations. The IAF continued to pound Egyptian positions and artillery batteries at the canal and to engage the EAF in dogfights. Israeli artillery continued to harass the Egyptians as before. The EAF lost twenty-six airplanes, mostly in dogfights but some to Hawk missiles. In retaliation for the sinking of an Israeli fishing boat by the Egyptian navy, the IAF sank an Egyptian destroyer and a missile boat in the Red Sea.[171]

To an Egyptian ambush at Ras el-Eish on 30 May the IDF responded most vigorously. First, the IAF launched a three-day offensive in the northern sector. Dropping four thousand bombs, it destroyed bunkers, bridges, roads, vehicles, and the Sweet Water Canal to Port Said. This city lost its land and bridge connections to Egypt, and its twenty-five thousand remaining citizens were left stranded without supplies.[172]

Then, on the night of 11 June, an Israeli infantry force crossed the canal in the same sector, cleared 2 kilometers of Egyptian frontline positions—killing more than twenty-one Egyptians—and disengaged. According to Dayan and other commentary, the operation was proof to the Egyptians that for all the "red thread woven into the Egyptian forces," the IDF maintained superiority, control, and the initiative along the front.[173] But this was a watershed operation, for after it the Israeli general staff decided the Israeli casualty figure (four dead and seventeen wounded) was too high and that such operations should not be repeated.[174]

During the last phase of the War of Attrition the IDF inflicted very large numbers of casualties on the Egyptians. Sources vary widely in their estimates, but the order of magnitude is astounding. Most sources, be they Egyptian or foreign, estimated between one thousand and three thousand Egyptian dead in the last four months. The *New York Times*'s Beirut correspondent wrote that in June and July alone there were ten thousand casualties.[175] But as we have seen, while the IDF was deciding to tone down its operations, Egyptian belligerence continued to increase, and Israeli casualty rates remained high.

On 19 June the United States proposed what became known as

171. Naor, *Hamilhama leachar ha-Milhama*, p. 115; *MER* (1969–70), p. 154.
172. Naor, *Hamilhama leachar ha-Milhama*, pp. 117–18.
173. *MER* (1969–70), p. 156.
174. Wallach, Lissak, and Shamir, *Atlas Carta: Assor Sheni*, p. 111.
175. For a number of these reports, see *MER* (1969–70), p. 172.

[167]

Rogers II, a modest plan entailing a ninety-day cease-fire and the resumption of talks under the auspices of Gunnar Jarring and within the framework of Resolution 242. One month later, on 22 July, Nasser agreed, and on 30 July, Israel followed suit. On 8 August 1970 the cease-fire went into effect.

Both superpowers were wary of the dangers of continued violence. The United States had been searching for a way to de-escalate since March, and the Soviets—once Egypt's defense was secure—saw no more potential gains in continued violence. According to a number of sources, Soviet leaders applied considerable moderating pressure on Nasser during a visit to Moscow in July, urging him to accept the Rogers initiative. Others, who claim that Nasser needed no prodding, agree that the Soviets supported his intention to accept.[176]

Nasser and Heykal explained that acceptance of the Rogers initiative was perfectly consistent with Egyptian strategy and principles, which they had been presenting all along. On 23 and 24 July addressing the Arab Socialist Union, Nasser announced and then explained Egypt's acceptance.[177] His main points were:

1. Reacquisition of the territories was a political-military enterprise with manifold stages. Now, having involved the superpowers *and* achieved military power, the time for political and diplomatic action had come. Negotiations would be useful, now that Egypt was in a position of strength.
2. Prepartion for further war would continue in the shadow of diplomacy, just as it had in 1967–68.
3. With the United States finally cognizant of, and motivated by, Egyptian power, it might be possible to pry her away from Israel by appearing conciliatory.
4. A *temporary* cease-fire would force Israel to start complying precisely because of the implicit threat that it would not be renewed. The Israelis could not use the interim to change the balance of power because their real source of strength was the IAF, which had been neutralized.

Other retrospective Egyptian explanations did discuss the pain that Egypt was experiencing at the canal toward the summer. According to

176. Karen Dawisha, *Soviet Foreign Policy towards Egypt* (London, 1979), p. 51; Breslauer, "Soviet Policy," p. 87; Eran, "Soviet Policy," pp. 37–38; Whetten, *Canal War*, pp. 106–7.

177. For summaries of Nasser's speeches and concurrent commentary, see *MER* (1969–70), pp. 69–71.

Heykal, Nasser told the Russians that "we need to give our army a break, and to cut down our civilian casualties. We need a cease-fire."[178] According to Chief of Staff Saad el-Shazli, in July the situation was a standoff. Accepting the cease-fire was to enable the Egyptians to make necessary preparations for a future assault. The critical preparation, adds Heykal, was to advance the "missile wall," a task to which they immediately turned.[179]

Israeli leaders made brave and ingenious attempts to portray the cease-fire as an Israeli achievement that reflected Israeli power.[180] In truth, Israel accepted Rogers II under substantial pressure—of the United States, of domestic fatigue, and of an increasingly deteriorating power position at the canal.

The Americans approached Israel with both inducements and pressure. The former included strong verbal support and promises by Nixon that the United States would not force any Israeli withdrawal not reached in bilateral negotiations. The administration also promised to increase economic and military aid, including the supply of electronic counter-measures (ECMs) to combat the SAMs. These promises were all conditional on Israeli compliance and were thus in themselves a source of pressure. They were a major consideration in Israel's decision to accept, for her leaders feared alienating the United States just as Israel was becoming so obviously dependent.[181]

Within the government there was a growing loss of confidence in the strategic prospects and in what remained to be gained from continued conflict. With the loss of air superiority in July, Israeli political and military leaders could not find an appropriate military response and found themselves in a real quandary. They realized that Egypt would probably use a temporary cease-fire to enhance her strategic position. At the same time, they did not know how to continue the military conflict without engaging in yet further substantial escalation. But this was unthinkable, for the extended war had undermined the national consensus supporting it. Having painted itself into a corner, with no satisfactory options to choose from, the National Unity Government accepted the cease-fire—and then dissolved.[182]

178. Heykal, *Road to Ramadan*, p. 95.

179. el-Shazli, *Crossing of the Suez*, pp. 14–15; Heykal, *Sphinx and the Commissar*, p. 201.

180. For example, see Bar Lev in *Bamahaneh*, 11 August 1970. For statements by others, see *MER* (1969–70), pp. 76–77, 162. See also Bar-Siman-Tov, *Israeli-Egyptian War*, pp. 192–93.

181. See "The International System" below.

182. Brecher, *Decisions in Israel's Foreign Policy*, pp. 494–96; Margalit, *Sheder meha-Bayit ha-Lavan*, pp. 156–83. See "Domestic Factors" below.

August–October 1970

A critical provision of the cease-fire accord was maintenance of the military status quo within a distance of 50 kilometers on either side of the canal. On the very night it went into effect (8 August), the Egyptians began to advance SAM-2 and SAM-3 batteries into the 50-kilometer band.[183] On 5 September the IDF spokesman announced that within the standstill zone forty new sites had been prepared and of these ten were newly occupied with operational batteries. Some of the new sites were within 10 kilometers of the canal, and coverage from them would extend over the east bank. By 26 September twenty batteries had been moved into the forbidden zone, and on 26 October the IDF intelligence chief reported that there were thirty-to-forty batteries within 30 kilometers of the canal. He described the deployed system as "one of the most advanced in the world." These were not mere tactical violations. By advancing a proven-efficacious SAM system toward the canal, Egypt was able to establish control of the air space over the east bank as well as their own. This accomplishment not only nullified Israel's single source of local superiority but actually tipped the balance of power in Egypt's favor.

Israel was powerless to arrest these violations. Try as they did, Israeli leaders could not convince the United States to confront the Egyptians over the issue. It took three weeks of Israeli political maneuvering, including cessation of the Jarring talks, to extract a State Department admission that violations had actually occurred. When Israel demanded that the United States act to rectify the situation, all she could elicit was an increase in military assistance, which included shipments of Shrike air-to-surface missiles and ECMs. As Ezer Weizman pointed out in 1971, these weapons could not restore Israeli superiority.[184]

Perhaps most striking is that Israel made no attempts to deter Egyptian violations directly. The IDF and Israel's political leadership had lost their nerve. Weizman later wrote, "They advanced their missile system to the Suez Canal—thus violating the explicit accord and under its protection. And the Israeli leadership had not the courage to order an attack to destroy this system, for it did not believe it could be done."[185] And so, admit it or not, and despite the appearance of a draw, Israel had lost her first war.

183. For various reports on the violations, see *MER* (1969–70), pp. 163–65.

184. Safran, *Israel*, pp. 449–50; *MER* (1969–70), pp. 83–85; Glassman, *Arms for the Arabs*, p. 81; Gazit, *Tahalikh ha-Shalom*, p. 74; Spiegel, *Other Arab-Israeli Conflict*, pp. 194–95.

185. Ezer Weizman, *Lekha Shamayim Lekha Aretz* [Thine is the sky, thine is the land] (Tel-Aviv, 1975), p. 319.

An Analysis

Relative Interests

A comparison of both intrinsic and power interests of the two main protagonists demonstrates that Egypt had the upper hand in this bargaining situation. She had an intense intrinsic interest in freeing the Sinai Peninsula from foreign occupation and an unambiguous power interest in continuous violence. Israel had few intrinsic interests in the Sinai. She did have power interests in the occupation of Sinai and some in violence, but these were more than offset by a dominant interest in pacification.

The intrinsic balance of interests in the Sinai qua territory was fairly evident to both sides in the conflict at the time. Nasser, Bar Lev, Heykal, and Dayan "agreed" that Egyptians were fighting for the "soil of the homeland,"[186] that Israel was a "thorn in the flesh of the Egyptians,"[187] and that "[Egypt] cannot sit on the far side of the Canal and accept the existing situation."[188] Nasser expressed it: "We swear to God that we shall be loyal to every inch of this territory at any cost and at any sacrifice."[189]

After the Six Day War, Israelis did discover national expansionism and an ideologically driven desire to retain captured territories, but such drives were mostly confined to Judah and Samaria. The Sinai was not part of Erets Yisrael (the Land of Israel), and the interests expressed in retaining all or part of it were strategic in nature. From the Israeli perspective, occupation of the Sinai and the east bank of the Suez Canal was a move in a bargaining process. Ultimately, territory was to be exchanged for direct negotiations and peace. Perhaps the best indication of Israel's disinterest in the Sinai is that, except for the Gaza area, Israelis did not settle it. This lack of substantial interest in the territory created severe difficulties for the Israeli government in demanding its youth's blood. According to Shabtai Teveth, as the war wore endlessly on, the public wanted to know, "Why fight and lose people over territories from which, in principle, Israel is willing to retreat?"[190]

186. Heykal, in *Al-Ahram*, 7 March 1969.
187. Dayan, *Mapa Hadasha*, p. 51; *Haaretz*, 20 October 1968.
188. Bar Lev, *Davar*, 13 May 1970.
189. *MER* (1968), p. 209.
190. Teveth, *Moshe Dayan*, p. 597. Most Israelis expected Gaza and Sharm el-Sheikh to remain under Israeli control in any future settlement, though both areas were of power interest. The Egyptians hinted that they had no great desire to reacquire Gaza and were amenable to its internationalization and to other arrangements. See Brecher, *Decisions in Israel's Foreign Policy*, pp. 460–62; *MER* (1967), p. 309; *MER* (1968), p. 210; Shamir, "Nasser and Sadat," p. 192.

For a number of reasons the Egyptian regime had a positive interest in violence in the post-1967 period. At the national political-cultural level there was a burning need to deny the defeat of June. The army, especially, felt and applied tremendous pressure to be allowed to prove its worth by fighting. There was a need at least, in Shazli's words, "to symbolize our refusal to remain defeated."[191] Acceptance of the defeat for what it was also entailed admitting the failure of fifteen years of socialist revolution. This helps explain the popular refusal to accept Nasser's resignation on 9 June 1967. As A. I. Dawisha wrote, "[Nasser's] resignation would have been synonymous with the defeat of 'Egyptian socialism' and 'Arab nationalism' by the forces of 'imperialism' and 'international Zionism.' "[192] It is in this sense that peace or even direct negotiations with Israel were so repugnant and refusing them a form of survival. Therefore, if the antiseptic solution of 1957 could not be repeated, violence was the only alternative.

Encouraging, tapping, and mobilizing these needs was in the regime's interests. Nasser was so personally identified with the debacle of June 1967 that he had no alternative but to try uncompromisingly to erase the traces of aggression and to prove that Egypt had not been defeated.[193] So, according to Mahmoud Hussein and Fouad Ajami, the regime both needed and recognized the potential for national integration inherent in continued armed conflict.[194]

There is little doubt that the Six Day War "marked the end of the Egyptian myth in Arab life," and it is true that the postwar period witnessed the beginning of the Egyptianization of politics and a movement away from Pan-Arab aspirations in Egypt.[195] But the break was not to be a clean one for two reasons. First, as I mentioned earlier, Nasser's entire program could not, after fifteen years, be abandoned with impunity overnight, especially as much of his domestic prestige rested on the *Arab* status he had bestowed on Egypt.[196] Second, an important element of Nasser's grand strategy was to mobilize Arab material resources and activate the Eastern Front. Violence against Israel was a key to mobilizing prestige, resources, and blood.

191. Shazli is quoted in Stein, "Calculation, Miscalculation, and Conventional Deterrence"; see also Lacouture, *Nasser*, pp. 327–28; O'Ballance, *Electronic War*, pp. 55–57; Dekmejian, *Egypt under Nassir*, p. 254.

192. A. I. Dawisha, *Egypt in the Arab World*, p. 51.

193. Shamir, "Nasser and Sadat," pp. 191–92.

194. Mahmoud Hussein, *La lutte de classes en Egypte* [Class conflict in Egypt] (Paris, 1971), pp. 313–23; Fouad Ajami, *The Arab Predicament: Arab Political Thought and Practice since 1967* (Cambridge, 1984), pp. 91–92.

195. Ajami, *Arab Predicament*, p. 81; Sela, *Achdut*, pp. 68–69.

196. Dekmejian, *Egypt under Nassir*, p. 265.

Belligerence was necessary to help diminish the blow to Nasser's prestige struck by the Palestinians. Especially after the Israeli-Fedayeen battle of Karameh in 1968, in which Israel suffered serious casualties, the Palestinians were emerging as the only force capable of and willing to challenge Israel physically.[197] Egyptian attrition made it possible to blur the distinction between those ("traitor") states (like Egypt) that had accepted U.N. Resolution 242 and those that remained loyal to the hard line. As long as Egypt fought the Zionists, the issue remained moot.[198] Indeed, continued violence and its attendant prestige enabled Egypt to realize some of her substantive interests in the Arab system. At Khartoum, Nasser managed to mobilize money from his archrival Feisal, and in late 1969 it enabled him to override Saudi Arabia's objection to an Arab summit.

Finally, we saw throughout the historical discussion that the heart of Egypt's grand strategy was offensive brinkmanship. Egypt required violence as a destabilizing mechanism. Of course it had to be substantial violence, but the military outcome was less important than the effect on the international system. Egyptian interests could only be hurt by nonviolence, which would signal acquiescence to the status quo and relieve the superpowers from pressure to intervene.

In contrast, to attain her goals of direct negotiations and peace without prior withdrawal, Israel depended on her ability to keep the situation pacific. After the Six Day War, Israel enjoyed strategic superiority in the region, the benefits of which she could only hope to reap if the superpowers stayed out. Escalation and destabilization would threaten global confrontation and bring the superpowers in to impose an undesirable order.[199] Nonetheless, there was constant temptation, as expressed by *Haaretz* in October 1969, to cause de-escalation by escalation: "If the Middle East is a powder keg, then the IDF should remove the fuse by a massive blow."[200]

Another more traditional interest provided pressure for military activism: the deterrence need to win every engagement by destroying the enemy's forces. In other words, there was a perceived need to act decisively in the present in order to perpetuate reputation into the future. Chief of Operations (and later Minister of Transportation) Weizman consistently pressed both the general staff and the government to

197. Kerr, *Arab Cold War*, pp. 131–32; Ajami, *Arab Predicament*, p. 91.
198. Daniel Dishon, *Inter-Arab Relations 1967–1973*, An Occasional Paper (Tel-Aviv, 1974), p. 5.
199. For a general discussion of this problem, see Evron, *Middle East*, pp. 79, 178–86.
200. *Haaretz*, 3 October 1969.

make a large crosscanal offensive. His operational purpose was to win, his strategic purpose to prevent future wars.[201]

In terms of Israeli interests Weizman may not have been completely wrong, but his analysis was partial instead of total, and when his suggestions were discussed in both the government and the general staff, the considerations they represented were seen as secondary to the central interest, which demanded greater passivity. This reasoning reflects a point made earlier. Just as the territorial interests being protected were in a sense luxuries and not vital, so was the reputation to be achieved by attacking Egypt. The reputation for successfully protecting Israel's vital interests had been established in 1967. The reputation in question in 1968–70 was for crazy-state proclivities, or for the willingness to undertake extreme actions on behalf of issues important but not vital to the question of immediate survival. While potentially useful, this interest could not compete with the projected real costs of achieving it or with the strategic interest in de-escalation.

This case is not useful in trying to assess the explanatory utility of ordering interests on the intrinsic-power axis. The reason is that Egypt had a fairly clear advantage in both. Nevertheless, as in earlier cases, the rather ambiguous notion of vitalness was helpful in comparing the power interests of Israel and Egypt. It was also helpful in sorting out competing interests, at least on the Israeli side.

Is there insight to be gained by considering the deterrence-compellence ordering? The case of Egyptian attrition is a good example of the difficulties in applying this terminology. Was Israel engaged in deterrence or compellence? And what about Egypt? The answer depends on two points: the level of analysis and who defines the status quo and how. At one level Israel treated the post-1967 lines as the status quo and was engaged in trying to deter Egyptian challenge of and at these lines. But for Egypt the only relevant status quo was the 4 June 1967 disposition, so Israel was engaged in compellence. And indeed she was, for at the *strategic* level Israel was threatening to occupy until Egypt made peace. Yet while occupying, she practiced *tactical* deterrence, to minimize ongoing violence. A possible conclusion is that tactical deterrence should be difficult when attempted in the context of strategic compellence.

Israeli demands for peace suggest that a territorial characterization of a status quo may be too narrow. Perhaps definition of a status quo

201. Weizman, *Lecha Shamayim Lekha Aretz,* p. 309; *Maariv,* 14 May, 4 June 1971; *Yediot Aharonot* (in the weekly supplement), 4 June 1971; Shlaim and Tanter, "Decision Process, Choice, and Consequences," p. 492.

should pertain to all aspects of a bilateral relationship that influence the security of the states involved. From this perspective, Israel did not recognize Egypt as a status quo power at all, for Egypt's pre-1967 occupation of the Sinai had only enabled Nasser to endanger her security; and Egypt's desire to force an Israeli surrender of the Sinai without renouncing the status belli was, from Israel's point of view, an act of Egyptian compellence. From this Israeli perspective, Israel was engaged not merely in tactical deterrence but in deterrence at the highest strategic level as well.

What is clear is that the parties could not agree on the nature of coercion involved. A central lesson may be that difficulties in deterrence are to be expected when opposing sides so disagree. In any event, the deterrence-compellence ordering is problematic, if useful at all, in explaining the bargaining outcome in this case.

Political Asymmetries

THE INTERNATIONAL SYSTEM

Basic underlying asymmetries in the nature of the actors' alliance relationships explain why Egypt was ultimately successful in mobilizing the support necessary to challenge, while Israel could not do the same for deterrence. Examining the sets of relationships reveals that, although neither had complete freedom of action and support, Israel's system placed increasing constraints on her just as—and *because*—foreign support for Egypt was increasing. The two alliance systems were interdependent in such a way that Egypt was more able than Israel to manipulate this interdependence to her advantage.

Egypt was largely unsuccessful in her attempts to mobilize the Arab system, especially in efforts to involve other states in the shooting war. Attempts in both 1968 and 1969 to activate the Eastern Front failed miserably. Wealth transfers were more forthcoming but even these within strict limits. After extracting income transfers at Khartoum, Nasser could not convene another Arab summit until December 1969 precisely because Saudi Arabia was not interested in transferring more resources. At the Rabat Summit itself Nasser was unable to elicit action or material for a major operation against Israel. At most, then, Arab support made it possible to keep the canal closed and to engage in limited violence. But the main effect of his failures in the Arab system was to push Nasser to exploit his other ally, the Soviet Union.

In 1967, Egypt was the key country in Soviet Middle East policy.[202] It

202. See expressions in the Soviet press, *MER* (1968), pp. 30–31.

was through Egypt that Russia had overcome American containment in the past, had pursued legitimacy as a nonimperialist friend in the Third World, and had built a bridgehead to influence in the Arab Middle East. Egypt had even been and still was an arena for Sino-Soviet competition within the communist world.[203] At a more immediate strategic level, as they pursued growth in their international military presence, Soviet leaders wanted to use Egyptian territory for air bases and to influence the opening and operation of the Suez Canal, their outlet to the Indian Ocean.[204]

The beachhead to all of these accomplishments had been seriously jeopardized in the June war, which cast serious doubt on the value of Russia as patron. The demise of the pro-Soviet regime, which seemed imminent in 1967, would have made the doubters certain and put at risk Soviet strategic goals. Having staked their prestige in Egypt and discovered its vulnerability, the Soviets were committed to protect their investment.[205]

Nasser clearly managed to extract Soviet assurance of his survival and support for attrition, but it appears that time and again the Soviets vetoed offensive action, whether by diplomatic pressure or through the control of quantities and types of weapons and ammunition they delivered. This behavior can be explained by Russian fear of the potential consequences of escalation and globalization of the conflict. Another explanation was their determination not to let Nasser fall. If Egyptian offensive action were to lead to another quick Israeli victory, then surely Nasser's regime and Russia's position and prestige would be doomed.[206]

The Soviets appear to have been unhappy even with Egypt's insistence on attrition. A number of times they were willing to go along with schemes for political solutions that fell short of their client's demands, and in 1968 they even advanced their own "December 30" proposal that suggested negotiated frontiers. Partially, this behavior is also explainable by their reluctance to tempt either superpower confrontation or Egyptian defeat. Robert Stephens adds to this a need, in the Third

203. Karen Dawisha, *Soviet Foreign Policy*, pp. 121–29; Rubinstein, *Red Star on the Nile*, pp. 6, 20, 28.

204. Eran, "Soviet Policy," pp. 30–31; *MER* (1968), p. 37; Schiff, *Knafayim me'al Suez*, p. 37; Rubinstein, *Red Star on the Nile*, p. 46.

205. On the danger to the Soviet position and the need to protect it after the Six Day War, see Evron, *Middle East*, p. 153; Safran, *Israel*, pp. 419–20; Eran, "Soviet Policy," pp. 29–32.

206. Karen Dawisha, *Soviet Foreign Policy*, p. 123; Safran, *Israel*, p. 419. See Heykal's appreciation of these limits, in Rubinstein, *Red Star on the Nile*, pp. 32–33.

World context, to show a "prospering" client, not just one involved in protracted fighting.[207]

Nasser may have had no choice but to live and act within the Soviet constraints on major offensive action, but he readily overruled their attempts to veto or dampen attrition. The Russians had to provide him with fairly large quantities of weapons just to make up for the 1967 defeat, to maintain Egyptian dependence, and to prove that the Soviet Union stood by its clients. They had declined Nasser's request in summer 1967 that Russia take over the defense of Egypt and therefore "had" to provide Egypt with the tools to defend herself. Because the technological requirements of attrition warfare are so simple, once Egypt had moderate amounts of weapons of any kind, she was free to wage low-level conflict.

Also, one imagines that the Soviets would have found it politically embarrassing to oppose low-level Egyptian belligerence because this would have branded them as at least implicit supporters of the Israeli occupation. In a sense, permitting low-level belligerence was an optimal Russian policy. It allowed the Soviets to reap the benefits of symbolic support for Egypt's continuing war with minimal risk.

Nasser was able to mobilize the Russians by threatening to lose. The desire to ensure Egypt's and Nasser's longevity helps explain the massive air and sea lifts in the immediate aftermath of the Six Day War and the intensive Soviet assistance in rebuilding Egypt's land, sea, and air defenses. Toward the end of the War of Attrition, Israel's strategic bombing enabled Nasser to make an immediate and credible threat to be defeated. In response, the Soviets decided to intervene directly, a historic departure from their traditional policy outside Europe.

Finally, Soviet behavior toward the end of the war was also motivated by Nasser's threat to defect. According to Heykal, direct Soviet intervention was extracted by Nasser's explicit threat to step down and hand over the regime to a pro-American president.[208] Throughout the 1967–70 period Nasser referred to the need to influence U.S. behavior, admitting that positive results would only come through Washington. In the spring of 1970 Nasser opened up to the United States. In April he welcomed a visit by Sisco, and in his May Day speech he made an explicit appeal to Nixon to try to resolve the conflict.[209] This behavior was quite threatening to the Russians and may explain, for example,

207. Stephens, *Nasser*, p. 521.
208. Heykal, *Road to Ramadan*, pp. 83–89.
209. Quandt, *Decade of Decisions*, p. 98; Rubinstein, *Red Star on the Nile*, pp. 116–17.

their support of Nasser's cease-fire violations of August–October 1970. It was their way to remain important to Egypt.

After the Six Day War, de Gaulle moved away from Israel, and the United States stepped in to replace France as Israel's primary patron. The relationship that developed between the United States and Israel was not to mirror Egypt's with Russia; Israel would have neither the freedom of action nor the ability to mobilize her ally enjoyed by Egypt.

In the bilateral context the United States had a substantive and ideological commitment to the survival and independence of Israel that was not motivated by global or other political considerations. At a more personal level, there seems to have been a strong social and cultural rapport between U.S. and Israeli leaders. Americans tended to see Israelis as "like us," and the two U.S. presidents during the 1967–70 period, Johnson and Nixon, had intense personal commitments to Israel and admiration for the Israeli character, guts, work ethic, and "moxie."[210]

In the global political context the United States saw the Middle East as an arena for superpower competition and had ejection of the Soviet Union as a primary interest. Unfortunately for Israel the U.S. theory of influence in the Middle East was not a reflection of the Soviet approach. Beginning in the late Johnson years and through 1970, U.S. policy was ambivalent, based on two competing approaches.[211]

The first of these approaches is normally associated with Dean Rusk, William Rogers, and the State Department. Briefly, they saw the correct path to influence through a regional conceptualization of the Middle East conflict. America could only hope to gain influence at Russia's expense when the local actors, and principally the Arabs, saw the United States as capable of resolving the local conflict to their satisfaction.

The second approach is generally ascribed to Henry Kissinger and Nixon. Their tendency was to bring the global confrontation into the Middle East, and hence their idiom was confrontational. Influence could be gained by demonstrating that allying with the Soviet Union bought defeat, that a U.S. ally with U.S. arms and support could prevail militarily over more numerous and seemingly powerful Russian proxies.

210. Spiegel, *Other Arab-Israeli Conflict*, pp. 123–25, 179; William B. Quandt, "The Arab-Israeli Conflict in American Foreign Policy," in Itamar Rabinovich and Haim Shaked, eds., *From June to October: The Middle East between 1967 and 1973* (New Brunswick, N.J., 1978), pp. 5–6.

211. The following discussion is based on: Spiegel, *Other Arab-Israeli Conflict*, pp. 178–81; Quandt, *Decade of Decisions*, pp. 60–61, 69, 79–81; Aronson, *Conflict and Bargaining*, pp. 94–95; Safran, *Israel*, pp. 417–19, 423–25.

Dichotomizing these theories between the State Department and the White House is an unhelpful oversimplification. Both presidents themselves seem to have been torn between the two approaches. Johnson and Nixon believed simultaneously that relations with the Arabs must be improved *and* that there were advantages, in the context of containment, to be had from Israeli military successes. Nixon reflects this thinking when he says, "Even handedness [between Israel and Egypt] is the right policy—but above all our interest is—what gives the Soviets the most trouble."[212]

In sum, then, whereas the Soviets may have had interests in one side of the conflict only, Israel's ally had substantial interests in both. But even such interests aside, the Americans were very unlikely to intervene directly in the Middle East. One constraint on U.S. action, which they shared with the Soviets, was a refusal to permit escalation to superpower confrontation. The second, in the context of the general backlash of Vietnam, was the reluctance to commit U.S. troops in regional conflicts, a constraint enunciated in the Nixon Doctrine of July 1969: "In cases involving other [nonnuclear] types of aggression, we shall furnish military and economic assistance when requested in accordance with our treaty commitments. But we shall look to the nation directly threatened to assume the primary responsibility of providing the manpower for its defense."[213] The Soviets clearly did not have this constraint.

It is important to understand that Israel's expectations from her patron were somewhat different from Egypt's. Emerging victorious and militarily superior from the Six Day War, Israel wanted a free hand to pursue the political benefits of her victory. What the United States could provide was arms and economic assistance, not involvement in the pursuit of imposed solutions. Later, in the spring of 1970, Israel revolutionized her position, demanding direct and active American deterrence of Soviet intervention. In the fall Israel again demanded U.S. intervention to arrest Egyptian-Soviet cease-fire violations.

The levers at Israel's disposal were also different in kind from those possessed by Egypt. The main one was *success* in independent action. Israel was free to act as long as she could demonstrate success in operations that did not carry a threat either of involving the United States directly or of leading to superpower confrontation. Another source of some leverage was Israel's strong relationship with the U.S.

212. Quoted in Spiegel, *Other Arab-Israeli Conflict*, p. 179. Nixon wrote this comment on a memorandum from Kissinger.
213. Quoted in John Lewis Gaddis, *Strategies of Containment: A Critical Appraisal of Postwar American National Security Policy* (New York, 1982), p. 298.

Congress—the special relationship. Unlike Egypt, Israel could not make either a threat to lose or a threat to defect. She was singularly dependent on the United States and had no real European alternative or Soviet option. Clearly, too, her survival was not at stake at any point in the 1967–70 period.

How successful was Israel in mobilizing and demobilizing the United States? Only partially, and less so as the War of Attrition progressed. Israel could not dissuade the United States from pursuing four-power and two-power talks, proposing the so-called Rogers I program in the fall of 1969, and initiating the process that led to Rogers II and the cease-fire. As long as the war was benign from the American perspective, Israel could and did ignore or openly reject the various U.S. initiatives, as she did with Rogers I. Rogers II she could not reject, a subject I return to presently.

Israel did poorly in eliciting arms transfers throughout the period. Immediately after the Six Day War, Johnson imposed an arms embargo in the hope of inducing the Soviets to follow suit. In October 1967, when the Soviet Union refused to cooperate, Johnson decided to unfreeze a 1966 accord for the delivery of forty-eight Skyhawk jets.[214] After this action Israel succeeded in concluding only one major arms deal (for Phantom F-4s) under Johnson, and not even one under Nixon in the relevant period.

Even the one new agreement signed under Johnson went through excruciating labor pains. Israeli Prime Minister Eshkol began the process in a visit to the Johnson ranch in January 1968. After a favorable but noncommittal reaction from Johnson it took Israel and her supporters until November actually to effect an accord. Obstacles raised were consistent with interests described earlier. Many in the State Department (and Secretary of Defense Robert MacNamara) were wary of the possible effects of such a deal on the prospects for a negotiated settlement. They believed a major sale would hurt U.S.-Arab relations while only further strengthening a militarily superior Israel and would exacerbate the superpower competition in arming their local clients.[215]

In overcoming these obstacles Israel had to appeal to her natural supporters in Congress and make a convincing case that at stake was her survival, or at least military parity, in light of Soviet transfers to Egypt. Israel and her supporters took advantage of their leverage in an

214. On the embargo and the decision in October to suspend it and supply the Sky-hawks, see *MER* (1967), p. 48; Quandt, *Decade of Decisions*, p. 61. On the history of the Skyhawk deal, see Weizman, *Lekha Shamayim Lekha Aretz*, pp. 300–5.

215. Spiegel, *Other Arab-Israeli Conflict*, pp. 160–61; Schiff, *Knafayim me'al Suez*, pp. 173–74.

election year, and even of Johnson's impending departure from office, to make "posterity" arguments.[216] The difficulty Israel had is striking when we consider that at the time Israel's aircraft inventory was considerably smaller than Egypt's, the war at the canal was quite tame with not even a hint of escalation, and there was no air war to speak of.

Israeli requests for additional Phantoms were presented to Nixon by Meir on the occasion of her first state visit in September 1969. This request coincided with the beginning of substantial Israeli escalation at the canal, a process that began to infringe on U.S. interests. Meir got no commitment. As Israel began its strategic bombing in January, Egypt was able to portray the United States as an enemy of the Arabs. After the Abu Zabal incident much Egyptian invective was aimed at the United States and the role of the Phantoms in the bombing. After a similar alleged incident at Bahr al-Baqar, the Egyptian government spokesman said that the problem was not to condemn Israel—which was a criminal state anyhow—but rather to reveal "the extent of the responsibility of the US."[217]

Arms transfers to Israel were thus making it impossible for Nixon to project an even-handed image of an outside power interested in peaceful resolution. In addition, Soviet intervention in mid-March was beginning to raise the specter of globalization. The sale of Phantoms was not approved; Nixon decided to "hold in abeyance" the Israeli requests, where they remained until September 1970.

Toward the end of the War of Attrition Israel failed in her attempts to mobilize the United States to deter the Soviets when they had intervened directly on behalf of Egypt. Israel also lost the ability to keep the United States from infringing on her freedom of action. Two results of direct Soviet intervention brought about these developments in U.S.-Israeli relations. Growing Soviet involvement created real concern in the United States. At the same time, confrontation with a superpower had revolutionized Israel's dependence on the United States and gave the latter a measure of control it had not previously enjoyed.[218] Nixon was finally in a position to impose a cease-fire, at least on the Israelis, in the form of Rogers II. Also, negotiating the cease-fire was a golden opportunity to reestablish America's credentials as the only power capable of producing positive movement in the conflict.

216. Spiegel, *Other Arab-Israeli Conflict*, pp. 161–62; Quandt, *Decade of Decisions*, pp. 66–67; Rabin, *Rabin Memoirs*, pp. 130–34. On the conclusion of this process, see *MER* (1968), pp. 82–83.

217. *MER* (1969–70), pp. 145, 149.

218. Evron, *Middle East*, p. 116; Brecher, *Decisions in Israel's Foreign Policy*, pp. 466–70; Bar-Siman-Tov, *Israeli-Egyptian War*, pp. 157–59, 173, 190–91; Weizman, *Lekha Shamayim Lekha Aretz*, p. 323.

Regarding the missile crisis of July–October 1970 two questions remain: (a) In a situation of potential superpower confrontation, why was the Soviet Union free to intervene and the United States not? and (b) After intervening successfully to save the regime, why did the Russians feel impelled and free to roll back Israeli air superiority first to the canal, and in August–October, even beyond?

The answer to the first question lies in the relative strategic condition of the two clients. Egypt was in an unambiguously inferior position, on the defensive, and with the integrity of her regime endangered. America's client was strategically secure and on a total offensive. Under such circumstances it seems a reasonable rule of intersuperpower behavior that the loser's patron be allowed to intervene.[219] What is interesting in this regard is that Israeli leaders tried to portray the Soviet challenge and the resulting Egyptian escalation as strategic, a prelude to general war. They even went so far as to portray the situation as a "Munich" and warn of the dangers of appeasing Egyptian-Soviet advances.[220] These were crocodile tears, shed in the unrequited hope of involving the United States directly.

An alternative interpretation is that Israeli concerns were sincere. If that is true, then what we have is a classic problem of alliance perception and buck passing. Israel, the state directly on the line, saw and portrayed the threat as immediate and acute. Her American ally, called upon to intervene, perceived and portrayed the threat as benign and hence not requiring immediate action.

Having saved the regime, why did the Soviets risk confrontation by rolling Israel back to the canal? In terms of the rules of intersuperpower behavior, it seems reasonable that the Americans and the Soviets could "agree" on the Egyptian right to control her own air space. Also, having intervened to protect the hinterland and observed the U.S. response, the Soviets may have felt confident that the rules were being adhered to. Another explanation is that having intervened, the Russians were anxious to arrest the fighting. The surest way to do so may have been to make it impossible for the Israelis to continue.[221]

219. On such "rules" guiding superpower intervention, see Barry M. Blechman, "Outside Military Forces in Third-World Conflicts," in *Third-World Conflict and International Security*, pt. 1 Adelphi Paper no. 166 (London, 1981); James M. McConnell, "The 'Rules of the Game': A Theory on the Practice of Superpower Naval Diplomacy," in Bradford Dismukes and James M. McConnell, eds., *Soviet Naval Diplomacy* (New York, 1979). In the same volume, see also Bradford Dismukes, "Large-Scale Intervention Ashore: Soviet Air Defense Forces in Egypt."

220. See Meir, in *Maariv*, 30 June 1970; Menahem Begin, in *Maariv*, 4 May 1970; Eban, in *Haaretz*, 30 May 1970; Bar-Siman-Tov, *Israeli-Egyptian War*, p. 156.

221. Given these calculations and advantages in intervention, the Soviets may also have enjoyed the aggressor's advantage in a game of Chicken. Once they were in first, they were in the position of having thrown out the steering wheel.

In the post–cease-fire period Egypt received at least tacit Soviet support for her violations, whereas Israel could not mobilize the United States to oppose them. We may explain this Soviet acquiescence as we did earlier intervention. Egyptian violations were occurring on Egyptian soil and were *not* strategically threatening to Israel. Furthermore, a cease-fire was in place, and the previous moves had so upset the local balance that the threshold of any Israeli military response must have appeared very high.

The U.S. refusal to respond may be explained by the vested interest in the "American" peace process set into motion with Rogers II. As a result, when "the Israelis complained almost immediately about Egyptian violations, U.S. officials were in no mood to listen."[222] And as Nixon later explained: even a violated cease-fire "established the United States as the honest broker accepted by both sides."[223] What we have here, again, is a classic problem of intra-alliance perception. Because interests diverged so acutely, the violated state could not get its ally even to admit that the violations had occurred.

DOMESTIC FACTORS

At the end of the Six Day War, Egypt's was a troubled polity under substantial stress. One could observe scheming and plotting within the military and government in 1967–68; student riots in February and November 1968; a precipitous loss of faith in the armed forces; and a decline of faith in, and deference to, the regime. Egypt's youth were demanding basic changes in the political culture: freedom of expression and the press, the right to participate, equality and distribution of power, and an end to governmental corruption. The domestic debate raged over questions of political economy, with competing sectoral demands for income, and over the more general questions of whether to favor consumption, security, or investment.[224] Symptomatic of the regime's difficulties were its decisions to bribe the middle class by promoting private consumption at the expense of investment.[225] Also telling were the appeals to Muslim traditionalists for the first time since the early 1950s—in order to "neutralize the appeal of counter-elites."[226]

Israeli countervalue threats and action only helped Egypt overcome these centrifugal forces and divert attention from domestic problems.

---

222. Spiegel, *Other Arab-Israeli Conflict*, p. 195.

223. Quoted in ibid.

224. On the regime's problems in the postwar period, see Dekmejian, *Egypt under Nassir*, chap. 13; Ajami, *Arab Predicament*, pp. 84–94; Stephens, *Nasser*, pp. 532–37; *MER* (1968), pp. 779–808.

225. On postwar economic policy see Mark N. Cooper, *The Transformation of Egypt* (London, 1982), chap. 4; Ajami, *Arab Predicament*, p. 91.

226. Dekmejian, *Egypt under Nassir*, p. 252.

Naturally, it is difficult to separate Israeli countervalue from counter-force actions. Israel's entire grand strategy was, in a sense, counter-value, depending as it did on occupation of Egyptian territory, closure of the canal, and the threat to the regime's integrity. But some of the actions were most explicitly and violently countervalue, such as deep commando raids against economic targets, shelling of the canal cities, and strategic bombing. These actions only helped integrate Egyptian society behind the regime. For example, the November 1968 riots, which were in large measure a demand for domestic change, were also a response to Israel's recent raid at Naj Hamadi; and many of the de-mands made through these riots were for a more active anti-Israeli posture.[227] Heykal later remarked of Israeli raids: "This threat to the irrigation system touched the deepest instincts of the Egyptians."[228]

Strategic bombing allowed Nasser to make a credible case that Israel's war was a total war against Egypt's national and political integrity. Avi Shlaim and Raymond Tanter describe the effects of the bombing: "Far from discrediting Nasser and undermining his credibility as the Israelis hoped, the raids helped to make Nasser the symbol of courageous resistance and an indispensible leader at a time of national crisis."[229] As for the shelling of the canal cities: the half million refugees turned their hatred against Israel instead of Nasser.[230] In any event, by 1969 the domestic crisis had entirely given way to preoccupation with the war.[231] Gen. (Res.) Mordechai Gur told me what he learned from the period: "Countervalue operations in the War of Attrition were a serious error. The effect [of countervalue actions] with conventional weapons is the opposite of that intended."[232] Given the lessons of strategic bombing in World War II and Vietnam we are not surprised that a nation did not disintegrate under countervalue pressure. But what we have here is even more extreme: a society in domestic trouble was actually pulled (or pushed?) together by this external pressure.

Several peculiarities of the Egyptian polity, society, and culture com-bined with this more universal process to exacerbate substantially Is-rael's deterrence problem. The authoritarian and centralized nature of the state made it possible, for example, to uproot over half a million

---

227. Mahmoud Hussein, *L'Egypte,* vol. 2, *1967–1973* (Paris, 1975), pp. 45–46.

228. Heykal, *Road to Ramadan,* p. 55.

229. Shlaim and Tanter, "Decision Process, Choice, and Consequences," pp. 498–99. See also Ajami, *Arab Predicament,* p. 92.

230. On Nasser's hopes that creation of refugees would frustrate the Egyptian people, creating even more hatred of Israel, see Schiff, *Knafayim me'al Suez,* p. 43.

231. *MER* (1969–70), pp. 1227, 1230–46.

232. Interviewed in Jerusalem, 14 November 1984. In 1968–69 Gur was commander, IDF forces, in Gaza and Northern Sinai. In 1974 he became IDF chief of staff.

residents of the canal cities, resettle them, find them employment, and set up or expand educational and health services for them where necessary.[233] The regime was also able to pick up and move intact part of the industrial plant from the canal zone. Thus, by explicit policy, Nasser was able both to signal his country's relative willingness to suffer and to remove whatever hostages Israel felt it had.[234]

The regime also had the capacity to impose perpetual military service. After the defeat in 1967 the Egyptians basically ceased discharging soldiers from active duty, a policy that continued until the Yom Kippur War. The advantages are obivous: the Egyptian army very rapidly returned to its prewar strength and continued to grow until it reached eight hundred thousand in 1973.[235]

Another monopoly the state enjoyed was of information. This created a serious obstacle to Israeli deterrence by demonstration, for the regime refused to show or advertise Israeli achievements through the national media. A cursory browsing of the press coverage during the period shows consistent Egyptian overstatement of their achievements and understatement of their casualties. A blatant example is the coverage of the first Naj Hamadi raid in October 1968. The Egyptians denied both that serious damage was done and that it was performed by a commando unit, insisting that it had been performed by "a lone plane."[236] In the air war the problem was as severe if not more so. For example, in all of the aerial encounters between March and July 1969, the IAF lost one plane, a spotter. The Egyptians reported that they had shot down twenty-nine! The EAF lost fifteen aircraft but reported only one damaged.[237]

Unfortunately, the problem was not confined to centralized and controlled disinformation. Behavior in the military reflected a deeper cultural problem: the Egyptian army and air force were lying to themselves and to the regime—pathological behavior that also obstructed Israeli communication. For example, in the spring of 1969 the Egyptian army reported that 60 percent of the Bar Lev Line had been destroyed. In March 1969, Egyptian scouts reported that the IDF was in a terrible state on the east bank. This may have influenced Nasser's decision to launch

233. For Nasser's hold on the instruments of power, see Dekmejian, *Egypt under Nassir*, p. 252; Lacouture, *Nasser*, pp. 314–18; Stephens, *Nasser*, pp. 542–44.

234. *MER* (1969–70), pp. 1238–39; *Al-Ahram*, 8 August 1969.

235. *MER* (1968), p. 817; el-Shazli, *Crossing of the Suez*, p. 22; Heykal, *Road to Ramadan*, pp. 204–5.

236. *MER* (1968), pp. 361–62. For similar behavior after an Israeli commando raid on high-tension wires in Upper Egypt on 30 June 1969, see *MER* (1969–70), p. 130.

237. *MER* (1969–70), pp. 128–29, 172–73.

his four-step program.[238] Egyptian Air Force behavior was similar. According to Schiff young pilots believed their more senior officers, who filed false reports of successful missions to the general staff. Also, some falsification was actually initiated at the top, as unearned medals were given out in the interest of general morale.[239]

Finally, instead of drawing conclusions about the strategic balance from various spectacularly successful Israeli operations, the Egyptians simply replaced the commanders who disgraced the homeland. In the three-year period we are considering, the EAF had four commanders. When the IAF buzzed Cairo in June, the Egyptians sacked EAF chief Mustafah Hinnawi and the commander of the anti-aircraft command.[240] After the armored raid in September 1969, Nasser dismissed his chief of staff, Ismail Ali, commander of the navy, and fifty other officers including the commander of the Red Sea Theater. Such a reaction is not unique to the Egyptian armed forces; I believe that it is universal. A large military organization is not likely to draw general conclusions about its overall quality and relative power from particular incidents in which one or some of its units perform poorly.

Israel emerged from the Six Day War powerful, confident, and unified. By the summer of 1970 she had drifted into loss of confidence and nerve and political disunity expressed in the disintegration of the National Unity Government. One difficulty in maintaining unity for this war was that it was just not a war of national survival or of vital interests. But there were also particular political, social, and cultural characteristics that made it extremely difficult to execute Israel's deterrent threats.

One such detrimental characteristic was Israel's democratic nature. With little patience for institutional deceit or excessive censorship, the Israeli public simply knew what was happening at the canal, of the successes and failures, of the numbers of casualties. In the free and open Israeli press, doubts were expressed, amplified, and made available to both the Egyptian challenger and the Israeli government.

As early as May 1969 sarcastic jokes and a new catchphrase made the rounds of the Israeli street and got into the press: "What will be the end?" or "When will it end?!" Writing in June 1969, Gen. (Res.) Uzi Narkiss described the atmosphere: "Things have reached a state where certain groups of our people have come to require constant injections of moral encouragement to prevent a sudden decline in their faith in our

238. See Dayan's direct warning to Nasser not to believe his army's reports: *Haaretz*, 19 May 1969. See also, Schiff, *Knafayim me'al Suez*, pp. 20–21.
239. Schiff, *Knafayim me'al Suez*, pp. 36–40.
240. Ibid., p. 119.

military strength. . . . It seems that we need to be assured every week that the difference between our strength and that of the enemy is as it always was and has not changed."[241]

There were other public phenomena unique to a democracy. In the spring of 1970 a number of protest movements became active; most prominent among these were the new-left radical movements, Siah and Matspen.[242] After Meir and the cabinet apparently refused to allow Nahum Goldmann to travel to Cairo to talk with Nasser, groups of high school seniors published letters to the prime minister. This was highly exceptional in the Israeli experience. One example:

> We, a group of high school students who are about to enter military service in Tsahal [IDF], protest the Government's policy in the Gold-mann-Nasser talks affair. Until now we believed that we were going to fight and serve our country for years because there was no alternative. This affair proved that, when there was an alternative, even the slightest one, it was ignored. In the light of this we and many others wonder whether to fight a permanent and endless war while our Government directs its policy in such a way that the chances for peace are missed. We call upon the Government to exploit every opportunity and every chance for peace.[243]

Such letters, signed by children of prominent political leaders, raised a public furor and caused shock and dismay among the political elite.

The goring of the sacred cow of defense and security was apparent in one more new phenomenon: the satiric, antiestablishment play. "The Queen of the Bathtub" was dramatized by the prestigious government-supported troupe the Kameri. The play was a broadside attack on everything hallowed: government decision making, the military, the treatment of Arabs, the imperative of the war.

Meir and Dayan as well as leaders of the right were taken aback by these expressions of disappointment and pressures to stop the war. Even if they did not represent majority views, it was the nature of an open society to amplify and dwell on these symptoms of a lost consensus.[244] According to Dan Margalit, these phenomena did not go

241. *Maariv*, 19 June 1969, trans. by Khalidi, "War of Attrition," p. 83.

242. Brecher, *Decisions in Israel's Foreign Policy*, pp. 462–63. These movements were the Israeli response to the European radical new-left of the 1960s.

243. Quoted in ibid., p. 463. See also *MER* (1969–70), p. 773. Nahum Goldmann was president of the World Jewish Congress. On the Goldmann affair, see Gazit, *Tahalikh ha-Shalom*, pp. 42–52; Margalit, *Sheder meha-Bayit ha-Lavan*, pp. 84–95.

244. See Dayan's comments on "The Queen of the Bathtub," in *Maariv*, 17 June 1970. For the intense pressure felt by the political leadership, see Margalit, *Sheder meha-Bayit ha-Lavan*, p. 96; Teveth, *Moshe Dayan*, pp. 596–97; Brecher, *Decisions in Israel's Foreign Policy*, p. 463; Safran, *Israel*, p. 442.

unnoticed in Cairo. He describes one meeting between Nasser and Western journalists where Nasser told them that a country whose newspapers publish the photographs of the previous day's casualties every morning cannot hope to win a low-level, protracted war.[245]

Except for the amplifying effect of the media and the society's openness, how do we explain the propensity for demoralization in this war? Especially because of the striking results of the Six Day War in 1967, Israelis had learned to expect decisive victory after short, intensive efforts that demanded few sacrifices. Israeli military doctrine has traditionally reflected an aversion to high casualty rates, a factor that became more important when survival was no longer the issue.[246] Heykal had been right, it seems, when he wrote in 1969 that one of Egypt's advantages in the coming war would be Israel's inability to handle a protracted engagement of continuous casualties. But even Heykal must have been surprised, for he had predicted that Israel would capitulate after sustaining 10,000 casualties.[247] In fact, Israel sustained 738 deaths in three years on all fronts together, only 375 of these on the Egyptian frontier.[248]

Weizman's accounts support the notion that the national elite had become spoiled as well, expecting easy and capital-intensive victories and unable to handle the efforts and sacrifices required in a "real" war. In discussing the decision to accept the cease-fire Weizman wrote, "It was the first time in the history of Israel and the IDF, that the inability to win a war or make any gains . . . was explained by technological deficiencies or the lack of this weapon or another. . . . From the great faith in our ability to defeat the Arabs even if we don't have this weapon or another . . . were left only the words."[249] Perhaps a more general case can be made that Israeli society is at a decided disadvantage in waging protracted war because of its Western and developed nature. The willingness of Israelis to kill and die and to suffer familial disruptions, tensions, and material deprivations is substantially poorer than that of her less Western and less developed (or industrialized) neighbors.[250]

The IDF also contributed to Israel's difficulties. The ethos of winning through offensive action was so ingrained and internalized that both at

245. Margalit, *Sheder meha-Bayit ha-Lavan*, p. 215.

246. For a general discussion of this point, see Ben-Horin and Posen, *Israel's Strategic Doctrine*, pp. 21–23.

247. *Al-Ahram*, 7 March 1969. At the same time, the Egyptian chief of staff claimed that seven Israeli deaths per day would put a rapid end to the war; see Zeev Schiff, *October Earthquake*, trans. by Louis Williams (Tel-Aviv, 1974), p. 10.

248. Wallach, Lissak, and Shamir, *Atlas Carta: Assor Sheni*, p. 103.

249. Weizman, *Lekha Shamayim Lekha Aretz*, p. 318.

250. See Khalidi's discussion in "War of Attrition," pp. 86–87.

the front and in the general staff there was constant and persistent pressure to attack, retaliate, escalate, and pursue victory. In Gen. Nathan Sharony's opinion, "much of the escalation was because of commanders in the field: Their need to react, to prevail, to reply. . . . the problem of prestige at the tactical level." Similar pressures were felt in Tel-Aviv.[251]

The effect of these structural and attitudinal attributes was to make Israel unable to pursue the two major principles of her deterrence strategy: frustration and pacification. Israel was incapable of simply sitting at the canal and taking a beating; so, when it hurt, her leaders strove to escape it. At first, the Israeli military and political leadership tried to escape the beating by escalating in search of victory, and they did so as long as this option appeared viable. In July 1970, when escalation had proven destructive and no longer seemed possible, the Israelis scrambled to escape the beating by capitulating and agreeing to an unfavorable cease-fire.

Power Asymmetries

At the end of the Six Day War the IDF sat on the banks of the Suez Canal. It had just destroyed seven hundred of Egypt's thirteen hundred tanks, and with them the integrity of most her ground force units. The IAF had destroyed 356 of Egypt's 431 combat aircraft.[252] The remaining Egyptian forces had to regroup just meters away from the Israelis and, together with the vast civilian population of the canal cities, sat within striking range of Israeli fire. The entire desert buffer now served Israeli defense. Unfortunately, the new disposition of forces undermined Israel's ability to deter low-level violence. This new geographic arrangement combined with Egypt's astounding ability to reconstruct and develop her forces and mobilize Russia's to render Israeli deterrent threats hollow or irrelevant.

Egypt had two major resources at her disposal in rebuilding and then sustaining and increasing her military power after the Six Day War: the Soviet Union and her own population. With massive Soviet capital transfers the Egyptians were able to reconstruct the pre-June army

251. Sharony is not implying that officers waged private wars, rather that the predisposition to active offense prevailed throughout the IDF and that senior officers were much influenced by the field commanders. In the mid-1970s Gen. (Res.) Sharony was chief of planning in the general staff. (Interviewed in Tel-Aviv, 23 November 1984.) Of a similar opinion was Gen. (Res.) Ahron Yariv. (Interviewed in Tel-Aviv, 18 November 1984.)

252. Dupuy, *Elusive Victory*, pp. 333, 337.

within one year. The immediate resupply was not always a one-for-one replacement, but the weapons sent were often newer. For example, not all of the lost tanks were replaced, but of the five hundred new tanks, four hundred T-54/55s replaced older T-34s. The EAF rapidly recovered its numerical strength; in the one year after the war its inventory of combat aircraft rose to about four hundred.[253]

Estimates of the monetary value of Soviet assistance between 1967 and 1970 vary and are complicated. But the orders of magnitude are in the billions of dollars, and as far as we know these transfers were free of (economic) charge or on long-term credit.[254] In trying to improve the quality of the Egyptian forces rapidly, the Soviets also transferred skills. In 1968 they provided advanced training to three hundred Egyptian pilots and two-to-three thousand advisers to the Egyptian ground forces.[255]

In discussing political asymmetries I noted that in the entire three-year period Israel received relatively little from the United States. The two agreements for arms sales during the relevant period were John-son's decision to execute a 1966 accord on forty-eight Skyhawks and his decision in late 1968 to sell fifty-eight Phantoms. Deliveries on both were slow. Phantom delivery only began in the fall of 1969 and had not been completed by late spring 1970.

One important effect of these transfers was that the two societies were required to shoulder highly disparate burdens. Egypt, with a GNP about one and one-half times as large as Israel's, was able to spend roughly as much as Israel on defense. Thus, the defense burden as a percentage of GNP was higher for Israel even though the Egyptian armed forces were undergoing rapid growth and the Israelis moderate growth at best (table 11).

Two more facts intervened to raise Israel's defense burden with but small power returns. The added territory with its blessing of strategic depth also created long internal lines of communication. The strategic implication was that it would be difficult in a future war to transfer troops rapidly between fronts. Israel had to start thinking in terms of fighting on at least two substantial fronts simultaneously. Thus, *effec-*

253. On the rearming of the Egyptians after the Six Day War, see Glassman, *Arms for the Arabs*, chap. 4; Rubinstein, *Red Star on the Nile*, pp. 29–31; Brecher, *Foreign Policy System of Israel*, pp. 87–89; *MER* (1967), p. 11; *MER* (1968), pp. 36–37.

254. For a discussion of the difficulty of assessing the value of Soviet aid, see Yair Evron, "Arms Races in the Middle East and Some Arms Control Measures Related to Them," in Gabriel Sheffer, ed., *Dynamics of a Conflict: A Reexamination of the Arab-Israeli Conflict* (Atlantic Highlands, N.J., 1975), pp. 100–1. See also Rubinstein, *Red Star on the Nile*, p. 81; *MER* (1967), pp. 11–12; *MER* (1968), pp. 36–37.

255. *MER* (1967), p. 12; *MER* (1968), pp. 35–36.

Table 11. Defense expenditures and burdens,
Israel and Egypt, 1966–1971

	In millions of U.S. dollars*		As % of GNP	
	Israel	Egypt	Israel	Egypt
1966	365	516	11	12
1967	562	718	16	12
1968	730	740	18	13
1969	955	836	22	17
1970	1278	1263	25	19
1971	1370	1450	24	21

Reprinted by permission of Transaction, Inc.,
from *From June to October: The Middle East between
1967 and 1973*, ed. Rabinovich and H. Shaked.
Copyright © 1978 by Transaction, Inc.
*At 1970 prices and 1970 exchange rates.

tively, the army had shrunk and would have to grow numerically to meet the same tasks as before.[256] In addition, after experiencing the French arms embargo in 1967, there was pressure in Israel to pursue self-reliance in arms production. The result was diversion of resources for investment in the local arms industry.[257]

Not only could Egypt outspend while underspending, she could do so while keeping virtually her entire army mobilized, a feat Israel could never match. The population difference between the two countries was tremendous: 32 million Egyptians versus 2.7 million Jewish Israelis. For Egypt, 200,000 people under arms represented 0.6 percent of the population, not an unreasonable burden for a state at war. For Israel an equivalent mobilization would have represented 7 percent of the population—a burden obviously untenable and therefore never attempted in the context of protracted war.

Turning our attention to the situation at the Suez Canal, we wonder: Why should Egypt have felt so confident in waging a protracted war of attrition or a shorter, limited offensive as planned in the spring of 1969? And why were they not dissuaded by experience? Looking at the local power balance, the Egyptians must have believed they had an absurd advantage (table 12). By early 1969 six Egyptian divisions organized into two army groups were deployed on the west bank. They had five hundred to six hundred artillery pieces and many hundreds of mortars.

256. Safran, *Israel*, p. 259; *Haaretz*, 7 June 1968. In his interview, Gen. (Res.) Gur complained that indeed this was the lesson but that Israel did not learn it very well.
257. Evron, "Arms Races in the Middle East," pp. 104–5.

Table 12. The Egyptian-Israeli military balance, 1967–1970

	July 1967*		July 1968		July 1969		July 1970	
	Israel	Egypt	Israel	Egypt	Israel	Egypt	Israel	Egypt
Total manpower	275,000†	140,000	275,000†	211,000	290,000†	207,000	300,000†	280,000
Ground forces								
Infantry brigades	4	Approx. 10	6	16	4	17 + 1‡	4	26
Commando battalions	—	10	—	10	—	10	—	18
Armor brigades	3	2	3	6	2	6 + 2‡	2	9
	(+22 reserve)§		(+24 reserve)§		(+26 reserve)§		(+26 reserve)§	
Tanks	990	370	800	700	1020	900	1050	1300(+)
Artillery	250 s.p.	650	250 s.p.	750	300 s.p.	700	300 s.p.	1500
Air forces								
Combat craft	230	225	270	400	275‖	400	330#	415**
SAM launchers	50 Hawk	120 SAM-2	50 Hawk	180 SAM-2	100 Hawk	180 SAM-2	~100 Hawk	250 SAM-2

Source: Institute for Strategic Studies (London). *The Military Balance* for 1967–68, 1968–69, 1969–70, 1970–71.

Note: All unit numbers are for regular forces except where stated otherwise.

*Represents the balance prevailing on 30 June 1967, including arms delivered after the Six Day War.

†Includes reserves.

‡In development.

§Combined armor and infantry.

‖Includes 48 Skyhawk A-4s.

#Includes 36 Phantom F-4s and 67 A-4s.

**Plus 22 SAM-3 sites manned by Soviets and 100 Soviet-flown MIG-21s.

Opposite them the Israelis deployed one to two brigades, with but a very small number of self-propelled guns and perhaps scores of mortars. In considering a protracted war, this balance of forces must have been even more tempting given that Israel could not upset it (by reserve mobilization) for any length of time. As Weizman remarked acidly, "It was impossible . . . when the Egyptians fired from 500 cannons, to return fire from 5—and say: 'The IDF returned fire to the sources of fire,' as though it were serious."[258]

This imbalance of forces must also have tempted the Egyptians to think in terms of a limited crossing. How could one Israeli division (in spring 1969) be expected to prevent crossing completely on a front 200 kilometers long?[259] Another temptation must have been the proximity of the forces. Getting into a position to engage the Israelis was not a major strategic or even tactical decision such as moving troops into or across the Sinai had been before June 1967. The enemy was "there," 150 meters away.

In considering a protracted war it was reasonable to conclude that Israel would not be able to utilize many of her outstanding advantages in overcoming the shear quantitative imbalance. The ability to mobilize quickly was meaningless because Israel could not remain mobilized for long, and the critical test was endurance. Accurate and real-time intelligence would not help in a static war of little troop movements, for there would be no real "main efforts" to detect. It would be extremely difficult to predict a limited crossing because no substantial troop movements would have to precede it. In a war of limited movement Israel's advantages in offensive mobile warfare—such as tactical flexibility, combined arms operations, initiative and intuition, and logistic competence—would not show up. Higher skill levels and advanced technologies were also less important in static warfare that relied on masses of firepower. The small Israeli artillery force may have been agile, accurate, and fast. What exactly could it do to six divisions and six hundred guns?

The Suez Canal as a barrier, together with Egypt's dense defense, helped maintain these Israeli disadvantages. As long as the war was kept at a low level it was guaranteed to remain static because casual Israeli crossings to conduct mobile warfare were highly unlikely. Israeli threats to inflict serious damage, to prevail, or to frustrate were therefore incredible. This situation created heavy pressure on Israel to take the highly escalatory step of introducing the IAF.

258. Weizman, *Lekha Shamayim Lekha Aretz*, p. 311.
259. Yaniv, "Harta'ah ve-Haganah ba-Estrategiya ha-Yisraelit," p. 36.

What of the Israeli threat to introduce its air force, and its effect once applied? The Egyptian expectation in 1968–69 that air power would not be decisive in the coming war was reasonable. Because they had such a quantitative advantage on the ground, they did not require freedom of aerial action over the canal. What Egypt needed was to deny the IAF that freedom. With three hundred new pilots, Soviet advisers, and a radar and SAM system in place, the Egyptians expected that in a standing war they would be able to prevent free IAF aerial action.[260] Furthermore, neither the Israelis nor the Egyptians believed initially that air power could be decisive or even very effective against well-dug-in ground targets.[261]

Once belligerence of a serious nature began, the Egyptians exhibited a remarkable ability to adapt to proven Israeli capabilities, especially air power. When the IAF concentrated on artillery in spring and summer 1969, the Egyptians substituted mortar and light arms fire, to great effect. Later, they simply learned to cope with IAF attacks and resumed and increased artillery activity. This underscores the technological and organizational simplicity of a war of attrition: even under considerable pressure it is possible to maintain the rather simple tasks of small-unit firing activities. When the IAF did become a serious problem and Egypt decided to evict it from the local air space, she sought and found a technological solution. Ultimately, after much experimentation, the dense-pack, ripple-fire approach proved effective.

Thus, for the most part the balance of immediate and mobilizable power and the geographic disposition rendered Israel's threats to frustrate, prevail, or even defend irrelevant to low-level and protracted violence. Further, the nature of protracted low-level violence made it possible for the Egyptians to experiment, learn, and design around Israeli attempts to prove the opposite.

So far I have presented Israel's deterrence disadvantages in a protracted low-level war. But Israel's traditional threat, at least between 1957 and 1967, was to act preemptively and mobilize, attack, and destroy the Egyptian (or any other Arab) army caught preparing a major challenge. Implicit was precisely a threat not to agree to a war of attrition. What happened to this threat after 1967? The answer lies to a large extent in the new geographic arrangement.

The major reason that a preemptive blitzkrieg was no longer a cred-

260. Schiff, *Knafayim me'al Suez*, p. 23.

261. On the Israeli astonishment at the effectiveness, see Bar-Siman-Tov, *Israeli-Egyptian War*, p. 89.

ible threat is that the Israelis themselves ceased to see in it a necessity. In the wake of the Six Day War a new concept came into Israeli strategic thinking: secure borders. Eban defined these in 1969 as "borders which can be defended without a preemptive initiative."[262] Although there was no consensus on the location of such borders, it appears that the Suez Canal was considerably further *west* than the future border envisioned by any significant political group, left or right.[263]

Even if Israel had insisted on applying the traditional doctrine she would have found much of its logic undermined by the new physical realities. What, for example, would be Israel's casus belli when facing an opponent whose forces are perpetually mobilized on her own territory and deployed so close to Israel's? The problem for intelligence I have already mentioned: how to know to mobilize, given no warning space? It is interesting to note that whatever warning time Israel had gained in the air she had lost on the ground.

The canal barrier and the dense and massive Egyptian deployment combined to render the prospect of a full-scale Israeli crossing highly unlikely. The Egyptians correctly believed that the Israelis would not try to negotiate a 150–200-meter deep-water obstacle with forces enough to overcome six divisions, only to fall into a nation of thirty million people. In any event, there was no way for the Israelis to effect a surprise attack. How do you secretly mobilize a number of divisions, transport them across the Sinai, and then surprise a permanently deployed army? The Israelis themselves believed in it so little that they did not really bother to develop amphibious, bridging, or water-crossing capabilities—a fact that surely did not go unnoticed.[264]

Enhanced security margins were also instrumental in Israel's failed attempt to deter Soviet intervention. With the battle taking place so far away from Israel proper, the rules of the game of superpower intervention were operative. Israel could not convince the United States that Soviet actions were placing her in strategic peril, and the Soviets, by limiting their intervention to SAMs and Mig-21 interceptors 300 kilometers from Israel, made it unambiguously defensive and nonthreatening. The Egyptians and Soviets would not have had this advantage were the confrontation taking place across the pre–June 1967 frontier.

262. *Maariv*, 6 June 1969. See Horowitz, *Israel's Concept of Defensible Borders*, pp. 13–14. On the demise of the offensive imperative in Israeli thinking after the Six Day War, see idem, *Hatfisa ha-Yisraelit shel Bitachon Leumi*, pp. 35–36.

263. Brecher, *Decisions in Israel's Foreign Policy*, pp. 460–62.

264. The IDF did not begin to develop its water-crossing capabilities seriously until 1971–72. Even in the Yom Kippur War the IDF's capabilities were still limited. See Adan, *On the Banks of the Suez*, chap. 21; Weizman, *Lekha Shamayim Lekha Aretz*, p. 305.

Escalation and Brinkmanship

We need devote but little attention to the problem of brinkmanship and downward convertibility, for it is clear that brinkmanship, in this case, was the tool of the challenger, not the defender. Egypt, and not Israel, was likely to gain by creating a risk of uncontrolled escalation. In the event of a credible or real risk, the superpowers, fearing a direct confrontation, could be expected to intervene directly, probably by forcing an unconditional Israeli withdrawal. Egypt's advantage was further enhanced by the distribution of risk. Escalation did not endanger Egypt, but rather the Soviets and Americans, and as far as Egypt was concerned directly, there was little risk in it. For Israel, though, uncontrolled escalation was anathema, and her leaders worked hard to communicate that the situation was under control.

In reality Israel did escalate, but the process only confirmed that things were well under control. Escalatory steps were gradual and deliberate, each taken after long and painful soul-searching. In a process that took three years Israel went slowly through the stages of counterforce reactive operations on the ground, countervalue reactive operations (first at the canal and then deep in Egypt), and initiated counterforce ground operations. Finally, Israel activated the air force, but even then the slow, methodical process continued: demonstrations of superiority in air battles over the gulf, tactical and reactive use at the canal, offensive and initiated use at the canal, and finally, strategic bombing. Even this last step was taken with considerable care: in-depth bombing was confined to counterforce targets and was not extensive, and after the mishap at Abu Zabal it was further restricted. All the while, Israeli leaders gave a running commentary to the effect that these escalations were only tactical and temporary and would eventually lead to de-escalation. This state was obviously neither crazy nor out of control.

Israel did try to "talk" brinkmanship after direct Soviet intervention in 1970, warning of the potentially dire outcome for world security of a Soviet-Israeli confrontation. The results vindicated the logic of her approach until then: the United States intervened to make sure that conflict would remain under control by imposing on Israel an unfavorable cease-fire.

Had she wanted to, Israel probably could have set in motion a process of rapid bilateral escalation against her own interests and despite superpower constraints, but most likely this would have been confined to operations with the regular army. Ultimately, she still would have reached the threshold of massive reserve mobilization, for without it the limits to threatening action were severe. Although a decision to mobi-

lize could have been made, it was not one Israel could have inadvertently slipped into. Reserve mobilization was too significant a step. And
finally, even if the threat of inadvertent escalation beyond the brink
could have been made credible, the Egyptians, for reasons of relative
power and geography, had little reason to fear the outcome of a general
war. Thus, as in the previous case, the process and destination of Israeli
brinkmanship would have to have been neither credible nor very threatening.

Undoubtedly, Israeli escalatory violence was painful to Egypt. But
the latter's response suggests severe limits to the deterrent use of incre-
mental escalation, which in this case both influenced and *immunized* the
Egyptians. Each new Israeli escalatory step did have a deterrent effect
on Egyptian behavior, but it quickly dissipated as the Egyptians learned
to live with whatever the new level or form of violence happened to be.

When in the summer and early fall of 1967 the IDF inadvertently hit a
number of civilian targets in the canal cities, the Egyptians ceased fire
for a month but at the same time decided to evacuate the cities. Then,
when the Egyptians sank the INS Eilat and Israel responded with a
premeditated shelling of the refineries and cities, the Egyptians, quite
taken aback, ceased fire for nearly a year, during which they continued
to evacuate the cities. By fall 1968 they were apparently willing to live
with Israeli countervalue shelling and restarted attrition. When Israel
then resorted to countervalue shelling and the Naj Hamadi in-depth
commando raid, it was the latter innovation that impressed the Egyptians, who ceased fire until March 1969. In March, willing to live with
both in-depth raids—"pinpricks," as Weizman called them—and shelling, the Egyptians began in earnest. When going back to shelling and
raids was unsuccessful and Israel resorted to air power, the Egyptian
army quickly learned to live with air raids. First it substituted mortar
and small arms fire for artillery, then later in the spring even the artillery
learned to operate under the IAF's wrath. Finally, when Israel turned to
strategic bombing, the Egyptian regime exploited that for national unification. As for the Egyptian people themselves, after a while they
became apathetic and simply learned to ignore the Israeli bombing.[265]

Because incrementalism serves to immunize a challenger and the
effect of escalation is but temporary, a defender may wish to consider
the following questions when formulating deterrence policy:

1. Would a massive escalation be preferable to a series of small and
   careful steps? and
2. If rapid and massive escalation is undesirable or impossible,

265. *MER* (1969–70), p. 1242.

[197]

would living with low-level violence be preferable to self-defeating gradual escalation?

A defender who opts for escalation should consider *ahead* of time:

3. How can the *temporary* disorienting and deterrent effect of escalation be taken advantage of, for example to pursue diplomacy or conciliation?

Deterrence, Spiraling, and De-escalation

Everything so far suggests that Israel was in a spiral with Egypt. In other words, all her attempts to deter were misplaced and led to greater violence. In a sense, Egypt felt the pressure of a security dilemma: every Israeli step to enhance or provide deterrence was threatening to Egypt and induced a greater, more violent, challenge. Ultimately, spiraling revolutionized the conflict when the Soviets intervened. A spiral implies the potential for constructive conciliation, for despiraling; and from a policy perspective the question of real interest is whether it would have been possible for Israel to induce cooperative or at least nonbelligerent behavior through de-escalation.

Actually, much of Israel's behavior can be interpreted and was intended as conciliation, and it is interesting to consider its failure. Does failure suggest that the only possible spiral direction was up? If not, what would it have taken to conciliate successfully? From the Israeli perspective the entire policy of slow and reluctant escalation reflected a desire to conciliate. Israeli leaders thought that if the IDF did the minimum necessary to protect and ensure the status quo, then it could induce either pacification or at least minimal belligerence. But it did not work. In General Sharony's words, "We tried everything: non-response to provocation, measured response, strong response and finally took the initiative—it made no difference."[266]

Most instructive in this regard is the action–reaction cycle surrounding the construction of the Bar Lev Line. The IDF built the line in response to Egyptian shelling so that it could hold on to the status quo. The Egyptians, in turn, saw the line as a concrete indication of Israel's intention to occupy the Sinai perpetually. According to a number of sources, this perception accelerated Nasser's decision to launch the offensive of spring 1969.[267]

266. Interview, 23 November 1984.
267. Haim Herzog, *War of Atonement*, p. 8. According to Schiff, *Knafayim me'al Suez*, p. 21, it was the near completion of the line that accelerated the Egyptian decision in spring 1969; Bar-Siman-Tov, *Israeli-Egyptian War*, p. 46.

The key word is "accelerated," for the real culprit was the status quo. From the Egyptian perspective, challenging it was ultimately unavoidable. Not only was it unavoidable, but the pressure to challenge was bound to grow with time, whose very passage was not neutral, as Heykal's words indicate: "The solution is more distant even if only due to the passage of time."[268] So, even had the Israelis merely sat at the canal and not fired a shot, they could not have avoided an Egyptian challenge. There was, in sum, no real option for *tactical* despiraling.

To be efficacious, concilation must appeal to an opponent's interests; to promise the Egyptians nonviolence was obviously no such appeal. Could Israel have reached basic Egyptian interests? Were there missed opportunities? One such was perhaps the 1968 Egyptian attempt to reopen the canal. Possibly, as Weizman and Yair Evron claim, Israel could have created an Egyptian interest in pacification by allowing the canal to reopen and the region to flourish.[269] But optimists beware. Indeed reopening the canal was an Egyptian and even a Soviet interest.[270] But as Nasser amply demonstrated, he was willing to sacrifice some interests for other, more vital ones: evicting Israel was worth the creation of half a million refugees. Had Israel allowed the canal to reopen and then merely continued to sit on its east bank, the quiet most probably would not have lasted long.

There are two arguments in favor of such an Israeli policy in the face of dismal prospects: First, measurement and comparison of interests is most difficult. Second, one can reasonably expect that as circumstances change so may interests. Therefore, it is conceivable that opening the canal would have created strong Egyptian and foreign, especially Soviet, interests in keeping it open. In any event, the potential costs of experimentation would seem to have been low. There was little to be lost by trying.

If the prospects of tactical conciliation seemed poor, did Israel have a real option for strategic constructive appeasement? The answer is yes. In a historically unique situation, Israel was in a position to relinquish enough territory to appease Egypt without incurring unacceptable risks for herself. With the Sinai to return, Yehoshafat Harkabi's earlier depiction of the situation, that "any concession which may weaken Israel is too big for her; for the Arabs it is too small if it leaves the existence of Israel intact,"[271] no longer held true.

As I indicated in describing Nasser's theory of stages, the Egyptians

268. Quoted in *MER* (1968), pp. 207–8.

269. See Weizman in *Maariv*, 4 June 1971; Evron, *Middle East*, pp. 92–94.

270. On the Soviet interest, see analysis in *Observer*, 27 October 1968, in *MER* (1968), p. 17; Evron, *Middle East*, p. 106.

271. Quoted in Jabber, *Israel and Nuclear Weapons*, p. 103.

had apparently lost interest in even discussing the destruction of Israel; they were interested in the return of their land. But more important, Israel was in a position to behave as though this were true, be found wrong, yet run almost no strategic risk. Israel could have recreated the pre-1967 situation: a demilitarized Sinai, operative casus belli, and the necessary spatial and temporal requirements to wage a preemptive blitzkrieg if necessary. Perhaps the most attractive aspect of the situation is that it lent itself to *unilateralism*. Because of the relatively low risk involved, Israel was in a position to get around the need to develop mutual trust and to dispense with lengthy negotiations and interminable attempts to assess true intentions. Israel could simply have withdrawn and announced her terms.

If the policy is so obvious, why was it not adopted? One level of explanation is domestic politics. Margalit has written that "a wide government must tread a narrow path,"[272] an apt characterization of Israel's National Unity Government at the time. Even though it could agree on the general principle of withdrawal, it could never have agreed on how far. Adopting the demand for direct negotiations and true peace in return for withdrawal was a way of avoiding concrete, disintegrating decisions.[273]

The decision to mobilize and activate conventional forces is a difficult one, as I have both asserted and observed. This inherent difficulty had two different effects on Israeli thought, both inimical to the idea of withdrawal, unilateral or otherwise. One was the determination, once having decided to mobilize and fight in June 1967, to make the most of it. Quoting Ben-Gurion, Heykal explained the Israeli leaders' dilemma: "If we withdraw and there is no peace treaty with the Arabs, what will we have gained from the Six-Day War? We will only have proved that Moshe Dayan is an efficient general."[274]

The other effect was to create Israeli insecurity about the credibility of her own commitments to react automatically and preemptively to casus belli, especially should the Egyptians engage in salami remilitarization of the Sinai. For the Israelis, a major lesson of the Six Day War may have been not that Israel preempted Egyptian aggression to protect her interests but that it took three weeks and much agony and political disruption to do so.[275]

272. Margalit, *Sheder meha-Bayit ha-Lavan*, p. 122.

273. On the decision-making problems of the National Unity Government, see Brecher, *Decisions in Israel's Foreign Policy*, p. 460; Aronson, *Conflict and Bargaining*, pp. 90, 103–9.

274. In Rubinstein, *Red Star on the Nile*, p. 54.

275. On the lengthy and messy political process leading to the Israeli decision in June 1967, see Michael Brecher, *Decisions in Crisis: Israel, 1967 and 1973* (Berkeley and Los Angeles, 1980), chap. 5; Safran, *Israel*, pp. 395–413.

Thus, as we have noticed before, in conventional contexts there may be a general preference to err on the side of deterrence. The danger in a low-level, protracted war that is *certain* but far away seems preferable to the risk of a strategic war close to home even with a high probability of no war at all.

Reputation and Knowledge

The Israelis and Egyptians lacked common knowledge in a number of important areas, but it would be wrong to argue that correcting these deficiencies would have enhanced deterrence. Both sides in fact attempted to improve the other's knowledge and understanding, but to no avail. Examination of what was (and was not) known and communicated shows that

1. knowledge was as useful for destroying deterrence as for its creation;
2. the Egyptians knew the critical facts necessary to decide in principle to challenge; knowing more would have induced a greater challenge sooner; and
3. had the Israelis known more, they could not have improved deterrence. Perhaps they could have decided to try appeasement instead.

Many were the gaps in Egyptian knowledge about Israeli capabilities and threats. At the strategic level, for example, they did not believe that Israel could survive and persist in such a long low-level war. They also did not seem to foresee any of the Israeli escalations and were surprised by each one. They were most astonished by the first shelling of the refineries, the first Naj Hamadi raid, and the introduction of the IAF. Finally, they did not suspect that the IAF could be as effective as it turned out to be against ground targets. Regarding their allies, the Egyptians were disappointed with their inability to mobilize the Arab system, for they had not expected such difficulties.

Israeli deterrence policy was largely education policy. The IDF set out to teach the Egyptians of its superiority in general and of specifics such as air power, IDF stubbornness, and Egyptian vulnerability. The Egyptians observed the lessons and instead of drawing the Israeli conclusions, drew their own, using the knowledge gained to alter their challenges where necessary. This propensity suggests that, had the Egyptians known ahead of time all that they learned gradually, they probably would have launched the Yom Kippur War *sooner* than they did. In other words, enhanced knowledge would have provoked deterrence failure sooner and at a higher level of challenge.

[201]

The reason enhanced knowledge of these particular facts could not have improved deterrence is that the Egyptians possessed the basic knowledge necessary for a decision to challenge. Interestingly, this knowledge was general, precision was unimportant, and Israel could not influence it. For example, the Egyptians may have underestimated the strength of Israel's power interest in the occupation but did understand that the general balance of interests favored Egypt. Perhaps they did not foresee the scenario of Soviet intervention, but they seem to have understood all along that the Soviets would simply not let them fall. They did not foresee Israel's ability to hang on for such a long war but understood that Israel was too sensitive to casualties and attrition to be able to outlast them. They also understood that Israel could not and would not wage a general offensive war across the canal.

Despite Egyptian attempts to educate, Israeli understanding of the Egyptians was poor. The Israelis never quite understood the significance of Egypt's willingness to sacrifice the canal cities, sustain thousands of casualties, keep the Suez Canal closed, and suffer deep raids. But even had she understood the signals, or even had she known in advance Egypt's reactions to her own moves, could she have used this knowledge to enhance deterrence? Searching for an alternative deterrence policy under the existing circumstances is a barren exercise. What could Israel have done with the knowledge that her small and gradual escalations were bound not to work, if with that knowledge came the fact of Soviet intervention and American abandonment in response to precipitous actions? Or how could Israel have adapted to a recognition of the strength of balance of interests? The only conceivable conclusion that could have come with a perfection of Israeli understanding is that deterrence was hopeless, that Israel had a choice—in the short run at least—between living with protracted war and appeasement and that, in the long run, the only way to avoid war was conciliation.

In this case as in the previous one, enhanced detailed knowledge on either side would not have improved the prospects of deterrence. In such circumstances defender and analyst naturally seek refuge in general knowledge, in threats made credible by reputation. Yigal Allon wrote in 1968 that "the victory of 1967 provides a new possibility for the IDF to sustain its credibility and enhances the hope that it will serve as a deterrent to prevent war or be decisive should the enemy opt for war."[276] Many Israeli leaders believed that the reputation for both willingness to go to war and the executive ability to win spectacular victories was finally in place by 9 June 1967.

They were to be severely disappointed. As after the 1948 war the

276. Allon, *Massakh shel Khol*, p. 397.

Table 13. Approximate land and air force strengths of participants, Six Day War (1967)

	Israel	Arabs	Egypt	Jordan	Syria
Mobilized operational manpower	250,000	328,000	210,000	55,000	63,000
Brigades	25	42	22	10	12
Artillery pieces	700*	960	575	263	315
Tanks	1,000	2,330	1,300	288	750
APCs	1,500	1,845	1,050	210	585
SAMs	50	160	160	0	0
Antiaircraft guns	550	2,000(+)	950	143	1,000
Combat aircraft	286	682†	431	18	127

Source: Trevor N. Dupuy, *Elusive Victory: The Arab-Israeli Wars, 1947–1974* (Fairfax, Va: HERO Books), p. 337. Reprinted by permission of HERO Books.
*This figure is from Wallach, Lissak, and Shamir, *Atlas Carta: Assor Sheni*, p. 56.
†Including 106 Iraqi aircraft.

game changed very rapidly, and the Egyptians were reluctant to learn general lessons from their most recent defeat. The reputation established served the new deterrence problem poorly.

First, why should the 1967 victory have been so impressive? The story is well known so I can be brief. In June 1967, Israel faced a mobilized armed coalition of three states: Egypt, Syria, and Jordan. The relative arsenals were most asymmetric, as table 13 shows. In the crisis that developed after mid-May it became readily apparent that Israel was on her own and unable to mobilize any outside balancers. Despite these disadvantages Israel managed virtually to destroy all three air forces and defeat the three armies in six days, while occupying vast tracts of her opponents' land, in effect quadrupling her territory. Any preexisting doubts about the professionalism of a reserve army, with which the Arabs surely had had no experience of their own, should have been dispelled by the demonstrated ability to mobilize a citizens' militia quickly and wage a complicated high-technology war of rapid movement.[277] Israel also demonstrated the ability to take advantage of short internal lines of communication and to move units between fronts as tactically required. Finally, Israel showed a willingness to go to war independently, despite the conditions set down by Ben-Gurion that major military action should only be initiated if supported by a major extraregional power.[278]

Of the three fronts, it was specifically against Egypt that Israel's reputation should have been made.[279] The spectacular preemptive air

277. Safran, *Israel*, p. 259.
278. Aronson, *Conflict and Bargaining*, pp. 16, 64.
279. The following discussion of the Six Day War is based on Dupuy, *Elusive Victory*, pp. 231–79; Herzog, *Arab-Israeli Wars*, pp. 145–66; Wallach, Lissak, and Shamir, *Atlas Carta: Assor Sheni*, pp. 54–66.

attack of 5 June was mostly against the EAF. In three hours the IAF flew five hundred sorties against nineteen air fields, destroying some three hundred aircraft on the ground. By the end of the war, the EAF had lost fifty more planes in air battles. On the ground, the Egyptians had deployed six regular divisions and assorted other forces. In these forces there were over one thousand tanks and six hundred artillery pieces. The IDF Southern Command consisted of three divisions and two independent brigades, with seven hundred tanks and 320 field guns.

The Israeli operation was a classic blitzkrieg in a number of respects. The divisions of Tal, Sharon, and Yoffe barreled across the Sinai in a three-pronged attack. The main operational principle was first to achieve maximum penetration in a short time. This was to cause disarray and collapse of the Egyptian forces (not their destruction) and to provide the IDF with control of territory. Once in control of the terrain the IDF could destroy the disorganized and retreating Egyptian forces at leisure. When attacking Egyptian units the Israeli forces relied on the indirect approach in large measure, often attacking at night, from behind, or across terrain considered impassable. Egyptian resistance was essentially broken by the end of the second day, when a hysterical chief of staff Abdul Hakim Amer ordered a general retreat. On 8 June after four days of fighting, the first IDF troops reached the Suez Canal. A day later the third Sinai Campaign was over.

The Egyptians immediately resorted to rhetorical and psychological denial of their humiliation by Israel. *Nakhsa* was the term preferred by Nasser to describe the outcome of the June War. It means "a setback," and its use instead of *hazima* ("defeat") was an attempt to impute a minimal and temporary character to the debacle.[280] Another psychological and semantic adjustment of the defeat was to portray Israel's war aims as having been far greater than her achievements. Heykal argued that "the military shock was intended to destroy the domestic front" and that Israel had desired to "crush the socialist revolution." But, went his argument, Egypt had successfully thwarted Israel's pursuit of these war aims and so could claim a victory of sorts.[281]

In examining the war itself, Heykal claimed that "the Arab force was compelled to suffer defeat without war," and that therefore "Israel gained a victory without justice."[282] As the Egyptian leadership portrayed the war, because of the preemptive air attack of 5 June,[283] the

280. Yehoshafat Harkabi, *Lekakh ha-Aravim mi-Tvusatam* [Arab lessons from their defeat] (Tel-Aviv, 1969), pp. 38–39.
281. *MER* (1967), p. 249.
282. Quoted in Harkabi, *Lekakh ha-Aravim mi-Tvusatam*, p. 42.
283. *MER* (1967), pp. 249–50.

hysterical retreat ordered by Amer, and the intrusion of the super-powers, there had been no land war to speak of and so no real Israeli victory.

Introduction of the superpowers as explanation, a definite echo of past apologies, was a convenient way to externalize guilt to factors exogenous to the bilateral relationship, thus making the outcome *not* a reflection of relative Egyptian-Israeli capabilities. During the war and immeditely thereafter, the Egyptians charged the United States with direct participation. Another complaint was that Egypt had lost the initiative because Nasser had heeded Soviet and American exhortations not to attack and had believed their promises to oppose whoever initi-ated hostilities.[284]

In explaining the defeat the Egyptians concentrated more on self-examination than on Israeli superiority. What they saw in the mirror was a set of specific, sometimes episodic, and always *correctible* deficien-cies, be they technological, behavioral, or organizational. A defeat caused by episodic or correctible problems, once those are rectified, is clearly not generalizable. According to Nasser, at the critical, basic, and most important level, nothing was wrong: "The men, when given an opportunity to fight, did so like men," and "the fighting qualities of our men were not a factor in the defeat."[285] Heykal wrote:

> If the reasons for the catastrophe of last June stem from the men and their capacity, there is no chance for us in this generation and perhaps for many generations to come. But if the reasons are the failure of methods, and the inability of the command to use its human and material resources, reform is possible. I do not believe . . . that it was a matter of human quality, for . . . the men fought heroically . . . whenever there was a chance of meeting the enemy on equal terms.[286]

At the episodic level of explanation we find references to such events as Amer's being in the air on a flight to Sinai precisely when Israel attacked.[287] At the behavioral level, the regime found fault in the deci-sions, actions, and general attitudes of officers at all levels. Com-manders were portrayed as having betrayed the revolution, sought privileges instead of duties, and being generally decadent.[288] Sadat explained the defeat: "It was all a question of negligence on the part of the command."[289]

284. Ibid., p. 253.
285. Quoted in ibid., p. 251.
286. Ibid.
287. Harkabi, *Lekakh ha-Aravim mi-Tvusatam*, p. 40.
288. *MER* (1967), pp. 250–51.
289. el-Sadat, *In Search of Identity*, p. 185.

Well, if officers were to blame, then they would have to go. After the war hundreds, including Amer and other generals, were forced to resign. In the autumn, in an act of scapegoating and national catharsis, leading commanders—especially of the EAF—stood trial for the negligence of June.[290] Blame was thus located, proven, and punished. With the guilty removed, a new beginning could be made.

In the fall Nasser began to effect the necessary organizational changes. The three services were combined under one staff, much greater emphasis than before was placed on training and exercises, and it was decided to draft university graduates into the army. In November 1967, Nasser said that "this reorganization was not a mere change of command, it was deeper and more thorough. The aim was that the armed forces would be truly armed forces."[291] In January 1969, Nasser could say, "The armed forces—and I am speaking on this matter from personal impression and from what I have seen—are now in a condition which cannot be compared to their condition before the 1967 War or after it."[292]

If there was a chance for Israel to develop a mythological reputation, it would have been for her air power. But instead of learning general lessons, the Egyptians immediately began to offset the specific advantages the IAF demonstrated in the Six Day War. The danger of losing the air force to surprise attack they minimized by building five hundred underground concrete bunkers for aircraft and dispersing the fleet to many air bases. In addition, they covered the country with radar and surrounded installations with SAM batteries.[293] Radar and SAMs had not really been tested in the 1967 war.

Weizman wrote in 1970 that "the ratio, in the case of a future war, between attacking enemy air forces on the ground and their engagement in the air, will be different. If in the Six Day War 90 percent of the airplanes were destroyed on the ground and 10 percent in the air, it is possible that in the future the ratio will be equal [1:1]. It is difficult to determine doctrine ahead of time for such a development."[294] But the relative aptitude for aerial combat had not really been established in the June war, and with three hundred newly trained pilots, the Egyptians, not unreasonably, felt confident in engaging the IAF in the air. Another

290. On the purge and trials, see *MER* (1967), pp. 557–58.
291. On the various changes mentioned, see *MER* (1967), pp. 572–73; *MER* (1968), pp. 815–18. Both Dekmejian, *Egypt under Nassir*, pp. 256–67, and Herzog, *War of Atonement*, pp. 13–14, remark that substantial behavioral changes were indeed effected.
292. Quoted in Harkabi, *Lekakh ha-Aravim mi-Tvusatam*, p. 44.
293. el-Shazli, *Crossing of the Suez*, p. 19.
294. Weizman, Preface to Schiff, *Knafayim me'al Suez*, pp. 15–16.

source of confidence was the growing imbalance of arsenals. While the Egyptian inventory of Mig-21 interceptors rose steadily and rapidly after the war, Israel did not receive a single supersonic jet until fall 1969.

Finally, given the different requirements of air power in a static war of attrition, the Egyptians, with their superior quantities of artillery and other ground forces, only really required that the IAF not be free to attack at will in a narrow, well-defined area west of the canal. Even in this discrete area, they did not need to control the skies in the classic sense.

How about Israel's capacity for preemptive blitzkrieg? It should suffice to recall, from the details of change, that in both will and skill the demonstration of June 1967 was irrelevant to the postwar situation. The will to mobilize and preempt could not be the same when the state's survival was not at stake. The ability and willingness to cross the canal and blitz across Egypt proper could not be deduced from the performance in the Sinai Desert in June.

What we have been observing is a process in which psychological denial, objective changes, and purposeful lesson learning and adaptation combined to render the postwar situation unique, not similar to that of the Six Day War. Israel's reputation, therefore, was not effective—except negatively in that the Egyptians did successfully play to Israel's reputational *disadvantages* such as her sensitivity to casualties.

The discussion of reputational effects yields conclusions similar to those of the discussion of despiraling. Israel could have extracted maximal utility from its 1967 reputation by recreating the pre-June conditions—by withdrawing. Naturally, the pre-June conditions could not be perfectly recreated because the war had obviously taught the Egyptians many lessons. But consider all the Egyptians would have had to learn and implement before they could feel confident in confronting the Israelis in another war of movement in the Sinai. Deterrence, one suspects, might have lasted longer than the ten weeks that it actually held after the Six Day War.

Success or Failure

Conclusions about the success or failure of Israeli deterrence in this case are highly sensitive to relativistic notions such as level of challenge or time frame. If the impression so far is of an unmitigated failure of deterrence, then it is time for some positive notes. There is little doubt that in the post-1967 period Israel successfully deterred any Egyptian challenge to her existence. Before 1967 the destruction of Israel, while not a primary item on Egypt's agenda, was also not considered impossible, and the challenge could be made, as in May–June 1967. No more. After the Six Day War, Egypt geared its entire national energy to recapturing the Sinai. Furthermore, Egypt did not consider herself capable of realizing even this limited aim in a purely military fashion and devised a *political*-military strategy. Thus, the persistent low-level challenge between 1967 and 1970—a deterrence failure—coexisted with success at the highest strategic level. Not only was the three-year war a concomitant failure and success, but within the period challenge (or failure) commuted across levels in response to Israeli deterrent activity. When, in 1969, Israel successfully and actively deterred Nasser's plan to launch a limited crossing, he adopted a static war of attrition. The latter, therefore, reflected both a deterrence success and failure.

Various Israeli moves of escalation throughout the 1967–70 period resulted in short-term pacification. Unfortunately, these pacific periods were exploited for digesting lessons and preparing for future violence. Also, these quiet periods became ever shorter. The shelling in 1967 produced a year of quiet; Naj Hamadi yielded four months. In 1969 and 1970, introduction of the IAF and the spectacular commando raids had but limited impacts on the volume of activity, effects that lasted days or at most two weeks. If we take a monthly perspective beginning in March 1969 (figure 2), the curve of Egyptian activity shows a nearly monotonic rise through July 1970.

Extending the discussion into the period between 1970 and the Yom Kippur War throws additional light on the effects of the level of armed conflict (or challenge) and the time frame. The historical study suggests that it would be wrong to consider the cease-fire of August 1970 a deterrence success, but we could argue that it was followed by three years of silence and hence should qualify. Such an argument would be bolstered by the fact that Egypt accepted the cease-fire when under substantial military pressure, attrited, and ready to stop. But if we look at the conditions created by the cease-fire and at how the Egyptians used the lessons of the War of Attrition in the next three years, we should conclude that the three-year break in the fighting was similar to the short-term pacifications during the period of attrition itself.

The Egyptians accepted the cease-fire in a position of local strategic superiority. In its wake they advanced the missile system to finalize and cap this achievement. Thus, in August and September 1970, silence at one level of belligerence was merely a cover for challenge at another, in this case higher and more significant. It is also interesting that the "cold" challenge was more serious than the apparently deterred "hot" challenge at the canal. Most important is that the cease-fire did not signal or reflect the surrender of Egypt's strategic goal or even a change

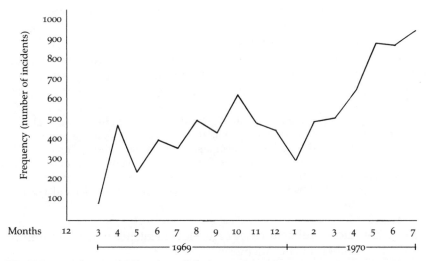

Figure 2. Frequency of incidents initiated by the United Arab Republic, March 1969–July 1970. From Daniel Dishon, ed., *Middle East Record,* vol. 5 (1969–70) (Jerusalem: Israel Universities Press, 1977), p. 167.

in its basic strategic concept. What it did was provide an opportunity for Egypt to learn the lessons of the War of Attrition and to prepare to implement them.

The Egyptians concluded that the next challenge should be one large, concentrated, and highly destabilizing operation. Their conviction was that attrition was not really useful because it did not provide a "victory" or sufficiently upset the local balance. Sadat believed that in order to be effective, the operation had to be large enough "to prove that the 'invincible Israel' was a mere illusion."[295]

The Egyptians also decided that the operation should also be sufficiently destabilizing to engage the United States. Explained strategist Hassan el-Badri, "One element of the Arab objective was to offer the United States the choice either of taking the long-delayed action on an implicit commitment to force Israel to evacuate the Arab territories or to expose U.S. interests in the Arab world to real danger."[296]

Failure throughout the 1967–70 period to activate the Eastern Front may also have taught the need for a large and concentrated operation. Israeli Gen. Dov Tamari has suggested that, even though Syria may

295. Quoted in John W. Amos, *Arab-Israeli Military/Political Relations: Arab Perceptions and the Politics of Escalation* (New York, 1979), p. 139.

296. Hassan el-Badri, Taha el-Magdoub, and Mohammed Dia el-Din Zohdi, *The Ramadan War, 1973* (Dunn Loring, Va., 1978), p. 17.

have been reluctant to go to war in 1973, as a leading rejectionist Assad could not afford to stand by while the "traitorous" Egyptians launched a major attack on the Zionists.[297]

Contributing to the decision to launch a major operation in 1973 was the deterrent effect of the attrition experience. Egyptian minister of war Gen. Ahmed Ismail explained:

> My view was that the War of Attrition had achieved its aims . . . and also that Israel would not acquiesce to its resumption, so that any attempt on our part to revert to it would meet a stronger reaction from Israel. This meant that I was faced with the possibility of engaging in small operations in which I should encounter a big reaction from the enemy—much bigger than was justified by their political and military value. So I ruled out a war of attrition.[298]

Thus, the successful deterrence of *low*-level violence may have contributed to a higher level challenge.

An important political lesson of the period of attrition was that the Soviet presence, while reassuring in defense, imposed serious constraints on offensive action. In July 1972, Sadat expelled the Soviets from Egypt, gaining in their departure the necessary independence.

The Egyptians also learned a number of more narrowly military lessons. One contributed to the decision for a large operation: attrition had not really allowed the Egyptians to take advantage of their quantitative superiority, the thinness of the Israeli deployment along the canal, and Israel's long internal lines of communication. Offensive action on a broad front would.[299] Also, the experience of commando raids had taught the Egyptians that it was possible to cross the canal between the Bar Lev strongholds and enjoy substantial freedom of action once on the east bank. On Yom Kippur they would cross between the maozim and not make their capture a precondition for crossing or advancing.

The question of air superiority remained critical, yet the War of Attrition had taught two important lessons: that (and how) the IAF could be neutralized by the use of SAMs and that soldiers, once dug in, could withstand air attacks. These lessons provided encouragement and guidance in devising the operational plans for the Yom Kippur War.[300]

Finally, the War of Attrition taught the Egyptians that Israel *does* indeed execute countervalue threats. In the three years before the Yom Kippur War, the Egyptians went to great lengths to extract from the

297. Interview, Ramat Hasharon, 3 November 1984.
298. Quoted in Amos, *Arab-Israeli Military/Political Relations*, p. 142.
299. el-Badri, el-Magdoub, and el-Din Zohdi, *The Ramadan War*, p. 23.
300. el-Shazli, *Crossing of the Suez*, pp. 6, 80.

Soviet Union weapons that could provide a countervalue threat against Israel. In 1973, Sadat finally obtained SCUD surface-to-surface missiles.[301] And it is a fact that in the war Israel attacked strategic targets in Syria but not in Egypt.

Whether we see in the entire six-year episode (of July 1967 through October 1973) a deterrence success or failure depends on how we view the Yom Kippur War. In the war's aftermath Israeli society was in trauma, believing that Israel had been on "the verge of total disaster."[302] In its wake, Chief of Staff David Elazar was fired, and in 1974 Meir's government fell. Israelis, I believe, misunderstood the Egyptian challenge.

True, Egypt waged a large campaign against Israel, committing ten divisions to the war. But examination of Egyptian war plans shows that even with ten divisions, and even when Syria assisted with an "Eastern Front," Egyptian plans were limited to capturing a narrow strip of land on the east bank of the canal.[303] This was no threat to Israel's survival, and she was on the verge of no disaster; Israel's strategic deterrence was secure and robust.

In sum, the Yom Kippur War reflects both deterrence success and failure. The particular magnitude of the Egyptian challenge was a deterrence failure securely in place between two successes: one at the highest strategic level, the other at the lower level of protracted attrition. Speaking about the Yom Kippur War to a group of officers in 1978, Rabin said, "For deterrence is not all or nothing. . . . There is no deterrence that can present in one 'blow' such potential power that would cause the other side to surrender; the question is whether it deflected him to a less dangerous [challenge]." It did.

301. el-Sadat, *In Search of Identity*, p. 220; Herzog, *Arab-Israeli Wars*, p. 228; Glassman, *Arms for the Arabs*, pp. 95–96, 101–2.

302. Safran, *Israel*, p. 185.

303. On the Yom Kippur War as a campaign with "limited aims," see Mearsheimer, *Conventional Deterrence*, pp. 155–64.

[5]

Conclusions

In this book I have undertaken two closely related tasks: to take a step in the development of conventional deterrence theory and to write part of a critical history of Israel's deterrence experience. My three-stage approach was to (a) develop a preliminary set of ideas, variables, and terms; (b) use these to execute a historical study; and (c) use the experience of historical application to assess the prospects for theory and draw specific and general conclusions about conventional deterrence. This chapter is the third stage.

I argued in chapter 1 that conventional deterrence is much more complex than its nuclear analogue. The logic and simplicity of mutual nuclear deterrence rest on the inescapability of the game of Chicken imposed by mutual fear of inadvertent escalation to Armageddon. The mere shared knowledge that two protagonists possess nuclear weapons greatly simplifies the rest of the knowledge requirements. Neither the details of capability nor rationality are important to the robustness of mutual deterrence. An aggressor's handicap prevails, and the status quo is preserved.

A number of attributes of conventional force and its application deny conventional deterrence this simple logic. It is difficult to inflict substantial punishment with nonnuclear forces: they are competitive in application, allow for discriminatory use, and are critically additive (highly sensitive to size), expensive and difficult to use, and constantly changing. These attributes lead to the conclusion that force may be useful at many levels and for many purposes, that a conventional relationship is not necessarily dominated by fear and therefore may have a structure different from a game of Chicken. The immediate implication is that details about will and skill of the protagonists dominate the analysis. In other words, defender and challenger must share immense amounts of detailed knowledge for deterrent threats to be relevant and credible. Because of the difficulty of generating and communicating so much information, scholars and policy makers need a framework for knowledge that will simplify the task.

Partly influenced by systems approaches, I suggested that structural analysis could provide such a framework. Because this study is a preliminary probe, I defined structure broadly, to include relative interests, external political relations and constraints, domestically rooted constraints and possibilities, and facts of geography and of physical and military power. Analyzing these produced specific propositions about conventional deterrence and the contribution of various structural arrangements to its success and failure. At times, naturally, deterrent threats are rendered irrelevant or incredible by the balance or nature of power, the balance of interests, or other structural conditions of a bilateral relationship. Furthermore, shared knowledge about these conditions is often elusive, and their effects on deterrence are often ambiguous. Perhaps most interesting is that there are strong incentives for both challenger and defender to create ambiguities and deliberately destroy common knowledge.

To overcome such problems, a defender has a choice of strategems: escalation and brinkmanship or reputation. Escalation is an instrument for intentionally altering the nature of a bilateral relationship or for clarifying and demonstrating ambiguous aspects of it such as the balance of interests or power. Brinkmanship is achieved through escalation, but its purpose is to simplify any relationship by converting it into a game of Chicken, with its robust status quo. Brinkmanship employs the threat of inadvertent and uncontrolled escalation to a conflict with unacceptable costs. Reputation should allow a defender to simplify the requirements of shared knowledge by creating a general appreciation of relative will and skill without depending on detail or specific circumstances. A given reputation must predate the crisis in which it would be useful.

An integral part of any theory should be its boundary: a definition of where or under what conditions it is not relevant or useful. I tried to establish the boundary of conventional deterrence theory by distinguishing spiraling from deterrence. If we follow this line of thought, a state has two basic choices in dissuading others from using violence against it: deterrence or appeasement. Misapplied deterrence of a potentially friendly state leads to an upward spiral of hostility; misapplied appeasement of an aggressor leads to defeat. By this reasoning, a spiral means deterrence has been applied when it is not relevant. Thus examining a spiral may be a good starting point for establishing the boundary of deterrence theory.

Finally, the dependent variable of interest in any study of deterrence must surely be success or failure. In conventional deterrence situations relativistic notions of success and failure should provide more insight than the yes/no options of the nuclear world. When we consider any outcome of conventional deterrence, assessment of success should vary with level of challenge and time frame.

This line of reasoning gave rise to a framework of analysis consisting of seven categories or sets of questions, to which I subjected each case. Here are some generalizations based on this experience. The excursion through Israeli experiences is a heuristic. At the highest level of analysis there are findings *about* the utility and structure of deterrence theory. At another, lower level there are a number of specific suggestions regarding the workings of deterrence and the application of the various variables—that is, findings *within* deterrence theory. Before presenting those detailed conclusions, let me first discuss the major findings about the utility of the theory developed here and its possible improvement.

FINDINGS ABOUT DETERRENCE THEORY

The boundary of deterrence theory was not identified by the model because deterrence and conciliation do not cover the universe of possible dissuasive choices in a conventionally armed world, at least not in a simple either/or manner, and not every challenger can be dissuaded. Because of the utility of force at various levels and for assorted purposes, different levels of conflict may occur at the same time. There are thus situations in which both deterrence and conciliation are simultaneously relevant and others in which neither is.

Ideally, I would have liked to find the "yellow brick road" toward parsimonious predictive theory. Alas, from this study it appears that the prospects for doing so are not good, at least from this approach. Parsimony was to be achieved by resorting for explanation to the structural variables of interests, political asymmetries, and power imbalances. The case studies show that these variables are most difficult to measure, their values ambiguous to analyst and protagonist alike. As predictors of deterrence failure or success, their utility is elusive because at times the causal relationship is reversed. Force is often used in a conscious effort to manipulate the structure of a relationship—to generate political support, alter alliance systems, or even to upset the balance of power.

[214]

Similarly, the strategies of escalation and reputation proved to be chained to the structural variables and incapable of completely escaping the latters' complexity, ambiguity, and density of detail. Hence these, too, fail to contribute meaningfully to parsimony or prediction. Despite limited utility of reputation, the case studies left little doubt as to its centrality to deterrence. Problems of knowledge associated with virtually every structural and choice variable constantly referred analysis to reputation. In the future a major area of study must be the creation and decay of reputations and the implications for deterrence in "virgin" conflicts, those with little or no histories of challenge and response.

Another obstacle to sharp predictive theory is the soft nature of the dependent variable, success. The study experimented with relativistic notions of success and failure and found them to be appropriate and even of critical importance to understanding conventional deterrence. Using various time frames of analysis or considering different levels of violent challenge within a given relationship greatly alters conclusions about success or failure. Also, the outcomes of deterrence at various levels of challenge and in different time frames are highly interdependent. Success at one level may actually cause failure at another; success now may cause failure later.

If the theoretical framework developed here is not likely to produce laws of deterrence success, it does contribute to the understanding of conventional deterrence. We have at least made some progress toward *explanation*.[1]

Deductive development of a framework of variables, and certain expectations about them and their application to historical cases, has provided an improved idea of how to use these variables and how much they explain. Application of the framework also produced some general policy implications and recommendations, presented in detail shortly.

The process of trying out the framework for analysis generated suggestions for its improvement, two of them significant. Discussions of interests, the international system, domestic politics, the efficacy of escalation, and reputation demonstrated that psychological or cultural analyses have the potential for explaining much of success or failure in conventional deterrence. There may be no escape from giving these a bigger part in such theory. Unfortunately, great dangers are involved, for undertaking rigorous and detailed psychological analysis in addition to the existing framework might render theory too rich, detailed, and, in the end, intractable. This issue must be sorted out in the future.

1. For a discussion of laws and theories in international relations, see Kenneth N. Waltz, "Theory of International Relations," in Fred I. Greenstein and Nelson W. Polsby, eds., *Handbook of Political Science*, vol. 8 (Reading, Mass., 1975), pp. 2–15.

The model looks at each of the three structural variables separately. There is room, it appears, for a more integrated approach. The discussions of interests constantly referred both to domestic and to international politics as generators of stakes and resolve. Analysis of power, too, rested to some extent on understanding domestic and international factors. It may be a helpful simplification to collapse the three structural variables to two—interests and power—and to use political and cultural analyses to help understand and evaluate them.

FINDINGS FROM APPLYING THE MODEL

To bring out the more significant findings in some detail, let me use again the seven categories of analysis to draw central lessons from all three cases, especially where such insight goes beyond the rather extensive analyses given in the case studies themselves.

Relative Interests

Although in the case of Egyptian harassment, relative interests, or resolve of the protagonists, were not a major determinant of deterrence success, in the cases of infiltration from Jordan and Egyptian attrition they were. In the War of Attrition the strength of Egyptian interests was the most dominant element of their bargaining advantage, and it rendered useless every Israeli threat and maneuver. But in trying to apply both intrinsic-power and deterrence-compellence schemes, there were severe obstacles to the ready ordering of interests in all three cases. These ordering difficulties, which affect practitioner as well as analyst, come about because not only do interests, or resolve, govern the use of force, but force is actually applied to demonstrate and alter resolve.

Infiltration from Jordan in the early 1950s raised an important analytic problem in ordering interests. Israel faced two major bargaining partners, causing uncertainty as to whose interests to compare: Israel's and Jordan's? Israel's and the Palestinians'? Jordan's and the Palestinians'? And which to compare: Israel's in frontier pacification and the Palestinians' in violence? Jordan's in domestic stability and Israel's in border pacification? Ultimately, after much experimentation, the Israelis (and with them this writer) stumbled onto the critical set: the relative interests of Jordan and Israel in the status quo. Deterrence depended on Jordan's developing a greater interest than Israel in border pacification.

A similar, rather tricky relationship prevailed across the Gaza frontier in the 1953–54 period, and again the relevant set of protagonists and interests for comparison had to be identified. Four actors were involved: the Palestinians of Gaza, the local Gaza authorities, Cairo, and Jerusalem. The actors whose interests determined the deterrence outcome were Israel and the local Gaza authorities. Again, as in Jordan, successful deterrence was possible when the Gaza authorities developed a greater stake than Israel in border pacification.

The Egyptian blockade of Israeli shipping in the early 1950s demonstrates that even in a more clearly bilateral competition, easy comparability of interests is not guaranteed. For the most part, the blockade served the interests of the Cairo regime in establishing its legitimacy and leadership in Pan-Arab and domestic contexts. Israel's interests were obviously in uninterrupted shipping. I have referred to this as a situation in which the object of violence is not really "between" the protagonists; it renders interests difficult to order.

A priori, one might have expected Israel's intrinsic interest in ship transit to outweigh Egypt's political or power interest in the blockade. If this was so, which is far from clear, it was not obvious to the players and did not receive appropriate expression in Israeli behavior. Most significant, Israel's strong interest in open shipping did not result in a lifting of the blockade, that is, in an Israeli bargaining advantage. Similarly, in the case of Egyptian harassment in 1955–56, one would have expected Israel's intrinsic interests in her territorial integrity to outweigh Egypt's mostly Pan-Arab–induced power or political interests in belligerence. If Israel did enjoy such an advantage, it was not reflected in successful deterrence.

The War of Attrition does provide some evidence for the utility of the intrinsic-power ordering of interests. The object in contention was a directly contested tract of land. One might have expected that Egypt's intrinsic interest would outweigh Israel's power interest in it as a means to direct negotiations and formal peace. In the end, this proved correct. But it is significant that the relative intensities of interests were not clear at the time. The Egyptians had a hard time understanding the strength of Israel's power interests and were thus surprised at her obstinancy, and the Israelis only really understood the lesser relative intensity of their own interests after six years and two wars.

The low-level and conventional arms nature of the confrontations did not oblige the protagonists in these cases to agree on a definition of the status quo. Therefore it was not always possible to decide whether deterrence or compellence was involved, much less to use the distinction to determine who had a bargaining advantage and so predict deterrence success or failure. Another difficulty arose from the simultaneous coexistence of deterrence and compellence within the same relationship but at different levels. At times, Israel was deterring at the tactical level while compelling strategically, or vice versa.

These problems of ambiguity plagued every one of the cases yet came together in the richest blend in the War of Attrition. Israel and Egypt could not agree on a definition of the status quo. For Egypt the relevant status quo was that which had existed before the Six Day War. From Egypt's perspective, therefore, Israel was *compelling* her to accept a revised status quo, be it a new territorial arrangement or formal peace. From Israel's perspective Egypt had proved in May–June 1967 that she herself did not really accept the previous status quo so that there was nothing viable to return to. Because Israel viewed the pre-1967 "arrangement" as merely a staging ground for Egyptian belligerence, she saw her attempt to define a new status quo as really an act of *deterrence*. One possible conclusion is that disagreement over what is involved may help explain failure of deterrence.

The War of Attrition is an excellent example of deterrence and compellence coexisting at different levels. One could argue that the Israelis were engaged in strategic compellence—compelling the Egyptians to redefine the status quo—while at the same time trying to deter Egyptian belligerence at a tactical level. A possible conclusion is that we should expect tactical deterrence to fail when attempted in the context of strategic compellence. This proposition deserves further examination and experimentation in other contexts and conflicts, if only because it restores the accepted order and could thus simplify analysis. If it is possible to ignore the nature of tactical interaction and identify deterrence and compellence by the nature of the strategic relationship, then we may actually have a significant theoretical tool in the deterrence-compellence ordering.

In all three cases Israel the defender was confronted with an intriguing problem: she had challengers whose violence was not aimed at capturing or acquiring—at least in the short run—an object in her possession. A challenger often pursued violence simply to prevent the status quo from becoming recognized or to influence his relationship with actors outside the bilateral context. Although there were disputed objects at times, none was immediately sought, and what had to be deterred was simply violence qua violence. Examples include Egyptian harassment and blockade as a means of improving internal and international legitimacy, Palestinian terrorism in the 1950s to delegitimize the status quo, and Egyptian attrition aimed at influencing Soviet and American thinking. In these examples, Israel had strong interests in nonviolence precisely to establish the legitimacy of the status quo. This put her in a tight spot from a deterrence perspective. Two propositions are suggested: (a) except by threatening very large retaliation, a defender has little hope of deterring by threat of violence a challenger who seeks violence; and (b) where a defender has a strong positive interest in pacification and his challenger has a strong positive interest in fluidity and violence, successful deterrence is unlikely.

Defender and challengers in these cases used force both to demonstrate their own interests and to alter those of opponents, thereby reversing the causal relationship between interests and force. Israel used retaliatory raids to manipulate Hussein's and then the Gaza authorities' interest in border pacification. In the War of Attrition Egypt attempted, in an exercise of controlled pressure, to alter Israeli resolve. Indeed, Israel's demands were devalued from "formal peace" to "cease-fire."

In the War of Attrition, Egypt also acted to raise her side of the interest balance by demonstrating how much she was willing to suffer for the return of the Sinai Peninsula. Nasser accomplished this by accepting destruction of the canal cities and by turning their population into refugees. For her part, Israel has been engaged since the 1950s in a process of education: teaching her neighbors through force just how seriously she takes her interests in freedom of navigation and the integrity of her borders. It is fair to say, I believe, that over time Israel's neighbors have learned well and have been increasingly more respectful of the integrity of Israel's frontiers.

This discussion gives cause both for optimism and for pessimism. On the one hand the fact that force is used to manipulate interests substantially complicates prediction. On the other hand the notion of teaching over time suggests the possibility of establishing a *reputation* for having and being willing to defend certain interests. If such education is indeed possible, then there may be hope of removing some of the ambiguities surrounding the balance of interests and enhancing the utility of this variable.

Political Asymmetries

THE INTERNATIONAL SYSTEM

There can be little doubt that alliances have a critical and visible impact on the success and failure of deterrence. But possession of allies does not represent a straightforward accretion of power to be wielded in deterrent threats, and actuating and mobilizing such power is severely proscribed by a number of rules of alliance behavior. At the extreme, the case studies demonstrate that even where alliances clearly enhance deterrence of one kind of challenge, they may simultaneously *undermine* the deterrence of others. In a given relationship the effect of alliances on deterrence is governed by (a) the structure of the competing alliance systems, including the interests of respective allies; (b) the nature of the defender's deterrent threats, and (c) the universal buck-passing nature of allies.

The dominant fact of all alliances in the Middle East has been the strong commitment of patrons to their clients' survival. This was true of Britain's commitment to Jordanian independence in the 1950s, the Soviet's guarantee of Egyptian integrity after June 1967, and the West's continued commitment to Israel's existence. At the same time, since the two superpowers began directly supporting opposing sides in the conflict in the late 1960s, a critical determinant of their behavior has been their refusal to be dragged into confrontation with each other. A third symmetrical characteristic of the alliance systems is the universal public goods problem: the allies of the protagonists have preferred to do as little as possible for their local allies, especially (but not only) when it might hurt their own interests.

This brings us to the major asymmetry in Middle East alliances: the West has had interests on both sides of the conflict, while the Soviet Union has had real interests only on the Arab—in our cases, Egyptian—side. As a result the Israelis have had no access to their opponents' ally and therefore but little control over the behavior of the United States. The Egyptians could severely influence both U.S. and Soviet behavior by threatening to defect from one to the other. The Soviets have had no access to Israel and hence been more subject to Egyptian control than the United States has been to Israeli leverage.

Divergent interests can also motivate significant perceptual discrepancies between allies. Israel could not convince the United States or Britain to support her exclusively or that her existence was in peril. The clearest manifestation of a perceptual divergence in the 1950s was Israel's failure to extract significant arms transfers or to be permitted to join with any Western nation in a formal alliance. Israeli alarm over the Baghdad Pact and the Czech arms deal was answered with promises that the local strategic balance was being carefully monitored and was in no danger of being upset. Years later in the War of Attrition, when the arming of Israel began to hurt U.S.-Egyptian relations, President Nixon decided to "hold in abeyance" Israel's requests for aircraft. He insisted the local strategic balance was in no danger of turning against Israel, an assessment not shared by Israeli leaders.

Such perceptual divergence raises serious obstacles to the downward convertibility of deterrence. From a Western and, later, U.S. perspective, infiltration and then attrition neither threatened Israel's existence nor were even serious strategic challenges, whereas to Israel they were strategic and of great import. In contemplating a deterrent threat Israeli leaders have been faced with a dilemma, for they have had to forego responding to low-level challenges in order to preserve Western guarantees of Israel's very existence. In sum, not only was high-level deterrence not convertible, but it even inhibited deterrence of low-level challenges.

The problem has been further exacerbated by the nature of Israel's deterrent threats. For reasons of size, economy, and domestic culture and politics, Israel has attempted to threaten *any* challenge with offensive and decisive war. But to do so is to threaten to respond to a low-level challenge, which may not mobilize her own allies, in a manner that *can* elicit alliance support for her challenger. Furthermore, such a response can even turn a defender's ally against him, as in Israel's deterrent activities toward Jordan in the 1950s. The same happened in the War of Attrition as Israeli deterrent escalation both endangered the Nasser regime and threatened to cause direct superpower confrontation. These dynamics also portend difficulties for the deterrence of salami tactics, which can be a high-level challenge in disguise.

The problem of divergent interests and perceptions has also undermined Israeli alliance-based deterrence of strategic challenge, again in interaction with the threat of preemptive war. The best example is the crisis of May–June 1967. If survival is guaranteed by patrons, how do we explain Israel's failure to elicit American action just before the Six Day War? In the prewar period Israelis held an apocalyptic vision of the future. But U.S. leaders remained confident that Israel would prevail even if attacked before she could preempt or, alternatively, that Israel could remain mobilized for months without undue damage to her economy. One reason for American-Israeli perceptual divergences in May–June 1967 is most likely the fact that the crisis period was one of mobilization and troop movements but *not* of violent action. It is more difficult for a patron to deny that a client-ally is in real danger when violent activity puts the client at tangible risk—a serious problem for a state whose deterrent threat is preemptive attack.

A similar problem affected Egyptian-Soviet relations. Egyptian-Soviet perceptual divergences plagued the entire course of the 1967–70 war until Israeli strategic bombing put the Egyptian regime at what appeared to be real risk. Then the Soviets intervened directly on Egypt's behalf. In the 1950s, Jordan was in a situation similar to Israel's. In the event of a major Israeli strike Hussein had no space to trade for time until his British ally could become convinced that he was in peril. This fact contributed to Israel's ability to deter infiltration from Jordan.

In the Yom Kippur War this logic played itself out in a revealing fashion. The Israelis decided not to preempt because they considered it imperative to demonstrate that *they* were being endangered by Syria and Egypt and not vice versa. Establishing this risk was, they assumed, vital for mobilizing American support; and indeed it was Egyptian and Syrian action on Yom Kippur 1973, together with an apparently poor Israeli showing, that elicited U.S. intervention (with arms transfers) on Israel's behalf.

For all the hubris of Pan-Arabism and anti-Zionist concerted action, the record of offensive Arab alliances against Israel has been poor. Alliances for declaration have risen, and resource transfers have been extracted, but alliance for action has been rare. Despite appearances, Israel's deterrence relationship has for the most part been with each Arab state individually. Arab alliances have generally followed the rules of coalition behavior: members pursue their individual interests and pass the buck whenever possible.

The 1948 war, once started, was basically an inter-Arab competition for spoils, with individual, uncoordinated campaigns against Israel. In the early 1950s, Jordan could not expect to receive Arab assistance in defense against Israel, nor could Hussein afford to risk allowing, say, Syrian troops on his territory to fend off an Israeli attack. In 1956, Egypt fought alone. In the early and mid-1960s, Syria could not induce Egypt to fight over Israel's diversion of water from the Jordan River to the Negev. In 1967, Jordan and Syria essentially left Egypt to fight alone, even though Syria had been the instigator of the May–June crisis. In the War of Attrition, Egypt could not induce Syria, Jordan, and Iraq to form an Eastern command and had to fight on her own for three years.

Some cite Egyptian-Syrian cooperation in 1973 as evidence of the ability to actuate an alliance for action and forceful challenge. To some extent the claim is valid, and this alliance demonstrates both the mobilizing power of Pan-Arabism and the damage to deterrence when a two-front alliance is formed. But two points should be made. Jordan refused to join, apparently remaining deterred by the bilateral power relationship with Israel, despite the potential power of a tripartite coalition. As for Syria and Egypt, the Yom Kippur War was a classic alliance due to a temporary convergence of primary national interests best served by cooperation. Because both countries were going to war for vital national interests and to achieve them required surprise, there was no potential gain from buck-passing; hence the close cooperation. Once the initial surprise was achieved, each belligerent went his own way down the military-political path of his choice.

Earlier I suggested that although the use of force is in large measure determined by alliances, at times this relationship is reversed and force is used in a conscious attempt to manipulate alliance systems. The cases include a number of attempts by both Israelis and Arabs to manipulate the behavior of extraregional actors by using force. In the 1950s a number of Israeli theories of action saw reprisals as a means of making it difficult for the United States and Great Britain to put forward unfavorable peace proposals. Reprisals were also used to demonstrate prowess and prove to the French that Israel was a worthwhile potential ally. In the War of Attrition, Egypt used violence in the context of offensive brinkmanship precisely to influence superpower behavior, especially to try to alter U.S. support of Israel. In the Yom Kippur War, Egypt used violence similarly, to change the superpower positions on a Middle East settlement.

Although within the region coalitions have had some effect on the ability to use force against Israel, Arab action against Israel has also been used to manipulate regional allies. In the 1954–56 period Nasser used blockade and direct harassment to enhance his leadership in the Arab system. In the War of Attrition, Egypt anticipated the following cause-and-effect chain: violence on the Western Front would "shame" the Eastern command into action, which would further enhance success on the Western Front. In 1968–69, Egyptian belligerence was in part an attempt not to lose Pan-Arab status to the extremely active Palestinians. In late 1969, Nasser was able to convene the Rabat Summit partly at least because of the Egyptian army's activism along the Suez Canal.

This discussion produces three general lessons about the effect of alliances on deterrence. First, where an ally's immediate interests are not also at risk, or when the ally also has a stake with the challenger, a defender will have serious difficulty in credibly threatening to involve him. Even when an ally does have interests at risk he prefers to pass the buck. In the 1930s, Hitler appears to have understood these principles when he challenged first Czechoslovakia, then Poland, and later France.

A second lesson is that reliance on alliance assistance may actually undermine the credibility and convertibility of deterrent threats. Where an alliance is effective in deterring one level of challenge, it may weaken deterrence at other levels. In the extreme, alliance considerations may force a defender to adopt less effective deterrent threats. France, again in the 1930s, resorted to object denial, instead of a threat to attack, on the theory that her ally, Great Britain, would intervene only if Belgium, France, and therefore Britain herself were in unequivocal danger.

The third lesson stems from the superimposition of superpower mutual nuclear deterrence on local conventional deterrence. When both superpowers are involved in a local confrontation, each backing a different client, constraints are placed on the allowable level of violence. If neither superpower will allow its client to go under, then both acceptable challenge and response are severely limited. For deterrence, this undermines the credibility of large or offensive threats and further dampens the naturally unlikely prospects of inadvertent escalation. In a sense, then, the effect of superpower involvement is to make it *safe* for violence—and so for challenges—of a limited nature.

DOMESTIC FACTORS

Examination of domestic cultures and political systems provides considerable understanding of Israel's deterrence difficulties in a way that suggests a number of universal or general lessons for conventional deterrence. Overall, the divergent internal political-cultural attributes of Israel and her Arab neighbors have undermined the credibility and efficacy of many of Israel's deterrent threats. Perhaps the aspect of Israel's political culture that has most weakened deterrence has been her Western democratic nature. This label subsumes a number of important attributes: decision making that is highly centralized yet subject to public and private debate and pressure; a highly disciplined army; a free and rather adversarial press; high social and political sensitivities to costs in resources, lives, and lifestyle; and political sensitivity to the breakdown of consensus on security questions.

The Israeli threat of reprisal for low-level harassment has been substantially undermined by the nature of decision making and execution. Most decisions on reprisals are made by the cabinet, or at least by the general staff, subject to constraints of the system and public sensitivity to casualties. The disciplined IDF rarely allows for "private" actions. Thus in all three case studies the number of Israeli reprisals turned out to be substantially smaller than the number of provocations. It is telling that the Qibya reprisal, the one most instrumental in creating deterrence, was effective precisely because it so departed from the norm.

The credibility of the Israeli threat to wage large-scale offensive war has been similarly undermined. The need for consensus, public accountability, and the sensitivity to costs have made Israel's few decisions to wage general war very difficult even under the most clear-cut strategic conditions. In 1967, for example, the Israelis spent three weeks building a consensus for war and overcoming the fear of sustaining an expected thirty thousand casualties.

The same traits have made it difficult to project a credible crazy-state image by threatening to respond irrationally to small-scale provocation, though some Israeli leaders and commanders may have tried to nourish just such a loose-cannon image. The most obvious Israeli attempt to cultivate a crazy-state reputation was the Lebanon war of 1982, but the domestic fallout and ensuing fall of Prime Minister Begin and Defense Minister Ariel Sharon testify that, though irrational escalation can occur, it is treated internally as an *error* and does not reflect a national trait.

Finally, as an open and Western democracy, Israel has been in a poor position to threaten frustration through protracted low-level war. The War of Attrition demonstrated how the society's inability to sustain costs, casualties, and extended disruption received public airing and led to a partial dissolution of the national consensus on security, leading in turn to escalation and ultimately capitulation. We might speculate that such a society should also have difficulty mobilizing to fight repeated large wars, especially if they occur close together. This last point strongly affects reputation.

Israel has confronted societies and polities very different from her own and from each other. What have been the effects of their outstanding characteristics on Israeli deterrence? In the War of Attrition, Egypt, a highly authoritarian regime, had a clear advantage in mobilizing resources, manipulating evidence to create support, and muting public debate. Together with lower expectations about quality of life, these attributes gave the Egyptian regime an ability to mobilize and stay mobilized. The Egyptians could suffer over time without being driven either to escalate or to capitulate. Clearly, then, Israel was not in a position to threaten Egypt with frustration. Israeli countervalue threats and actions against Egypt had little if any coercive effect. In the 1950s this inefficacy may have derived from Egypt's disinterest in Gaza, but in the War of Attrition the values at stake were integral to Egypt: population, cities, and economy. Israeli countervalue actions in fact not only failed to deter but counterproductively caused Egyptian society to unify behind Nasser. In Vietnam the United States discovered similar limits to forceful coercion and countervalue action.

In two of the case studies countervalue threats and actions were effective deterrents: in Jordan in 1954–55 and in Gaza in 1953–54, before Cairo's involvement. What was special about these cases? Outstanding in both was the extreme alienation of a regime from a population with its own agenda. Also in both cases the regime was in a special power position: strong enough to confront its own population but too weak to confront Israel. In these rather special circumstances Israeli countervalue reprisals stirred up the local population to an extent that endangered the integrity of the polities and induced the regimes to stop infiltration. When Hussein became too weak to confront his Palestinian population reprisals ceased to be useful. When Cairo became involved

[225]

and interested in Gaza, and harassment became "Egyptian," Israel faced a regime strong enough to confront her, and again reprisals became useless.

Thus the conditions necessary for countervalue deterrence to work are special and narrow. If a regime is not alienated from the target population or too weak to control it, or if it is strong enough to confront the defender, deterrence should fail. The lesson has ongoing importance for Israel. In the late 1960s, Israel again faced the problem of harassment from Jordan. Hussein's kingdom was once again beset by the disintegrating pressure of a large Palestinian presence bent on harassing Israel and difficult to control. Israeli countervalue actions against Jordan helped Hussein decide to put an end to Palestinian "independence" within Jordan and to pacify the frontier. But Lebanon illustrates the narrow limits. For many years Israel has faced the problem of Palestinian infiltration and sabotage from across its Lebanese border, but operations aimed at solving it have been to no avail. The Lebanese governments have simply been too weak to stop the Palestinians or to confront the Israelis. From this perspective, Israel's Lebanon campaign of 1982 can be seen as an attempt to put a government in place in Lebanon that would be just strong enough to be coercible into controlling the Israeli-Lebanese frontier.

Another Israeli deterrence instrument that has consistently failed for internal reasons has been low-level demonstration of general superiority. First, as in the War of Attrition, the Egyptian political-military culture refused to acknowledge what it saw. Self-delusion was rampant at all levels. Second—a more universal reason—a large military organization is not likely to decide that it is inferior to an opponent simply because that opponent successfully slaps around a number of its units. In both cases involving Egypt this organizational characteristic was apparently an important impediment to Israeli communication of superiority. Behavior of the Arab Legion in the early 1950s suggests an even broader proposition. Despite very poor showings by the IDF in the early reprisals, Comdr. John Glubb refused to draw the conclusion that the legion was therefore superior. Low-level demonstrations simply appear to be irrelevant to assessments of the general balance of power, positive or negative. In sum, domestic factors place severe limits on the *upward* convertibility of conventional deterrence—a nice counterpoint to the obstacles to *downward* convertibility anchored in alliance behavior.

Power Asymmetries

Conventional deterrence is extremely sensitive to the physical determinants of power—quantitative, qualitative, or geographic. Sheer quantitative balance—numbers—appears to have an almost decisive effect on deterrence, especially in interaction with other physical, political, and interest factors. Finally, not only are decisions to use force affected by physical asymmetries, but the reverse is also true: force may be used purposefully to influence the balance of power. Relative power, then, is an endogenous variable.

In the Jordan case the power differential was so skewed in Israel's favor that questions of doctrine, quality, or mobilization were irrelevant. In the confrontation with Egypt in the mid-1950s, leaders on both sides were most impressed with the Egyptian advantage in both putative and actualized power. Even Israeli leaders and analysts, looking at the raw size differences, were pessimistic about the outcome of an Israeli-Egyptian confrontation in either the long or short run.

Israel's reliance on a reserve army undermined her ability to deploy a level of power that might have been meaningfully threatening to Egypt in the 1950s. This, combined with Israeli reluctance to bear the costs of mobilization, made low-level harassment by Egypt most difficult to deter. In the crisis of May–June 1967 both sides were again greatly influenced by sheer differences in quantities. Despite the IDF's perfection after 1956 of a first-rate blitzkrieg army and the knowledge that the IAF could destroy the Arab air forces on the ground, when the crisis developed, Israeli leaders lost their confidence. Nasser, in contrast, was apparently self-assured as he surveyed the orders of battle of the opposing forces.

In confronting its major opponents, Israel has relied on a large number of intangibles for battlefield superiority, such as the quality of the individual soldier, technological proficiency, superior organization, the ability to mobilize a reserve army quickly and then operate it, and the tactical ability to substitute the movement of force for its accumulation. Although these components of superiority may make for battlefield victory, they may also render deterrence difficult; with conventional forces, victory and deterrence can be mutually exclusive. The more the details of these components are hidden from an opponent, the better the chance of winning and the less of deterring him. The more he knows, the better the prospects for deterrence.

This appears to create a policy choice of how much information to divulge, depending on whether the purpose is victory or deterrence. Unfortunately such a choice cannot escape the following dilemma: Because conventional forces are adaptable, divulging information in the hope of enhancing deterrence gives an opponent an opportunity to design around the revealed capabilities, so that eventually deterrence is undermined by knowledge. Yet, if the opponent knows too little, he will also remain undeterred.

The case studies provide examples of the consequences of challengers knowing either too much or too little. In the crisis of May–June 1967, Israel failed to deter violations of casus belli because Egypt did not understand the sources of Israeli superiority. In the War of Attrition the IDF taught the Egyptian army and air force much about its capabilities, thus contributing to the deterrence failure of October 1973. This discussion suggests that a defender whose deterrent threats depend on detail-intensive intangibles should seek to establish a more general appreciation of his superiority—a reputation.

The geographic arrangement of opposing forces can also prove critical in determining deterrence outcomes. Geography interacts with other systemic factors to enhance or undermine the credibility and efficacy of deterrent threats and may be most critical when deterrence depends on specific doctrines and other intangibles, as does Israel's. Deterrence of infiltration from Jordan in the 1950s was made possible in part by the dimensions of the West Bank and the fact that it was surrounded by Israel. Geography together with an overwhelming power asymmetry in Israel's favor created the implication that Israel would require almost no time to conquer the West Bank. Because time would have been critical in mobilizing potential British intervention, Jordan was indeed coercible.

The Egyptian blockade in the early 1950s was executed partially *within* Egypt—at the Suez Canal—and partially very far from Israel—at Sharm el-Sheikh—which made Israeli access to the critical points difficult. The geopolitical arrangement at the time also favored Egyptian harassment across the Gaza frontier. With Egypt's indifference to the safety of the Gaza residents, the situation was such that Egypt's forces were close to Israel's population, while Israeli forces were far from Egypt's. Because Israel's blitzkrieg army had not yet emerged, the Egyptians enjoyed substantial freedom of action.

After the Six Day War the geographic disposition greatly undermined Israeli deterrence. The occupation of the Sinai changed the nature and intensity of Egyptian interests in the conflict. In terms of alliance behavior, the fact that the War of Attrition was conducted at the canal enabled the Egyptians to drag in the Soviets and made it possible for the latter to intervene without fearing a collision with the United States. Deployment at the canal placed the rather tiny regular formations of the IDF in a static confrontation with a relatively enormous army. In trench warfare the IDF was powerless to exploit most of its qualitative sources of superiority, and Israel's deployment at the canal also neutralized the threat of offensive blitzkrieg. In effect, then, the local balance of power became the total balance of power, and Israeli deterrence was doomed to fail.

[228]

The experience of the War of Attrition suggests that we think of deterrent threats in terms of their sustainability, which in turn depends on a certain congruence among the various systemic factors and the deterrent threats. Deployment at the canal forced Israel to make threats she could not support. The defender in this kind of situation must ask: which factors can I manipulate to bring them into line with the others and the wielded threat? In the event, the only element Israel could have manipulated was her own deployment; even a small redeployment back from the Suez Canal and the creation of a demilitarized zone would have improved Israeli deterrence. Then, had the Egyptians stayed on the west bank, the threat to deter by frustration would have been unnecessary because the constant friction could have been avoided. The threat to wage offensive war could have been made credible because it would have been offensive war on the *east* bank. Of course the Egyptians conceivably could have attrited the Israelis with repeated small crossings. Alternatively, Israel could have redeployed essentially to the Negev, which might have made her deterrent threats even more sustainable and hence credible. After the 1973 war the Israelis began to understand this. It is significant that many members of the national security establishment welcomed the separation of forces and, later, the complete Israeli withdrawal from the Sinai.

There are numerous examples in which force has been used to alter power asymmetries, reversing the expected causal relationship between power and deterrence. This is the essence of preventive war, in which both Arabs and Israelis have engaged. In the War of Attrition, Egypt used force in conscious attempts to alter the balance of power. The Egyptian four-stage program of March 1969 was a kind of preventive war: Nasser was afraid that if he waited too long the Israelis would solidify their positions and be unassailable on the east bank. His plan was to preempt this development and then to shift the balance of power against Israel—by force—to the point where it could be translated into political achievements.

Escalation and Brinkmanship

In the Israeli experience the efficacy of escalation has been bound by the same constraints as any threat. Escalation is nothing but movement from one level of activity to another. At any level, once there, the structural conditions determine the effectiveness of active deterrence. Thus, escalation against Jordan by reprisal was deterring because of her clear military inferiority, domestic political fragility, and internationally imposed constraints. Escalation to engage Egyptian interests in 1954–55 failed because of the nature and distribution of interests and asymmetries of geography and physical power. Escalation to demonstrate superiority in the War of Attrition and in the mid-1950s confronted cultural and organizational barriers. It seems, then, that the efficacy of escalation should usually be evaluated not separately but within the study of the three basic structural categories.

One special characteristic of escalation has important policy implications. The act itself, the dynamics of movement from one level to another, can have a deterrent effect of its own. It appears that right after an escalatory move one's opponent may be disoriented, without an appropriate response, and unclear as to the implications. This effect may be but temporary, while the opponent learns to cope with the new reality. In the War of Attrition each Israeli escalatory move had an initial deterrent impact on the Egyptians, followed by adaptation and renewed challenge. In Jordan the initial large escalation at Qibya had a much greater disrupting effect than the later large raid at Nahleen. President Kennedy had the same kind of phenomenon in mind when, discussing the possibility of U.S. involvement in Vietnam, he warned, "The troops will march in; the bands will play; the crowds will cheer; and in four days everyone will have forgotten. Then we will be told we have to send in more troops. It's like taking a drink. The effect wears off, and you have to take another."[2]

Assuming a decision to escalate, there are two policy implications here. First, because the deterrent effect of escalation may be temporary, one should act concomitantly and rapidly on the political and diplomatic fronts to take advantage of the temporary effect. Second, and not exclusive of the first, one needs to maximize the disorienting (and hence deterrent) effect by escalating in large and rapid steps.

One purpose of escalation is brinkmanship, which operates on both the process of escalation and its destination (the expected damage). In the nuclear world, a very small probability of the process getting out of control is enough to put off a confrontation because the expected destination is Armageddon. It is also inherently easy to lose control when the distance to maximal exchange of blows is from the eye to the command button. The relationship is basically symmetrical because the expected damage is mutual destruction. In a conventional setting it is possible to lose control of events, as demonstrated by the crisis of May–June 1967. It is also possible for the expected damage to be significant and threatening. But both probability and damage are inhibited, so that conventional brinkmanship is a much less useful tool than its nuclear cousin. In the Middle East probability and expected damage have been

2. Quoted in Arthur M. Schlesinger, *A Thousand Days: John F. Kennedy in the White House* (Boston, 1965), p. 547.

further dampened by the expectation of superpower intervention and control. Furthermore, because the expected damage is asymmetrically distributed in conventional confrontation, brinkmanship should favor one of the protagonists, but not necessarily the defender, regardless of relative will.

Israeli attempts to apply brinkmanship in deterring Egypt in 1954–56 and again in the War of Attrition faltered on a number of systemic factors. Centralized and considered Israeli decision making and a highly disciplined military made it impossible to project the prospect of imminent loss of control. The highly visible national debate over general war made it abundantly clear that Israel, though surely capable of errors, was not likely to stumble inadvertently into a general war. Furthermore, Israel could not really escalate to general war without the deliberate act of mobilization of the reserves. In the War of Attrition a salience that could not be inadvertently crossed was the Suez Canal. The 1956 Sinai Campaign taught the Egyptians that unexpected, if not quite inadvertent, escalation to general war *can* occur, but the course proved reversible, a possibility demonstrated again in the War of Attrition and yet again in 1973.

So much for the process. As for costs, relative size and geographic disposition in 1954–56 conspired to render the damage Egypt could expect quite small even in a full-scale war, an expectation borne out by events. In the War of Attrition alliance considerations made the expected damage of escalation asymmetric. It was clear to both Israelis and Egyptians that the probable result would be superpower intervention and the imposition of a solution unfavorable to Israel. The brinkmanship advantage belonged to Egypt.

In the confrontation with Jordan in the mid-1950s brinkmanship was effective and the advantage belonged to Israel. The probability of inadvertent escalation to general war was small but not quite as small as it was vis-à-vis Egypt. Israel could strike a lethal or at least highly damaging blow to Jordan rapidly and without reserve mobilization. This made violence strategically significant at a relatively low level and automatically raised its probability. Deterrence through brinkmanship, then, was effective only where the infliction of significant damage required relatively minor violence; the probability of reaching it was reasonable; and the advantage, should it be reached, was with the defender.

Reputation and Knowledge

Deterrence problems associated with knowledge all point to reputation as an instrument of deterrence that provides a way around these problems. Reputation allows a defender to substitute general for detailed knowledge so that a challenger knows *that* the defender will react and prevail but not quite *how*. The cases demonstrate three barriers to the effective establishment of reputation and its utility for deterrence. First, the lessons a defender would like to teach have to be learned—by people and organizations. Both are naturally biased and motivated to draw self-serving conclusions from defeats. They do not necessarily see what a defender wants to show. Second, lesson-teaching events occur under *specific* structural circumstances. Because structural conditions influence the use of force, a challenger can reasonably expect different outcomes under different circumstances and will try to alter those circumstances. Third, because reputation has to be established by force, its creation may be economically and socially costly. These costs may inhibit future readiness to execute threats, so that a defender, in trying to enhance deterrence by reputation, may actually diminish it.

Personal and organizational resistance to generalizing negative experience is nicely illustrated by the Nasser regime's attitude to defeat. Nasser and the Free Officers came to power in 1952 and the army remained a keystone of their rule. Therefore, the 1948 defeat was explained in terms of exogenous or passing phenomena unrelated to Israeli superiority: the corruption of Farouk and his court, the traitorous behavior of Jordan's King Abdullah, and Western imperialism. After the defeat of June 1967 the regime could not very well blame itself and still needed the army's loyalty, so responsibility was ascribed to individual officers (who could be replaced), again to the behavior of Western powers, and even to the Soviet Union. Low-level demonstrations of capability or interests can be interpreted as attempts to create reputation within a crisis, and such attempts can meet with similar responses: extreme and understandable reluctance to draw general conclusions of inferiority from specific and especially *minor* events.

The effect of changing circumstances is demonstrated by the impact of the Czech arms deal of 1955. By so completely altering the quantitative balance of power, it dissipated much of Israel's qualitative reputation of 1948. Egyptian military reforms after 1952 and again after 1967 were aimed specifically at correcting the deficiencies that had led to defeats. Changes in organization, training, manpower policy, and doctrine allowed the regime and the army to believe after a number of years that the qualitative balance of power had been corrected as well.

In the 1967–70 period the disposition of forces was dramatically different from that of June 1967. In consequence, many aspects of the unquestionable reputation developed by Israel in 1967 were rendered irrelevant. In the War of Attrition Egypt acted explicitly to develop and exploit dimensions in which Israel had not established superiority in

1967. The war itself provided the Egyptian forces with excellent on-the-job training. The protracted conflict gave them repeated opportunities to evaluate Israeli capabilities and experiment with ways around Israeli aptitudes. Thus, attempts to teach general superiority through specific lessons led the challenger to adopt a policy aimed at altering, also through specifics, the relevant balance.

The cost of establishing reputation and the effect of that cost were most clearly visible in the War of Attrition. In the extended attempt to demonstrate resilience to pain, Israel at first succeeded but ultimately faltered. By succumbing to costs Israel actually established a negative reputation.

Note that the Jordan case played no role in illustrating barriers to establishing reputation. This is because reputation was of minor importance to the Israeli-Jordanian relationship in the 1950s. Israeli superiority did not depend on intangibles of quality, brinkmanship was effective, and no problem of detail undermined deterrence. Also, the most relevant threat, reprisal, was cheap to execute. In short, there were no problems of knowledge that needed overcoming through reputation.

All of this is not to say that reputations are impossible to establish or useless for deterrence. Clearly, over the long haul, Israel has caused her interests to command considerable respect from her neighbors. The 1948 war established the Jewish State and the Israeli soldier as worthy institutions. Israeli reaction to the blockade and harassment in the 1950s established the seriousness of her regard for her borders and rights of maritime passage. The 1956 Sinai Campaign made known an unexpected Israeli propensity to escalate precipitously and a military aptitude Nasser admitted to taking seriously after the war. In the Six Day War, Israel demonstrated her ability to decide independently and then wage and win a three-front offensive lightening war. True, the reputation of 1967 could be (and was) got around by means of limited and local war, but we should be just as impressed by Egypt's refusal to entertain any idea of a major offensive despite an overwhelming quantitative advantage. It appears from Jordan's behavior in 1973 that the 1967 reputation also put to rest Hussein's remotest hope of challenging Israel. Syria's care since 1967 to avoid and prevent low-level violence across her frontier is also most striking. Note that all of these reputation-creating operations were full-scale campaigns.

What are the policy implications? The most important, perhaps, is attitudinal. To the extent that deterrence depends on reputation, it cannot be expected to cover all possible challenges or be effective at all levels. A reputation cannot be timeless, for with time circumstances will change; force will probably have to be used and reused from time to time to "buy" periods of deterrence. To extend the reputational effects of violent action over levels and types of challenge and over time, large-scale and highly damaging operations are preferable. Finally, because of the sensitivity of reputation to specific circumstances, a defender needs to maintain or recreate the conditions under which reputation became established.

Spiraling and De-escalation

The simple deterrence-spiral formulation recognizes two possible errors: a defender may appease a hungry revisionist aggressor or deter an otherwise friendly state and possibly cause a spiral. Where a spiral occurs, conciliation *could* have been an effective dissuasive instrument. Where appeasement leads to aggression and escalation, deterrence would have been appropriate. Dissuasion, by this formulation, is possible one way or the other.

The case studies show that in fact the conventional world is substantially more complicated than suggested by this framework. Because force is useful at various levels and for assorted purposes, sometimes there is simply no dissuasive option, and disputes may have to be settled by fighting it out or ignoring challenges. Because of the layer-cake nature of conventional confrontations, it is also possible for both deterrence and conciliation to be relevant simultaneously, each at a different level of a relationship. The defending decision maker may have to identify not the nature of the opposing state, but the critical level of interaction, and then decide whether deterrence or appeasement is relevant at that level.

In trying to arrest infiltration from Jordan in the early 1950s, Israel attempted appeasement but found it irrelevant. At times deterrent escalation met the same fate. The Palestinians' immediate objective was to maintain a fluid status quo by perpetuating violence. Threatening violence could not deter them, and Israel did not have a conciliatory option—save surrendering her existence. At first Hussein was coercible through violent threats, but as he became weaker he could no longer be influenced by escalation or appeasement. In trying to deter Egyptian harassment across the frontier and her shipping blockade, Israel faced a similar predicament. With no relevant conciliatory option and with deterrence ineffective, Israel had the choice of living with harassment and blockade, which she did for a long time, or waging war, which she eventually did in 1956.

In the War of Attrition, Israel and Egypt could not agree on the

[234]

classification of Israeli actions as either defensive (and conciliatory) or offensive (and deterrent). The most prominent example was the Bar Lev Line. Israel constructed it partly as a *defensive tactical* response to Egyptian shelling, but to the Egyptians it was an offensive, *strategically escalatory* move, proof of Israel's intention to stay put. Actually, at the strategic level it was an integral component of Israeli deterrence by frustration. Thus the correct evaluation of a particular move as escalatory (and deterrent) or conciliatory depends first on identifying the level at which it is significant to one's opponent.

All of this should inject some hope for salvaging the deterrence-spiral framework. If the relevant level of interaction is correctly identified, then the notion of a spiral may help in identifying the boundaries within which deterrence is relevant and give guidance to decision makers in choosing policy.

Success and Failure

The importance of a relativistic definition of deterrence success is confirmed by the study of Israel's experience. The question Was deterrence successful? can only be answered by first answering the question Deterrence of *what* and in what time frame? In all three cases one can identify deterrence failure at a tactical level concurrent with success at a strategic level, and at times vice versa. But Israeli deterrence exhibited an even more complex relativism: at times success or failure at one level or in a given time frame directly influenced the fortunes of deterrence at other levels and periods. These characteristics of the dependent variable are not an encouraging finding in the search for parsimonious and predictive theory.

Interlevel influence may work in either direction. For example, successful strategic deterrence of Egypt after 1967 led Nasser to adopt the low-level attrition of 1967–70. But by 1970 the Egyptians were deterred from further attrition, and they decided to raise the challenge. Deterred simultaneously from total war and low-level harassment, the Egyptians devised a compromise: the Yom Kippur War.

Events in the 1950s and in the post-1957 period also demonstrate possible inimical effects of time's passage. First, periods of calm were often merely covers for organizing challenges. The Palestinians in the mid-1950s and the Egyptians in the War of Attrition used temporary truces in this manner. Second, passage of time can have a frustrating effect, actually exacerbating a relationship and shifting the balance of interests in the challenger's favor, as in the 1970–73 period in Egypt. To the strategist these dynamics are an important warning. A defending strategist should look vigilantly beneath apparent deterrence success to examine the underlying structural features of the relationship and their direction of change. Most important, he should ask What is happening to the balance of interests? and Are the political and power factors or the nature of the intended challenge changing (or being manipulated) in ways that render deterrence inherently fragile or an existing reputation less efficacious?

Because appeasing is often not an alternative possibility, this analysis implies that a defending decision maker who would pursue deterrence may face a rather uncomfortable set of choices, not between war and peace, but rather, between a small war now and a larger one later, or vice versa. The latter kind of choice is precisely the idea of reputation, which requires violence *now* to prevent greater violence *later*. I noted that there is some hope for reputation as a deterrent instrument, so that the relativism uncovered here may actually be a source of guarded optimism: in the conventional world of nonabsolute deterrence, it may be possible for a defender to engineer the conflict and make conscious choices about the nature and timing of violence and deterrence failure, much as the challenger normally does.

Bibliography

BOOKS

Abidi, Aqil Hyder Hasan. *Jordan: A Political Study, 1948–1957*. New York: Asia Publishing House, 1965.

Adan, Avraham (Bren). *On the Banks of the Suez*. Novato, Calif.: Presidio, 1980.

Ajami, Fouad. *The Arab Predicament: Arab Political Thought and Practice since 1967*. Cambridge: Cambridge University Press, 1984.

Allon, Yigal. *The Making of Israel's Army*. New York: Bantam, 1971.

———. *Massakh shel Khol* [Curtain of sand]. Tel-Aviv: Hakibbutz Hameuchad, 1959.

Amos, John W. *Arab-Israeli Military/Political Relations: Arab Perception and the Politics of Escalation*. New York: Pergamon, 1979.

Arad, Yitshak, ed. *Elef ha-Yamim, 12 Yuni 1967–8 August 1970* [1000 days, 12 June 1967–8 August 1970]. Tel-Aviv: Ministry of Defence Publishing House, 1972.

Aronson, Shlomo. *Conflict and Bargaining in the Middle East: An Israeli Perspective*. Baltimore: Johns Hopkins University Press, 1978.

Avnery, Arieh. *The Israeli Commando: A Short History of the Israeli Commandos—1950–1969*. Vol. 4, *The War of Attrition*. Tel-Aviv: Sifriat Madim, [1970?].

el-Badri, Hassan, Taha el-Magdoub, and Mohammed Dia el-Din Zohdi. *The Ramadan War, 1973*. Dunn Loring, Va.: T. N. Dupuy Associates, 1978.

Bar-Siman-Tov, Yaacov. *The Israeli-Egyptian War of Attrition, 1969–1970: A Case Study of Local Limited War*. New York: Columbia University Press, 1980.

Bar-Zohar, Michael. *Ben-Gurion* (in Hebrew). 3 pts. Tel-Aviv: Am Oved, 1977.

Bartov, Hanoch. *Daddo: Arba'im ve-Shmoneh Shanah ve'od Essrim Yom* [Daddo: 48 years and 20 more days]. Tel-Aviv: Maariv, 1979.

Ben-Gurion, David. *Israel: Years of Challenge*. New York: Holt, Rinehart & Winston, 1963.

———. *Yechud ve-Ye'ud* [Uniqueness and destiny]. Tel-Aviv: Ma'arachot, 1972.

Ben-Horin, Yoav, and Barry Posen. *Israel's Strategic Doctrine*. R-2845-NA. Santa Monica, Calif.: Rand Corporation, September 1981.

Berger, Earl. *The Covenant and the Sword: Arab-Israeli Relations, 1948–1956*. London: Routledge & Kegan Paul, 1965.

Blechman, Barry M. "The Consequences of the Israeli Reprisals: An Assessment." Ph.D. diss., Georgetown University, 1971.

——. *Military Event Data Set*. Computer Tape 0489. Inter-university Consortium for Political and Social Research, 1972.

Brecher, Michael. *Decisions in Crisis: Israel, 1967 and 1973*. Berkeley and Los Angeles: University of California Press, 1980.

——. *Decisions in Israel's Foreign Policy*. New Haven, Conn.: Yale University Press, 1975.

——. *The Foreign Policy System of Israel: Setting, Images, Process*. New Haven, Conn.: Yale University Press, 1972.

Brodie, Bernard. *Strategy in the Missile Age*. Princeton, N.J.: Princeton University Press, 1959.

——. *War and Politics*. New York: Macmillan, 1973.

Burns, Eedson L. M. *Between Arab and Israeli*. New York: Obolensky, 1963.

Clark, Ian. *Limited Nuclear War*. Princeton, N.J.: Princeton University Press, 1982.

Cohen, Yohanan. *Umot be-Mivhan* [Small nations in times of crisis and confrontation]. Tel-Aviv: Ma'arachot, 1985.

Cooper, Mark N. *The Transformation of Egypt*. London: Croom Helm, 1982.

Davis, Morton D. *Game Theory: A Nontechnical Introduction*. New York: Basic Books, 1973.

Dawisha, A. I. *Egypt in the Arab World: The Elements of Foreign Policy*. New York: Wiley, 1976.

Dawisha, Karen. *Soviet Foreign Policy towards Egypt*. London: Macmillan, 1979.

Dayan, Moshe. *Avnei Derekh* [The story of my life]. Tel-Aviv: Dvir, Yedioth Ahronoth Edition, 1976.

——. *Mapa Hadasha: Yakhasim Akherim* [A new map: New relations]. Tel-Aviv: Sifriat Ma'ariv, 1969.

——. *Yoman Ma'arekhet Sinai* [Sinai Campaign diary]. Tel-Aviv: Am Hasefer, 1965.

Dekmejian, R. Hrair. *Egypt under Nassir: A Study in Political Dynamics*. Albany: State University of New York Press, 1971.

Deutsch, Morton. *The Resolution of Conflict: Constructive and Destructive Processes*. New Haven, Conn.: Yale University Press, 1977.

Dishon, Daniel. *Inter-Arab Relations 1967–1973*, An Occasional Paper. Tel-Aviv: Shiloach Institute, 1974.

——. ed. *Middle East Record*. Vols. 3–5. Jerusalem: Israel Universities Press, 1971–1977.

Doriel, J. *Habitakhon ha-Leumi shel Yisrael: Mavo le-Gisha Hadashah* [The national security of the Jewish people]. Tel-Aviv: Reshafim, 1974.

Dupuy, Trevor N. *Elusive Victory: The Arab-Israeli Wars, 1947–1974*. New York: Harper & Row, 1978.

Evron, Yair. *The Demilitarization of Sinai*. Jerusalem Papers on Peace Problems, No. 11. Jerusalem: Leonard Davis Institute for International Relations, Hebrew University, 1975.

——. *The Middle East: Nations, Superpowers and Wars*. New York: Praeger, 1973.

Eytan, Walter. *The First Ten Years: A Diplomatic History of Israel*. New York: Simon & Schuster, 1958.

Feldman, Shai. *Israeli Nuclear Deterrence: A Strategy for the 1980s*. New York: Columbia University Press, 1982.

Freedman, Lawrence. *The Evolution of Nuclear Strategy*. New York: St. Martin's, 1983.

Gaddis, John Lewis. *Strategies of Containment: A Critical Appraisal of Postwar American National Security Policy*. Oxford: Oxford University Press, 1982.

———. *The United States and the Origins of the Cold War, 1941–1947*. New York: Columbia University Press, 1972.

Gazit, Mordechai. *Tahalikh ha-Shalom (1969–1973)* [The peace process (1969–1973)]. Tel-Aviv: Hakibbutz Hameuchad, 1984.

George, Alexander, and Richard Smoke. *Deterrence in American Foreign Policy: Theory and Practice*. New York: Columbia University Press, 1974.

Gilpin, Robert. *War and Change in World Politics*. New York: Cambridge University Press, 1981.

Glassman, Jon D. *Arms for the Arabs: The Soviet Union and War in the Middle East*. Baltimore: Johns Hopkins University Press, 1975.

Glubb, John Baggot. *A Soldier with the Arabs*. London: Hodder & Stoughton, 1957.

Green, Phillip. *Deadly Logic: The Theory of Nuclear Deterrence*. Columbus: Ohio State University Press, 1966.

Hamroush, Ahmed. *Nasir wil'Arab* [Nasser and the Arabs] Beirut, 1976.

Handel, Michael I. *Israel's Political-Military Doctrine*. Occasional Papers in International Affairs no. 30. Cambridge, Mass.: Harvard University, Center for International Affairs, 1973.

Harkabi, Yehoshafat. *Arab Attitudes to Israel*. Jerusalem: Keter, 1972.

———. *Lekakh ha-Aravim mi-Tvusatam* [Arab lessons from their defeat]. Tel-Aviv: Am Oved, 1969.

Herzog, Haim. *The Arab-Israeli Wars: War and Peace in the Middle East*. New York: Random House, 1982.

———. *The War of Atonement: October 1973*. Boston: Little, Brown, 1975.

Heykal, Mohammed. *The Road to Ramadan*. New York: Quadrangle/New York Times Book Co., 1975.

———. *The Sphinx and the Commissar: The Rise and Fall of Soviet Influence in the Middle East*. New York: Harper & Row, 1978.

Higgins, Rosalyn. *United Nations Peace-Keeping 1946–1967. Documents and Commentary: The Middle East*. London: Oxford University Press, 1969.

Horowitz, Dan. *Hatfisa ha-Yisraelit shel Bitachon Leumi: Hakavua veha-Mishtaneh ba-Khashiva ha-Estrategit ha-Yisraelit* [Israel's concept of national security: The constant and the dynamic in Israeli strategic thought]. Jerusalem: Levi Eshkol Institute for Research of the Economy, Society and Policy in Israel, Hebrew University of Jerusalem, 1973.

———. *Israel's Concept of Defensible Borders*. Jerusalem Papers on Peace Problems, no. 16. Jerusalem: Leonard Davis Institute, Hebrew University, 1975.

Hussein, Mahmoud. *L'Egypte*. Vol. 2, *1967–1973*. Paris: Maspero, 1975.

———. *La lutte de classes en Egypte* [Class conflict in Egypt]. Paris: Maspero, 1971.

Hutchison, Elmo H. *Violent Truce: A Military Observer Looks at the Arab-Israeli Conflict, 1951–1955*. New York: Devin-Adair, 1956.

Ikle, Fred Charles. *Every War Must End*. New York: Columbia University Press, 1971.

Jabber, Fuad. *Israel and Nuclear Weapons: Present Options and Future Strategies*. London: Chatto & Windus, 1971.

Janis, Irving L., and Leon Mann. *Decision Making*. New York: Free Press, 1977.

Jervis, Robert. *Perception and Misperception in International Politics*. Princeton, N.J.: Princeton University Press, 1976.

Jervis, Robert, Richard Ned Lebow, and Janice Gross Stein, eds. *Psychology and Deterrence*. Baltimore: Johns Hopkins University Press, 1985.

Kerr, Malcolm H. *The Arab Cold War: Gamal Abd al-Nasser and His Rivals, 1958–1970.* 3d ed. New York: Oxford University Press, 1971.

Knorr, Klaus. *The Power of Nations.* New York: Basic Books, 1975.

Lacouture, Jean. *Nasser.* Trans. Daniel Hofstadter. New York: Knopf, 1973.

Landau, Eli. *Suez: Fire on the Water.* Trans. from Hebrew by R. Ben-Yosef. Tel-Aviv: Otpaz, 1970.

Lavon, Pinkhas. *Benetivei Iyun uma-Avak* [Reasoning and challenge]. Tel-Aviv: Am Oved, 1968.

Lewy, Guenter. *America in Vietnam.* New York: Oxford University Press, 1978.

Maoz, Zeev, and Avner Yaniv. "Game, Supergame and Compound Escalation: Israel and Syria 1948–1984." Haifa University, 1984.

Margalit, Dan. *Sheder meha-Bayit ha-Lavan: Aliyatah u-Nefilatah shel Memshelet ha-Likud ha-Leumi* [Message from the White House: The rise and fall of the National Unity Government]. Tel-Aviv: Otpaz, 1971.

Maxwell, Stephen. *Rationality in Deterrence,* Adelphi Paper No. 50. London: International Institute for Strategic Studies, 1968.

Mearsheimer, John. *Conventional Deterrence.* Ithaca, N.Y.: Cornell University Press, 1983.

Meir, Golda. *My Life.* New York: Putnam's, 1975.

Milstein, Uri. *Milhamot ha-Tsankhanim* [Wars of the paratroopers]. Tel-Aviv: Ramdor, 1968.

Morgan, Patrick. *Deterrence: A Conceptual Analysis.* Beverly Hills, Calif.: Sage, 1977.

Naor, Mordechai. *Hamilhama leachar ha-Milhama* [The war after the war]. Tel-Aviv: Ministry of Defense Publishing House, [1970?].

Nasser, Gamal Abdel. *The Philosophy of the Revolution.* Buffalo, N.Y.: Smith, Keynes & Marshall, 1959.

Nutting, Anthony. *Nasser.* London: Constable, 1972.

O'Ballance, Edgar. *The Electronic War in the Middle East 1968–1970.* London: Archon, 1974.

Peres, Shimon. *Hashlav haba* [The next phase]. Tel-Aviv: Am Hasefer, 1965.

―――. *Kela David* [David's sling]. Jerusalem: Weidenfeld & Nicolson, 1970.

Posen, Barry. *The Sources of Military Doctrine: France, Britain, and Germany between the World Wars.* Ithaca, N.Y.: Cornell University Press, 1984.

Quandt, William B. *Decade of Decisions: American Policy toward the Arab-Israeli Conflict, 1967–1976.* Berkeley and Los Angeles: University of California Press, 1977.

Quester, George. *Deterrence before Hiroshima.* New York: Wiley, 1966.

Ra'anan, Uri. *The U.S.S.R. Arms the Third World.* Cambridge, Mass.: MIT Press, 1969.

Rabin, Yitzhak. *The Rabin Memoirs.* Boston: Little, Brown, 1979.

Rhodes, Edward J. "Nuclear Weapons, Irrational Behavior and Extended Deterrence." Ph.D. diss., Princeton University, 1985.

Ro'i, Ya'akov. *From Encroachment to Involvement: A Documentary Study of Soviet Policy in the Middle East, 1945–1973.* Jerusalem: Israel Universities Press, 1974.

Rubinstein, Alvin Z. *Red Star on the Nile: The Soviet-Egyptian Influence Relationship since the June War.* Princeton, N.J.: Princeton University Press, 1977.

el-Sadat, Anwar. *In Search of Identity: An Autobiography.* New York: Harper & Row, 1978.

Safran, Nadav. *From War to War: The Arab-Israeli Confrontation, 1948–1967.* New York: Pegasus, 1969.

―――. *Israel: The Embattled Ally.* Cambridge, Mass.: Harvard University Press, 1981.

―――. *The United States and Israel.* Cambridge, Mass.: Harvard University Press, 1963.

Schelling, Thomas. *Arms and Influence*. New Haven, Conn.: Yale University Press, 1966.

———. *The Strategy of Conflict*. Cambridge, Mass.: Harvard University Press, 1980.

Scheuftan, Dan. "Harta'ah Yisraelit be-Sikhsukh Yisrael-Arav: Haperspektiva ha-Aravit [Israeli deterrence in the Israeli-Arab conflict: The Arab perspective]. December 1982.

———. *Optsiah Yardenit: Yisrael, Yarden veha-Palestina'im* [A Jordanian option: the "Yishuv" and The State of Israel vis-à-vis the Hashemite regime and the Palestinian national movement]. Tel-Aviv: Hakibbutz Hameuchad, 1986.

Schiff, Zeev. *A History of the Israeli Army (1879–1974)*. San Francisco: Straight Arrow, 1974.

———. *Knafayim me'al Suez* [Phantom over the Nile: The story of the Israeli Air Corps]. Haifa: Shikmona, 1970.

———. *October Earthquake*. Trans. by Louis Williams. Tel-Aviv: University Publishing, 1974.

Schiff, Zeev, and Eitan Haber, eds. *Lexikon le-Bitahon Yisrael* [Israel, army and defense: A dictionary]. Tel-Aviv: Zmora, Bitan, Modan, 1976.

Schlesinger, Arthur M. *A Thousand Days: John F. Kennedy in the White House*. Boston: Houghton Mifflin, 1965.

Sela, Avraham. *Achdut betoch Perud ba-Maarekhet habein-Aravit* [Unity within conflict in the inter-Arab system]. Jerusalem: Magnes, 1983.

Sharett, Moshe. *Yoman Ishi* [Personal diary]. 8 vols. Tel-Aviv: Sifriat Ma'ariv, 1978.

el-Shazli, Saad. *The Crossing of the Suez*. San Francisco: American Mideast Research, 1980.

Shimshoni, Daniel. *Israeli Democracy: The Middle of the Journey*. New York: Free Press, 1982.

Shimshoni, Jonathan. "Conventional Deterrence: Lessons from the Middle East." Ph.D. diss., Princeton University, 1986.

Snyder, Glenn. *Deterrence and Defense*. Princeton, N.J.: Princeton University Press, 1960.

Snyder, Glenn, and Paul Diesing. *Conflict among Nations*. Princeton, N.J.: Princeton University Press, 1977.

Sorley, Lewis. *Arms Transfers under Nixon: A Policy Analysis*. Lexington, Ky.: University Press of Kentucky, 1983.

Spiegel, Steven L. *The Other Arab-Israeli Conflict: Making America's Middle East Policy, from Truman to Reagan*. Chicago: University of Chicago Press, 1985.

Steinbruner, John. *The Cybernetic Theory of Decision*. Princeton, N.J.: Princeton University Press, 1974.

Stephens, Robert. *Nasser: A Political Biography*. London: Allen Lane, Penguin Press, 1971.

Stock, Ernest. *Israel on the Road to Sinai, 1949–1956*. Ithaca, N.Y.: Cornell University Press, 1967.

Teveth, Shabtai. *Moshe Dayan: Biographia*. Jerusalem and Tel-Aviv: Schocken, 1971.

Totah, Khalil. *Dynamite in the Middle East*. New York: Philosophical Library, 1955.

Touval, Saadia. *The Peace Brokers: Mediators in the Arab-Israeli Conflict, 1948–1979*. Princeton, N.J.: Princeton University Press, 1982.

Vatikiotis, P. J. *The Egyptian Army in Politics: Pattern for New Nations?* Bloomington: Indiana University Press, 1961.

———. *Politics and the Military in Jordan: A Study of the Arab Legion 1921–1957*. London: Cass, 1967.

Wallach, Jehuda, Moshe Lissak, and Shimon Shamir, eds. *Atlas Carta le-Toldot Medinat Yisrael: Assor Sheni* [Carta's atlas of Israel: The second decade]. Jerusalem: Carta, 1980.

Waltz, Kenneth N. *Theory of International Politics.* Reading, Mass.: Addison-Wesley, 1979.

Weizman, Ezer. *Lekha Shamayim Lekha Aretz* [Thine is the sky, Thine is the land]. Tel-Aviv: Sifriat Ma'ariv, 1975.

Wheelock, Keith. *Nasser's New Egypt: A Critical Analysis.* New York: Praeger, 1960.

Whetten, Lawrence. *The Canal War: Four-Power Conflict in the Middle East.* Cambridge, Mass.: MIT Press, 1974.

Ya'ari, Ehud. *Mitsrayim veha-Fedayeen, 1953–1956* [Egypt and the Fedayeen, 1953–1956]. Givat Haviva: Center for Arabic and Afro-Asian Studies, 1975.

Yaniv, Avner. *Deterrence without the Bomb: The Politics of Israeli Strategy.* Lexington, Mass.: Lexington Books, 1987.

ARTICLES

Allon, Yigal. "The Soviet Involvement in the Arab-Israel Conflict." In Michael Confino and Shimon Shamir, eds., *The U.S.S.R. and the Middle East.* Jerusalem: Israel Universities Press, 1973.

Amiel, Saadia. "Deterrence by Conventional Forces." *Survival* 20 (March/April 1978).

Aronson, Shlomo. "The Nuclear Dimension of the Arab-Israeli Conflict: The Case of the Yom Kippur War." *Jerusalem Journal of International Relations* 7, nos. 1–2 (1984).

Aronson, Shlomo, and Dan Horowitz. "Ha-Estrategiya shel Tagmul Mevukar: Hadugmah ha-Yisraelit" [The strategy of controlled reprisal: The Israeli example]. *Medinah Memshal ve-Yakhasim Bein-Leumim* 1 (1971).

Art, Robert. "To What Ends Military Power." *International Security* 4 (Spring 1980).

Ayalon, A. "Bitkhonah ha-Leumi shel Yisrael be-35 Shnoteyhah" [Israel's national security throughout her 35 years]. *Skirah Hodshit*, nos. 2–3 (February/March 1983).

Baldwin, David A. "The Power of Positive Sanctions." *World Politics* 24 (October 1971).

Blechman, Barry M. "Outside Military Forces in Third-World Conflicts." In *Third-World Conflict and International Security*, pt. 1. Adelphi Paper no. 166. London: International Institute for Strategic Studies, 1981.

Breslauer, George W. "Soviet Policy in the Middle East, 1967–1972: Unalterable Antagonism or Collaborative Competition?" In Alexander George, ed., *Managing U.S.-Soviet Rivalry: Problems of Crisis Prevention.* Boulder, Colo.: Westview, 1983.

Brilliant, Moshe. "Israel's Policy of Reprisals." *Harper's Magazine* 210 (March 1955).

Dayan, Moshe. "Israel's Border and Security Problems." *Foreign Affairs* 33 (January 1955).

———. "Mishalav el Shalav" [From stage to stage]. *Maarachot* 118–19 (May 1959).

———. "Pe'ulot Tsva'iyot bi-Ymei Shalom" [Military actions in times of peace]. *Maarachot* 118–19 (May 1959).

———. "Why Israel Strikes Back." In Donald Robinson, ed., *Under Fire: Israel's Twenty Year Struggle for Survival.* New York: Norton, 1968.

Dismukes, Bradford. "Large-Scale Intervention Ashore: Soviet Air Defense Forces in Egypt." In Bradford Dismukes and James M. McConnell, eds., *Soviet Naval Diplomacy.* New York: Pergamon, 1979.

Dowty, Alan. "Israel and Nuclear Weapons." *Midstream* 22 (November 1976).

Eran, Oded. "Soviet Policy between the 1967 and 1973 Wars." In Itamar Rabinovich and Haim Shaked, eds., *From June to October: The Middle East between 1967 and 1973*. New Brunswick, N.J.: Transaction Books, 1978.

Evron, Yair. "Arms Races in the Middle East and Some Arms Control Measures Related to Them." In Gabriel Sheffer, ed., *Dynamics of a Conflict: A Reexamination of the Arab-Israeli Conflict*. Atlantic Highlands, N.J.: Humanities Press, 1975.

———. "Israel and the Atom: The Uses and Misuses of Ambiguity." *Orbis* 17 (Winter 1974).

———. "The Relevance and Irrelevance of Nuclear Options in Conventional Wars: The 1973 October War." *Jerusalem Journal of International Relations* 7, nos. 1–2 (1984).

———. "Two Periods in the Arab-Israeli Strategic Relations: 1957–1967; 1967–1973." In Itamar Rabinovich and Haim Shaked, eds., *From June to October: The Middle East between 1967 and 1973*. New Brunswick, N.J.: Transaction Books, 1978.

Goren, Asher. "Kavim u-Megamot" [Political summary]. *Hamizrah he-Hadash* 7, no. 1 (1956).

Gray, Colin. "Nuclear Strategy: The Case for a Theory of Victory." *International Security* 4 (1979).

Jervis, Robert. "Cooperation under the Security Dilemma." *World Politics* 30 (January 1978).

———. "Deterrence and Perception." *International Security* 7 (Winter 1982/83).

———. "Deterrence Theory Revisited." *World Politics* 31 (January 1979).

———. "Systems Theories and Diplomatic History." In Paul Gordon Lauren, ed., *Diplomacy: New Approaches in History, Theory, and Policy*. New York: Free Press, 1979.

Khalidi, Ahmed S. "The War of Attrition." *Journal of Palestine Studies* 3 (Autumn 1973).

Knorr, Klaus. "Threat Perception." In Klaus Knorr, ed., *Historical Dimensions of National Security Problems*. Lawrence: University Press of Kansas, 1975.

Kreps, David, and Robert Wilson. "Reputation and Imperfect Information." *Journal of Economic Theory* 27 (August 1982).

Kreps, David, Paul Milgrom, John Roberts, and Robert Wilson. "Rational Cooperation in the Finitely Repeated Prisoners' Dilemma Game." *Journal of Economic Theory* 27 (August 1982).

Lanir, Zvi. "Political Aims and Military Objectives: Some Observations on the Israeli Experience." In Zvi Lanir ed., *Israeli Security Planning in the 1980s: Its Politics and Economics*, A JCSS (Jaffee Center for Strategic Studies, Tel-Aviv University) Book. New York: Praeger 1984.

Lebow, Richard Ned. "The Deterrence Deadlock: Is There a Way Out?" *Political Psychology* 4, no. 2 (1983).

McConnell, James M. "The 'Rules of the Game': A Theory on the Practice of Superpower Naval Diplomacy." In Bradford Dismukes and James M. McConnell, eds., *Soviet Naval Diplomacy*. New York: Pergamon, 1979.

Mishal, Shaul. "Conflictual Pressures and Cooperative Interests: Observations on West Bank–Amman Relations, 1949–1967." In Joel S. Migdal, ed., *Palestinian Society and Politics*. Princeton, N.J.: Princeton University Press, 1980.

O. Y. "Mishtar ha-Hafikhah ve-Otsmatah shel Mitsrayim" [The revolutionary regime and Egypt's potential]. *Hamizrah he-Hadash* 7, no. 3 (1956).

Quandt, William B. "The Arab-Israeli Conflict in American Foreign Policy." In

Itamar Rabinovich and Haim Shaked, eds., *From June to October: The Middle East between 1967 and 1973* (New Brunswick, N.J.: Transaction Books, 1978.

Rabinovich, Itamar. "Seven Wars and One Peace Treaty." In Alvin Z. Rubinstein, ed., *The Arab-Israeli Conflict: Perspectives* New York: Praeger, 1984.

Shamir, Shimon. "Nasser and Sadat, 1967–1973: Two Approaches to a National Crisis." In Itamar Rabinovich and Haim Shaked, eds., *From June to October: The Middle East between 1967 and 1973.* New Brunswick, N.J.: Transaction Books, 1978.

Shapiro, Carl, and Steve Salop. "A Guide to Test Market Predation." Princeton University, n.d.

Shlaim, Avi, and Raymond Tanter. "Decision Process, Choice, and Consequences: Israel's Deep-Penetration Bombing in Egypt, 1970." *World Politics* 30 (July 1978).

Snyder, Jack. "Perception and the Security Dilemma in 1914." In Robert Jervis, Richard Ned Lebow, and Janice Gross Stein, eds., *Psychology and Deterrence.* Baltimore: Johns Hopkins University Press, 1985.

Stein, Janice Gross. "Calculation, Miscalculation, and Conventional Deterrence. I: The View from Cairo." In Robert Jervis, Richard Ned Lebow, and Janice Gross Stein, eds., *Psychology and Deterrence.* Baltimore: Johns Hopkins University Press, 1985.

Swift, Richard N. "International Peace and Security." In Clyde Eagleton, Waldo Chamberlin, and Richard N. Swift, eds., *1954 Annual Review of United Nations Affairs.* New York: New York University Press, 1955.

——. "Peace and Security in the United Nations." In Clyde Eagleton and Richard Swift, eds., *Annual Review of United Nations Affairs 1955–1956.* New York: New York University Press, 1957.

Tal, Israel. "Torat ha-Bitakhon, Reka u-Dinamikah" [The principles of security, background and dynamics]. *Maarachot* 253 (December 1976).

Waltz, Kenneth N. "Theory of International Relations." In Fred. I. Greenstein and Nelson W. Polsby, eds., *Handbook of Political Science,* vol. 8 (Reading, Mass.: Addison-Wesley, 1975).

——. "Toward Nuclear Peace." In Robert Art and Kenneth N. Waltz, eds., *The Use of Force,* 2d ed. Washington, D.C.: University Press of America, 1983.

Watkins, Sharon. "Deterrence Theory: Expectations and Illusions." *Journal of Strategic Studies* 5 (December 1982).

Yaniv, Avner. "Harta'ah ve-Haganah ba-Estrategiya ha-Yisraelit" [Deterrence and defense in Israeli strategy]. *Medinah Memshal ve-Yakhasim Bein-Leumim* 24 (1985).

Yona, Lt. Col. "Mediniut ha-Maavak shel Abd Al-Nasser" [Nasser's policy of (for) struggle]. *Maarachot* 223 (June 1972).

Index

Library of Congress Cataloging-in-Publication Data

Shimshoni, Jonathan.
    Securing Israel's borders.

    (Cornell studies in security affairs)
    Bibliography: p.
    Includes index.
    1. Israel—National security. 2. Israel—History,
Military. 3. Deterrence (Strategy) I. Title.
II. Series.
UA853.I8S49 1988   355'.095694   87-47965
ISBN 0-8014-2120-9 (alk. paper)

LUIS.